# Critical Mission

## Democracy and Rule of Law Books from the Carnegie Endowment

Aiding Democracy Abroad: The Learning Curve
*Thomas Carothers*

Democracy Challenged: The Rise of Semi-Authoritarianism
*Marina Ottaway*

Open Networks, Closed Regimes: The Impact of the Internet
on Authoritarian Rule
*Shanthi Kalathil and Taylor C. Boas*

The Third Force: The Rise of Transnational Civil Society
*Ann M. Florini, Editor*

Funding Virtue: Civil Society Aid and Democracy Promotion
*Marina Ottaway and Thomas Carothers, Editors*

Assessing Democracy Assistance: The Case of Romania
*Thomas Carothers*

---

To read excerpts and to find more information on these and other publications from the
Carnegie Endowment, visit **www.CarnegieEndowment.org/pubs**.

# Critical Mission

## *Essays on Democracy Promotion*

Thomas Carothers

CARNEGIE ENDOWMENT FOR INTERNATIONAL PEACE
*Washington, D.C.*

Carnegie Endowment for International Peace
1779 Massachusetts Avenue, N.W., Washington, D.C. 20036
202-483-7600, Fax 202-483-1840
**www.CarnegieEndowment.org**

*To order, contact Carnegie's distributor:*
The Brookings Institution Press
Department 029, Washington, D.C. 20042-0029, USA
1-800-275-1447 or 1-202-797-6258
Fax 202-797-2960, Email bibooks@brook.edu

Composition by Stephen McDougal
Printed by Edwards Brothers, Inc.

*Library of Congress Cataloging-in-Publication data*

Carothers, Thomas, 1956–
   Critical mission : essays on democracy promotion / Thomas Carothers.
     p. cm.
   Includes bibliographical references and index.
   ISBN 0-87003-209-7 (pbk.) — ISBN 0-87003-210-0 (hc)
   1. Democracy. 2. Democratization. 3. Economic assistance. I. Title.

   JC421.C2462 2004
   321.8—dc22                                  2004012798

10 09 08 07 06 05 04          1 2 3 4 5          1st Printing 2004

# Contents

# Foreword

FOR YEARS, DEMOCRACY promotion sat on the sidelines of American foreign policy. Foreign policy specialists paid ritualistic deference to it, respecting the ideal, but invested little close attention to the actual practice. Now that has all changed. Over the last year and a half the entire world has watched the unfolding drama of the United States and its coalition partners struggling to transform Iraq into something resembling a working democracy. Moreover, the United States and Europe are in the early phase of what they declare to be a historic new commitment to helping the entire Middle East find a democratic future. And central to the global war on terrorism is the idea that promoting freedom where authoritarianism now reigns is critical to eliminating the roots of political extremism and violence. Democracy is front and center on the international stage and the consequent need for knowledge and expertise about democracy promotion is enormous.

There is no greater expert on this subject than Thomas Carothers. During the last ten years as founder and director of the Democracy and Rule of Law Project at the Carnegie Endowment, he has produced an unmatched body of research and writing on this subject. Simultaneously tackling the dual questions of how democratization occurs around the world and what the United States and other interested actors can do to promote it, he has led the way in crystallizing an incipient field of inquiry into a mature body of knowledge.

Tom's work has several signal characteristics. It is always searching and incisive. He instinctively challenges underlying assumptions and accepted frameworks, pointing the way to new, better approaches. He has a truly unusual ability to synthesize specific insights gleaned from field research into powerful conceptual findings. He is startlingly broad in reach, ranging across every region of the world, yet never lapsing into superficialities or generalizations. And he has consistently demonstrated an uncanny ability to see beyond current trends and mindsets, to anticipate the issues still only just visible on the horizon.

*Critical Mission* draws together a substantial collection of the many seminal articles and papers he has written over the past ten years at Carnegie. It is an extraordinarily rich set of writings, covering the gamut of issues in democracy promotion, always in elegant, accessible prose. Many of these articles changed the way people think about the issues in question, and they are cited again and again in the press, policy circles, and academic journals.

Tom's contributions at Carnegie are scarcely limited to these articles, impressive as they are. In addition to authoring or editing three other books during his time here he has overseen the growth of a large research team, and for a five-year period starting in 1997 he made a huge contribution as Carnegie's director of research and later vice president for studies. In addition to his remarkable productivity he is the best of colleagues, always generous with his time, a pleasure to work with, and modest well beyond due.

Given the crucial nature of the challenge that democracy promotion presents to the United States and the democratic community more broadly, it is a great pleasure for Carnegie to offer this book as a source of deep learning and practical guidance that I know will add immensely to decisions that lie ahead.

Jessica T. Mathews
*President*
*Carnegie Endowment for International Peace*

# SECTION ONE

---

# *Introduction*

---

DEMOCRACY PROMOTION IS much in the news these days. The strenuous effort by the United States and its coalition partners to carry off a democratic transformation of Iraq has provoked a fierce, global debate over the legitimacy and limits of Western democracy promotion. The broader U.S. and European commitment to supporting a democratic transformation of the Middle East—rooted in the hope that positive political change in that region can be an antidote to radical Islamist terrorism—has stirred up vivid emotions in the Arab world and many other quarters. Democracy promotion has in a short time become fused with "high policy" on the world stage, with the result that it is receiving an unprecedented level of public attention, as well as substantial new resources. This is of course hardly the first time Washington has invoked the idea of a democratic mission as a response to a crisis of American security. But the seriousness of the September 11, 2001, attacks against America, the spread of Islamist terrorism to Europe, and the threat of future attacks give this new push on democracy promotion a special intensity.

Democracy promotion is at a critical juncture not only because of the new attention to the Middle East. In many parts of the developing and postcommunist worlds, where political freedom and pluralism made notable gains during democracy's recent "third wave," political blockage, malaise, and backsliding are now common. Complete lapses back to outright authoritarianism are, fortunately, relatively rare. But many attempted transitions have sputtered to a stop as strongmen leaders in the former Soviet Union, Africa, Asia, and elsewhere have

1

consolidated semi-authoritarian regimes in which they obey some of the formal niceties of democracy but keep a firm grip on the main levers of power. In other places, including much of Latin America, but also in parts of South and Southeast Asia, Southeastern Europe, and Africa, real political pluralism has been achieved but is falling into or teetering on the edge of dysfunctional patterns of corruption, fecklessness, and shallowness that produce poor socioeconomic performance and deeply disillusioned, alienated citizens. Very generally speaking, it is remarkably difficult to travel to any of the dozens of "new democracies" around the world today without being met by a chorus of negativism from ordinary citizens about the grievous shortcomings of the politicians who rule the country and the lack of perceived tangible benefits of democracy.

These enormous challenges—trying to help initiate a democratic trend in the Middle East and supporting the embattled trend in the rest of the developing and postcommunist worlds—throw into sharp relief a disjunction that has long afflicted the democracy promotion domain. The array of organizations involved in democracy building around the world, public and private, multilateral and bilateral, specialized and generalist, continues to grow. Approximately $2 billion per year (roughly half from public and private sources in North America and half from largely public sources in Europe) now goes for democracy-related aid projects. And at the diplomatic level, the governments of many established democracies, as well as various multilateral organizations, devote ever-increasing attention to democracy-building challenges. Yet even though democracy promotion activities keep multiplying, the amount of distilled, accumulated, and organized knowledge about this domain remains quite limited.

Many reasons for the gap between ambition and know-how can be identified. Democracy promoters tend to be activists who focus intently on the challenges at hand and are often impatient with backward-looking, learning exercises, especially ones with a critical bent. Most of the institutions for which they work are under much pressure to show quick, impressive results and have few incentives to invest heavily in research and reflection. Moreover, some of the persons who have in the past several years rushed to embrace the cause of democracy promotion out of the perceived connection with the war on terrorism give short shrift to the complexities of the endeavor and to the fact that there is now a long record of experience in diverse regions on which it is important to draw.

The academic world has not stepped up to the plate to fill this gap. Democracy promotion is only weakly present in scholarly research circles. It sits awkwardly in between the disciplines of international relations, comparative politics, development studies, and law—related to all four but not finding a home in any one. And being a practical domain, carried out in distant countries where easily obtainable numerical research data are scarce, the subject is not a tempting target for the many academic researchers who are either preoccupied by theoretical concerns or rely primarily on quantitative methods.

All this is not to say that learning about democracy promotion is nonexistent. It does exist, especially in the organizations that specialize in the subject and have been at it for years. But the bulk of this learning resides in the minds of practitioners and is not committed to paper. A small flow of reflective writing on the topic has started appearing in recent years. The Office of Democracy and Governance at the U.S. Agency for International Development (USAID) has set a valuable example for all aid organizations in producing a series of well-researched overview studies of different areas of democracy aid. Various public and private institutes, including for example the International Institute for Democracy and Electoral Assistance and the National Democratic Institute (NDI), have published practitioner-friendly handbooks on electoral issues and other core elements of democracy building. A growing number of young political scientists, often persons who worked in democracy promotion organizations before going back to graduate school, are starting to produce valuable work on the subject, above all, on the topic of civil society development. Yet overall, democracy promotion remains remarkably understudied, and the gap between what we want to accomplish and what we really know about how to accomplish it remains dauntingly wide.

When I joined the Carnegie Endowment in 1993, democracy-building work was mushrooming. Aid providers were hurriedly setting up camp all over Central and Eastern Europe, grappling with the challenge of starting up in the former Soviet republics, responding to the unexpected wave of transitions away from one-party rule in Africa, finding new opportunities in East and Southeast Asia, and continuing to operate in many parts of Latin America. I had worked in the second half of the 1980s on U.S. democracy programs in Latin America, written a book analyzing the effects on Latin American democracy of the Reagan administration's policies there, and participated as a consultant for NDI in some of the new democracy aid initiatives in Eastern Europe, Africa, and Asia. The time seemed ripe for an effort to engage in some reflection on what was being learned about this burgeoning field and to do so from the standpoint of someone sympathetic to the task yet willing to be critical. I set about to do so. A decade later I find myself still at that task, with the demand and need for such work only growing. Along the way I wrote two more books and co-edited another, all aimed at constructing an analytic framework for democracy promotion and drawing together at least a first layer of accumulated knowledge about such work. In the same years I have also written various essays, articles, and papers, sometimes trying to go deeper into a specific area of democracy aid and sometimes venturing into related topics, particularly the place of democracy promotion in U.S. foreign policy and the state of democracy worldwide. Though written and published one by one, these writings nevertheless represent several continuous lines of inquiry, and so prompted by my ten-year anniversary at Carnegie I decided to gather some of them together in a book in the hope that they can be useful to persons looking for insights into the pressing challenges of democracy promotion at hand today.

The essays herein are connected to each other not only by several subject themes but also by some common elements of my basic outlook on the subject. Perhaps most striking to many readers will be the consistent tone of critical caution, some would probably say skepticism, that colors these writings. I have always been deeply wary of the overstated claims that seem endemic in the democracy promotion domain, whether it is rose-tinted triumphalism about the tide of democracy in the world, inflated declarations by U.S. officials about America's unbending commitment to supporting democracy worldwide, or unrealistically grand claims of impact by democracy promoters. I believe it is quite possible, in fact preferable, to be fully committed to the cause of democracy yet also be relentlessly realistic about democracy's difficulties in many countries, the often partial or conflicted place of democracy in America's foreign policy, and the generally modest impact of most externally sponsored democracy-building efforts. Put differently, I have pursued my work in the belief that the critical mission for the United States and other established democracies of promoting democracy abroad can be facilitated by tough but constructive criticism of such efforts as they unfold.

Moreover, I am often struck how democracy promotion is hurt by the habitual tendency of its practitioners toward overstatement. One of the fundamental challenges that democracy promotion faces as an organized endeavor is credibility—credibility on the part of people both in countries that are the recipients or targets of such activity and in countries that sponsor such work. Most people on the receiving end have an instinctive and wholly understandable suspicion about anyone who comes to their country claiming to be sincerely dedicated to helping build democracy there. This is glaringly evident in the Middle East today but has been and often still is the case in many other parts of the world. And within the United States and other established democracies, most people outside that small world of democracy promoters know little about the issue and tend to be dubious about it. Convincing people that democracy promotion is a credible enterprise is a slow, incremental task. It requires consistency and seriousness of purpose, skill, and capability in execution, and sobriety in evaluation and credit taking. Some progress has been made on the credibility front, both within established democracies and recipient societies, but it is at best only a start.

I also harbor an admittedly prickly antipathy toward fads in the democracy domain. As is common in the broader development aid world, many democracy aid organizations have a weakness for fads. Every few years some new idea is embraced as the key to unlocking the democracy puzzle. Since the late 1980s, one enthusiasm after another has enjoyed a brief, intense run—including elections, civil society, rule of law, decentralization, and anticorruption. As a fad takes hold, aid groups rush to create programs in that area, often shifting resources from other work and investing the new activities with great expectations. In parallel fashion, enterprising people in recipient countries demonstrate a newfound interest in the topic and quickly start up work on it, or strategically re-label what they were already doing to fit the new fashion. A boom period follows, but then within a few years the hoped-for dramatic results do not appear and cracks in the edifice start to show. Restless aid providers move on in search of a new romance.

Each fad rests on some degree of insight. Elections are indeed an irreplaceable element of democracy; civil society development can bring big benefits for pluralism and participation; the rule of law is vital; and so forth. But the urge to embrace fads reflects an unhelpful attachment to the idea that democratization is amenable to magic bullets and the lack of a well-grounded and well-accepted base of knowledge about the process.

A third fiber in the connective tissue of these essays is a focus on local realities. Every set of "lessons learned" on democracy-building programs includes the admonition to "be sensitive to local realities." But no golden rule of aid work is more frequently practiced in the breach, and I have discovered that there often seems to be something intrinsically subversive about conveying to Western aid providers or policy makers critical accounts and insights directly gathered from recipients of democracy aid. I have tried hard to understand democracy promotion work from "the other end of the telescope," primarily by basing my research on a core method of listening as carefully and systematically as possible to what a wide range of people in developing and postcommunist countries say about the experience of being on the receiving end of democracy promotion policies and programs. Much of this research has been, by necessity, exploratory and highly qualitative. Even the basic concepts and terms that practitioners use still represent a rather tenuous projection of frameworks and expectations on unruly foreign realities. Precisely defined operational hypotheses and fine-grain empirical research are only starting to come along. For now we are still largely groping in the semidarkness, bumping into a lot of things, gradually discerning the outlines of the major pieces of furniture in the room, and hoping to do more good than harm.

I am extraordinarily fortunate to have had the Carnegie Endowment as my professional home for the last ten years, and I wrote all the essays in this volume while working here. Under its current president Jessica Mathews, and its former president Morton Abramowitz, who originally hired me, the Endowment has embodied the key values of what I believe a think tank should be: analytically rigorous, policy relevant, stubbornly independent, willing to take risks, and able to give close attention to the crises of the day without losing sight of crucial long-term trends and problems. It has been an honor and a pleasure to try to live up to these high standards, and I thank both Jessica and Mort for having given me the chance. I also thank two invaluable colleagues at the Endowment, Paul Balaran and Marina Ottaway, for having helped so much along the way.

# The Place of Democracy Promotion in U.S. Foreign Policy

ASSESSING THE PLACE of democracy promotion in U.S. foreign policy is a complex undertaking. The story stretches back across most of the previous century and has long been subject to sharply conflicting interpretations, ranging from glowing portrayals of America as a uniquely noble, pro-democratic force in the world to dark portraits of a sinister superpower, habitually backing tyrannies and other forces of oppression. The essays in this section examine the most recent chapter of that story—the period from the end of the Cold War to the present day. And they aim for what I hope is a balanced view. I identify some changes in the role of democracy promotion in U.S. policy that occurred in the transitions from the George H. W. Bush administration to the Clinton administration and from the Clinton administration to the George W. Bush administration. But I find a strong line of continuity connecting all three. All of these administrations ended up making democracy promotion the rhetorical framework of their foreign policy. Yet, at the same time, all three pursued what might be described as a semirealist policy in practice: Where supporting democracy in another country or region was consistent with U.S. economic and security interests, the United States stood up for democracy; but where policy makers saw strong economic or security reasons for staying on friendly terms with authoritarian or semi-authoritarian regimes, Washington almost always downplayed its democracy concerns. The set of countries where America's hard interests conflicted with democratic goals changed over time, especially after the end of the Cold War and then again after the launching of the war on terrorism. But the gap between lofty, pro-democratic rhetoric and much more instrumental realities has been wide all along. I have never been especially surprised by that gap, but my various efforts to point it out and analyze it have consistently met with objections from U.S. officials in the various administrations who felt that their policies were much closer to the rhetorical aspirations than I judged them to be and much more pro-democratic than those of any of their recent predecessors.

The first essay in this section, "Promoting Democracy and Human Rights: Policy Allies or Rivals?" explores a divergence I found puzzling back in the early 1990s—although human rights and democracy are clearly closely linked, the policy subcommunities devoted to the promotion of human rights and of democracy are surprisingly separate and even sometimes suspicious of each other, particularly the human rights advocates toward democracy promoters. Even though the essay is ten years old, the division persists today. The next two pieces look at the Clinton administration's approach to democracy promotion. The first, "Democracy Promotion under Clinton," published in 1995, takes the measure of the Clinton administration's early embrace of the democracy theme and evaluates the degree of change in the shift from George H. W. Bush to Clinton. The second, "The Clinton Record on Democracy Promotion," written in 2000, is a late-term portrait that attempts an overall assessment of the Clinton record in this domain. In "Ousting Foreign Strongmen: Lessons from Serbia," written shortly after the fall of Slobodan Milosevic, I examine the impact of democracy aid used as a method of regime change. The next article in the group, "Promoting Democracy and Fighting Terror," written a year after the September 11 attacks, scrutinizes the double-edged impact of the war on terrorism on U.S. democracy policies—the combination of the new push for democracy in the Middle East and the simultaneous pursuit of closer security ties with various strongmen rulers in different parts of the world. Paula Dobriansky, Undersecretary of State for Global Affairs, took objection to my analysis. Her reply is included here as well as my reply to her in turn.

# CHAPTER ONE

# Democracy and Human Rights: Policy Allies or Rivals? (1994)

FOR MANY PEOPLE involved in the field of democracy promotion, the relationship between U.S. efforts to promote democracy and to promote human rights abroad is simple—the two areas of activity are two sides of the same coin. This view is based on the assumption that human rights, or more particularly, political and civil rights such as the rights to free expression, free association, freedom of movement, and equality before the law, are defining elements of democracy. It follows from this assumption that *by definition* promoting democracy entails promoting human rights and conversely that promoting human rights is a form of promoting democracy. The persons who subscribe to this view tend to believe that the essential complementarity or even identity of democracy promotion and human rights promotion is self-evident, and they are often mystified by the notion that there might be any contrary view.

But there is in fact a contrary view. Some members of the U.S. human rights community do not see any natural or inevitable complementarity between U.S. efforts to promote democracy and to promote human rights. These persons tend to be deeply skeptical of U.S. democracy promotion policies and programs. As Aryeh Neier wrote in his previous capacity as executive director of Human Rights Watch, "by and large the human rights movement would prefer not to be associated with a global crusade to promote democracy."[1] Some members of that movement believe that democracy promotion policies pursued by the U.S. government differ from human rights promotion in fundamental ways, that those policies sometimes involve the forsaking of human rights goals, and that the programs they generate sometimes actually work against human rights.[2]

This rift between at least some members of the U.S. human rights community and what may be called the U.S. democracy community dates back to the beginning of the current wave of democracy promotion activity, that is, to the early 1980s. It has its origins in the early association of democracy promotion policies with President Ronald Reagan's fervent anticommunism and his related desire to reverse the Carter administration's human rights policies. Somewhat surprisingly, the rift has not substantially healed during the intervening years, despite the evolution of the world away from the Cold War and of U.S. foreign policy away from anticommunism. If anything the rift gained a certain renewed intensity in 1993 with the arrival of the Clinton administration. The new administration is attempting to emphasize both democracy promotion *and* human rights in its foreign policy. The democracy community favors the idea of such a dual approach and sees it as confirmation of the view that promoting democracy and promoting human rights go hand in hand. At least some members of the human rights community, however, are uncomfortable with a dual approach and argue that human rights alone, not democracy promotion, should be the centerpiece of the Clinton administration's foreign policy.

The Clinton administration has not really tried to resolve the rift between the two communities but has proceeded instead on the probably mistaken assumption that the rift will gradually disappear if the administration tries to be all things to all people, that is to say, if it swears equal fidelity to the agenda of each group. In fact, however, the first step toward resolution of this division is not to try to assume it away but to air it thoroughly and submit it to a systematic analysis—analysis that has been notably lacking in the rhetorical salvos and sloganeering that have dominated both sides of the debate to date. This article attempts to identify and analyze the main points of the debate and to suggest various lines of rethinking necessary on both sides if movement toward a middle ground is to occur.

Throughout this article repeated reference is made to the "democracy community" and the "human rights movement," two shorthand concepts that in this context can be defined as follows. The democracy community is a loose amalgam of people who work on democracy assistance programs either at the small but growing set of quasigovernmental and nongovernmental organizations exclusively devoted to promoting democracy abroad,[3] or at the very large number of nongovernmental organizations, including many major U.S. universities, foundations, and policy institutes, that have established at least some activities aimed at promoting democracy abroad. The democracy community also includes various academic specialists and policy commentators who publicly advocate democracy promotion. Depending on how one defines the borders of the community, it can also be said to include the growing number of persons in the U.S. government who work on democracy promotion policies and programs, primarily at the U.S. Agency for International Development, the State Department, and the U.S. Information Agency, but also at the Defense Department and the Justice Department.

The U.S. human rights movement is the semi-organized network of persons in the United States who work in domestic and international human rights organizations,[4] or who work at development institutes, universities, law firms, or other organizations but devote some significant amount of their time to human rights work. Again, depending on how the borders of the movement are defined, it may also include those persons in the U.S. government who work on human rights issues. The democracy community and the human rights movement overlap somewhat but are nonetheless identifiably distinct communities. The human rights movement is by no means unified in its view of U.S. government efforts to promote democracy abroad. Some persons in the movement share the view of the democracy community that there is a very close relationship between U.S. efforts to promote democracy and to promote human rights. Others, however, do not. Although those who are critical of U.S. democracy promotion efforts do not necessarily represent the whole movement, they are an influential and vocal group.

## Points of Difference

The democracy community and the human rights movement differ on several specific points. Some are practical, others theoretical. Some concern the value of the U.S. government's democracy promotion efforts; others the question of whether democracy promotion and human rights promotion are closely related endeavors. Five points of difference, constituting a representative but by no means exhaustive list, are examined here.

### Law versus Politics

For many in the human rights movement there is a very significant difference in formal status between human rights and democracy: human rights are international legal norms, whereas democracy is a political ideology. In their view, U.S. government pressure on a foreign government to improve its human rights behavior is a form of entirely legitimate intervention in the internal affairs of that country because human rights norms are binding under international law on all states. By contrast, they consider that U.S. pressure on a foreign government to become democratic is of questionable legitimacy because democracy is just one of a number of competing political ideologies, not a binding obligation. Democracy promotion by the U.S. government, they hold, constantly runs the risk of veering off into neo-imperialism.

Some members of the democracy community reject the assertion of a law-politics divide between human rights and democracy. They point to a small body of recent international law scholarship in the United States that contends that democracy is in the process of attaining the status of a right under international law.[5] Other members of the democracy community accept that there is a difference in formal status between human rights and democracy but do not believe the difference is particularly significant. When confronted with the distinction between human rights as law and democracy as ideology, they tend to respond that the U.S. government legitimately promotes, with both positive and negative inducements, numerous policies and principles abroad that do not have the status of international legal norms. Along with the World Bank and the International Monetary Fund, for example, it promotes free market economic principles around the world even though such principles are not international legal norms. The legitimacy of U.S. government efforts to promote democracy abroad is ensured, in the view of many in the democracy community, by their strongly felt but not clearly defined notion that democracy is a universal aspiration and a universal good.

There is no simple resolution of this point of difference between the human rights movement and the democracy community. The human rights movement is certainly justified in being wary of any easy assumptions about the legitimacy of U.S. government efforts to change other countries' political systems. The human rights movement must also, however, be wary of overplaying the law-politics distinction between human rights and democracy. It is true that many human rights have attained the status of international law and are therefore binding on all states regardless of the ideological configuration of any particular government. The fact remains, however, that the internationally established set of political and civil rights, and even some of what are considered the fundamental human rights, developed out of and are still intimately linked with liberal democratic ideology. Human rights advocates may believe that a viable distinction can be drawn between the U.S. government on the one hand pressuring another government to respect political and civil rights such as the rights to freedom of expression, thought, association, and movement, equality before the law, due process, and political participation, and on the other hand pressuring another government to move toward liberal democracy. From the point of view of many foreign governments, however, such a distinction is likely to appear formalistic at best.

Human rights advocates should also be cautious about overstating the significance of the distinction between human rights as international legal norms and democracy as political ideology because the boundary between international law and politics is both porous and evolutionary. A major source of international legal norms is the customary practice of nations. Although it is premature to state that democracy is an international legal norm, the active promotion of democracy may over time help engender the practices and beliefs that lead to the emergence of an international right to democracy. Human rights advocates should be particularly aware of this because international law in the human rights field has evolved greatly over the past 50 years and human rights advocacy contributed significantly to that evolution.

The weakness of the democracy community's position on this issue is an over-reliance on the rather facile assumption that democracy is a universal aspiration in order to ward off charges of political interventionism or neo-imperialism. The democratic trend has certainly spread to many parts of the globe. In many cases, however, democratic undertakings in previously undemocratic societies appear more to be either pragmatic or desperate experiments rather than expressions of deeply felt aspirations of "the people." Even if it could be said that democracy is clearly a universal aspiration, it would not necessarily follow that external actors such as the United States could automatically assume that they are entitled to interpret for other societies what form democracy should take and to attempt to influence its development in them.

*Relative Urgency of Human Rights versus Democracy*

A second point of difference between the human rights movement and the democracy community concerns the relative importance of U.S. government efforts to promote democracy versus its efforts to promote human rights. Some human rights advocates assert that human rights promotion is fundamentally more important than democracy promotion. They argue, for example, that systematic torture or murder by a foreign government should surely command the U.S. government's attention more than should the denial of free and fair elections. The idea of "lower order" and "higher order" rights is sometimes advanced in this vein. Some human rights advocates argue that "lower order" rights such as the right to freedom from torture are building blocks to "higher order" rights, such as the right to political participation, and that these categories should form a natural sequence for U.S. policy.

In response, some members of the democracy community argue that the most dramatic reductions in human rights abuses in different countries during the past 15 years have not occurred because of changes in human rights policies per se. They have occurred, according to this argument, because of transitions to democracy. In Eastern Europe and South America, for example, the human rights situation, although still flawed, has greatly improved since the late 1970s, particularly with respect to gross human rights abuses. In both regions, democracy promotion advocates argue, the primary cause of the improvements is the shift to democracy that has occurred. In their view, efforts by the U.S. government to promote democracy may have less immediate impact on people's well-being than human rights efforts but may in the longer term have much more wide-reaching and long-lasting impact. Neither side is completely correct in this debate over the relative importance of democracy promotion versus human rights promotion. Some human rights advocates have been overly skeptical of the democratic trend. They have underestimated both the possibility of dramatic democratic change in many parts of the world and the significance of such change for improving human rights conditions. Quick to point to the continuance of serious human rights abuses in some countries that have made transitions to democracy, these human rights advocates have been sometimes too grudging in their acknowledgment of the human rights improvements that democratic transitions have brought. And as a result they underestimate the at least potential contribution that democracy promotion efforts may make to the human rights objectives of U.S. policy.

At the same time, however, some proponents of democracy promotion have been too quick to move from the observation that in numerous countries, democratization has led to significant reduction in human rights abuses to the conclusion that democracy promotion is therefore more essential or important than human rights promotion. In most of the countries that have undergone democratic transitions in recent years, during the generative period of the transitions (generally the late 1970s and early to mid-1980s), the emphasis of external actors was on human rights advocacy rather than democracy promotion per se. Therefore, just as human rights advocates should not overlook the fact that democratization has advanced the cause of human rights in many countries, democracy promotion proponents should not ignore the contribution of human rights advocacy to democratization.

### Elections

A third point of difference concerns elections. Human rights advocates are often critical of the U.S. government and the democracy community for placing what they consider undue emphasis on the importance of elections in democratization processes or more simply equating elections with democracy. They argue that elections in transitional societies sometimes do not establish a representative government with genuine authority, that elections sometimes constitute only superficial political maneuvering that leaves underlying antidemocratic forces intact. Human rights abuses often continue even after the transitions from dictatorships to elected governments, they emphasize, and the U.S. government gives too much credence to the fact of elections while paying too little importance to the continuing human rights problems.

The democracy community, including those parts of the U.S. government that sponsor democracy promotion programs, does put a strong emphasis on elections in transitional situations, for several reasons. First, the community believes that national elections are the best way of concentrating the energies and attention of a society in transition away from nondemocratic rule and toward a broad, participatory act of political self-definition. Second, it views the establishment of an elected government as the keystone of any emerging democratic process. Third, it sees regular elections as the essential method for ensuring the accountability of the leaders of a country.

The critical view of some human rights advocates toward the place of elections in U.S. democracy promotion policies was primarily formed during the 1980s, particularly in reaction to the Reagan administration's policies in Central America. The human rights movement fought bitterly against that administration's dual tendency to proclaim as full-fledged democracies countries such as El Salvador or Guatemala that had held elections but were still controlled by underlying antidemocratic forces and to ignore the continuing human rights abuses in those countries. As discussed in more detail below, however, the U.S. government's Cold War habit of using democracy promotion as a rhetorical cover for policies aimed at quite distinct security interests has greatly faded in recent years. And with that change has come a marked reduction in the government's previous tendency to accept a country as democratic merely because it has had elections. The Clinton administration appears to be interested in promoting democracy abroad as an end in itself and to be aware of the pitfalls of simplistically equating elections with democracy.

Despite this evolution, the democracy community must guard against the tendency to overestimate the significance of elections in transitional societies. Many persons in the democracy community still harbor at least signs of this tendency, not because of an interest in using democracy promotion as a cover for other policy goals, but because of an American habit of conceiving of democracy in procedural rather than substantive terms and of failing to get beyond the most tangible level of political activity in a complex transitional society to the underlying realities of power and tradition.

*Strengthening Governing Institutions*

A fourth point of difference between the democracy community and the U.S. human rights movement concerns what has been a common feature of U.S. policies to promote democracy—programs that involve assistance to governing institutions in transitional societies aimed at rendering those institutions more effective and more democratic. Some human rights advocates have criticized the general idea of such programs, arguing that they risk strengthening governing institutions that are not generally under democratic control and increasing the capacity of some institutions to enforce nondemocratic practices or to commit human rights abuses. To support this argument, human rights advocates frequently point to police aid programs, particularly U.S. police aid to El Salvador in the 1980s. Such aid, they argue, strengthened politically tainted police forces that were not under the control of the elected Salvadoran government, thereby associating the U.S. government with human rights abuses and increasing the capacity of those forces to commit such abuses.

Those involved in police aid programs that are part of democracy promotion initiatives respond to such criticisms in two ways. In the first place they distinguish between police aid that is specifically designed as democracy assistance and other police aid programs, such as police aid that is part of antiterrorism or security assistance programs. They acknowledge that those other types of police aid may well conflict with democratic and human rights goals. They insist, however, that the assistance they give is specifically designed not to strengthen existing operational patterns, but rather to train police to commit fewer human rights abuses, both by teaching human rights directly and by training police in investigative techniques that will steer them away from abusive interrogations and other wrongdoing.

Police aid proponents also respond by noting that human rights groups seem to focus only on possible negative effects and never on the positive effects of such programs. These groups, they assert, seem to believe that one wrong committed by the U.S. government outweighs any number of rights. They argue that although police aid aimed at improving the human rights performance of police may entail some risks, the benefits of such assistance greatly outweigh any negative effects. In their view, the choice presented by police aid is that between working directly to try to change the institutions that have been responsible for many wrongs in the past or simply standing back in a critical mode without offering any assistance for change.

A definitive answer to this debate over democracy-related police aid would involve considerable empirical inquiry into the full range of effects of such aid and is beyond the scope of this article. It is certainly the case that given the troubled history of U.S. efforts to reform military and security forces in various parts of the world throughout this century, the burden of proof regarding the overall positive balance for the recent democratic police aid programs in Central and South America lies with the proponents of such aid. As a general argument against programs aimed at building the institutions of democracy, however, the critical assertions regarding police aid are not especially powerful. It may be that some of the democracy-related police aid of the past 10 years has in El Salvador and several other Latin American countries had some negative human rights effects. Police aid is, however, only a small part of the overall set of U.S. assistance programs aimed at strengthening democratic institutions. There is little evidence that the other forms of institution-building assistance—constitution-writing projects, parliamentary training, judicial training, and the like—entail any broad risk of increasing human rights abuses. The harder question is whether externally sponsored training and reform programs can have any lasting effect at all on poorly functioning parliaments or judicial systems in countries with long histories of nondemocratic rule and the absence of the rule of law.

## U.S. Funds and Foreign Political Processes

A fifth point of difference concerns the effect of U.S. government funds on foreign political processes. Some human rights advocates are uncomfortable in general with projects funded by the U.S. government that directly involve foreign political processes, no matter how pro-democratic the intent. They believe that in many cases local organizations that accept such funds will be contaminated by their link to the U.S. government and unable to maintain any credibility as legitimate democratic political actors. They also hold that U.S. funding of organizations involved in politics and governance will almost inevitably deform the local political process, giving too much weight to some actors and robbing the process of its own internal coherence.

The democracy community contends that with appropriate caution and line-drawing the U.S. government can legitimately carry out assistance projects related to foreign political processes without unduly influencing them. In countries where a nondemocratic regime is being challenged by a rising group of pro-democratic political actors, for example, the democracy community believes that U.S. assistance to a wide range of the pro-democratic actors legitimately "levels the playing field" and promotes democracy without preselecting a particular part of the emerging democratic spectrum. In countries that have made a transition from a nondemocratic regime to a democratically elected government, the democracy community holds that assistance both to strengthen the fledgling governing institutions and to foster the broad development of civil society promotes democracy without deforming the process.

There is no easy resolution to this difference of views over the role of U.S. government funds in foreign political processes. The end of the Cold War has made it somewhat easier for the U.S. government to involve itself in political development assistance, although, as noted below, the democracy community sometimes gives too little attention to the negative legacies of past U.S. involvements in the internal political processes of many countries. And the successful work of organizations funded by the U.S. government, European governments, and Western nongovernmental organizations in the many transitional elections around the world in recent years has given credibility to the idea that external actors can support democratic elections without trying to influence their outcome. Nonetheless, any U.S. government assistance related to foreign political processes is very sensitive, and its effects on those processes are likely to be scrutinized and debated by local political actors. The question of what is development versus what is deformation of a local political process is exceedingly complex and cannot be assumed away or answered in anything other than a case-by-case fashion.

## Toward a Middle Ground

As the above discussion illustrates, there is no simple resolution of any of these various points of difference between the democracy community and the human rights movement over U.S. government efforts to promote democracy abroad and the relation of such efforts to the promotion of human rights. Nonetheless, in each case a middle ground is at least visible if each side is willing to acknowledge the merit of some of the other side's arguments and avoid ritualistic positioning. In general, some broad rethinking on both sides could make convergence toward a middle ground possible. This middle ground would reject the contending notions that U.S. government democracy promotion and human rights policies are either inherently consistent or sharply at odds. It would hold rather that such policies can and should enjoy a significant overlap of both methods and goals but that some theoretical and practical differences between them are nonetheless inevitable.

For the human rights movement, three broad lines of rethinking can be suggested. To start with, for some in the human rights movement, U.S. government efforts to promote democracy abroad are still viewed through a Cold War lens and are strongly associated with the Reagan administration. The human rights movement formed a deeply negative view of democracy promotion policies in its various battles with the Reagan administration, particularly over the administration's militant anti-Communist policy in Central America. From those experiences, some human rights advocates came to see U.S. democracy promotion policies as self-righteous, rhetorical covers for the pursuit of other interests, particularly anti-Communist security interests. They also grew mistrustful of the U.S. government's apparent tendency to equate elections with democracy and to downplay the human rights violations committed by supposedly democratic allies.

Those policies, that administration, and even significant aspects of that historical period have passed. The human rights movement should leave behind its reflexively negative view and its Cold War lens and confront the subject in today's terms and realities. Current U.S. democracy promotion policies and programs are not crafted as rhetorical covers for underlying goals. For the most part the Clinton administration is promoting democracy as an end in itself. Although it asserts that democracy promotion is helpful to U.S. security interests, it does so out of the belief that democracies tend to be more peaceful than nondemocracies rather than out of the habit of using democracy promotion as a pleasing cover for less publicly presentable security goals. Similarly, the emphasis on elections has faded somewhat in U.S. policy. Although, as discussed above, the habit of overestimating the importance of elections has not disappeared, the Clinton administration does not simplistically equate elections with democracy and focuses much of its democracy-related attention on the need to help countries go from the achievement of an elected government to the consolidation of full-fledged democracy.

Another issue for reconsideration is the general view of some human rights advocates that U.S. democracy promotion is a highly self-centered activity rooted in the United States' habit of trying to transform the world in its own image. It is true that some democracy assistance programs embody too much of this tendency, yet considerable progress has been made in the past few years toward programs that impart a comparative perspective and promote the sharing of information and experiences *between* countries in transition to democracy.

Although an instinct to remake the world in its image has been part of the international outlook of the United States for generations, the current emphasis on democracy promotion cannot be explained—or dismissed—simply as an external manifestation of that reflex. The German political foundations have been carrying out large-scale democracy promotion assistance in many parts of the world for decades. The British government has recently established the Westminster Foundation for Democracy, an organization devoted to promoting democracy abroad. The Japanese government and the European Union are both seriously exploring the possibility of creating democracy promotion organizations. A number of international organizations, including the United

Nations, the Organization of American States, the Organization of African Unity, and the Conference on Security and Cooperation in Europe have established democracy promotion units or election units. Some of the international financial institutions, such as the World Bank and the Inter-American Development Bank, are approaching political development assistance through the concept of governance. Democracy assistance today is not so much the product of U.S. self-centeredness as a spreading global practice.

A final point of possible reconsideration by the human rights movement concerns the relationship between democracy assistance and the overall state of relations between developed countries and developing countries. Although developing countries are still quite concerned about preserving their sovereignty and continue to feel aggrieved in many ways about their treatment by developed countries, the anti-imperialist, politically relativistic Third Worldism of the 1960s and 1970s has given way quite dramatically in many parts of the developing world to a hunger for information, knowledge, and skills relating to both the economic and political practices of the developed world. Democracy assistance from the United States and other developed countries and international organizations is not, as some human rights advocates seem to think, unwanted intrusive assistance being forced on reluctant recipients. Rather in many cases it is a hurried and still insufficient response to a powerful demand.

Both the democracy community and the human rights movement need to rethink certain assumptions and approaches to achieve convergence on a middle ground. In the first place, the democracy community must beware of a facile universalism in its view of the global democratic trend. Some persons in the democracy movement see other countries primarily in terms of a simple continuum of democracy versus nondemocracy and are satisfied with an almost completely ahistorical and even acultural approach to working in other countries. In the belief that democratization is a universal and therefore easily comprehended phenomenon, they make little effort to bring to their assistance efforts any real understanding of the societies they are working in other than certain barebones information about the current political situation. The result is often shallowness, in both the design of the specific democracy assistance projects and the understanding of their actual effects.

Second, the democracy community should give more due to the human rights movement's strong sensitivity to some of the negative legacies of past U.S. involvements in different parts of the world. Some in the democracy community do not seem to bear in mind that despite increasing demands in many developing countries for Western political and economic cooperation, they retain a deep skepticism about the potential value of any role played by the United States in their domestic affairs. In many countries the United States is still associated with the support of nondemocratic regimes and the use of both covert and coercive means of political influence.

Some persons involved in democracy promotion projects funded by the U.S. government tend to ignore such negative legacies. Others are aware of them but tend to see the policies that caused them as part of the distant past (that is, pre-1989) and to assume that the foreigners they are working with will simply accept the idea that the U.S. government's approach to such matters has changed. These negative legacies are not permanent obstacles to democracy promotion. They cannot, however, be ignored or assumed away. They will only be overcome through patient, consistent efforts to gradually replace the repositories of distrust with goodwill.

Third, the democracy community needs to reconsider some of its work methods and here, too, take a page from the human rights movement. The best human rights organizations approach their mission in a manner that is long-term, labor-intensive, and marked by strict adherence to well-defined goals. Democracy assistance organizations would do well to emulate such an approach. They have shown some tendency to pursue short-term projects and to move rapidly from one to the next while drawing little overall connection between them. And as funds for democracy assistance have mushroomed in recent years, the projects generated have started to become more dollar-intensive than labor-intensive. The rapid obligation and disbursement of money has begun to take precedence over careful planning and strategic thinking. Furthermore, most democracy assistance organizations tend to assume that the definition of democracy is self-evident and that therefore the goals of democracy assistance organizations do not require extensive elaboration. The result in many transitional countries has been multiplication of quite disparate projects, all being carried out under the rubric of democracy assistance. The danger is both that the impact will be diffused by weakly focused objectives and that the concept of democracy assistance will become associated with a wide range of activities of dubious relevance or merit.

A cooperative, productive middle ground between the democracy community and the human rights movement is possible if both sides show a willingness to rethink some of their positions, to move away from the past, and to learn from each other. It is important that both sides make the effort to narrow the differences between them. The differences divert the scarce resources and energies of the two groups away from their essential tasks abroad. The differences also weaken the general effort to bolster wavering U.S. public support for a sustained U.S. commitment to helping people in other countries lead better lives. If the Clinton administration wishes to succeed in crafting a coherent foreign policy that combines a bold emphasis on democracy promotion with a vigorous renewal of concern for human rights, it must attempt both to define and seize a middle ground between these two groups. It will do that only if it abandons its apparently instinctive tendency to paper over differences between competing constituencies and present as a seamless whole what is in fact a hesitant alliance. The administration should acknowledge the practical and conceptual tensions that exist between democracy promotion and human rights advocacy and attempt to forge a reconciliation based on the rethinking outlined above. In this way the seemingly natural but not yet existent partnership of democracy and human rights in U.S. policy may become a reality.

## Notes

The Carnegie Endowment gratefully acknowledges the permission of MIT Press Journals to reprint this article, which originally appeared in *The Washington Quarterly*, vol. 17, no. 3 (Summer 1994).

1. Aryeh Neier, "Asia's Unacceptable Standard," *Foreign Policy* 92 (Fall 1993): 47.
2. Some of these views are expressed in Holly Burkhalter and Juan Mendez, "Rights, Wrongs, and U.S. Foreign Policy," *Legal Times*, July 19, 1993, pp. 27–28, and Jack Donnelly, "Human Rights in the New World Order," *World Policy Journal* 9 (Spring 1992): 249–277.
3. These include the National Endowment for Democracy and its four core grantees (the International Republican Institute, National Democratic Institute for International Affairs, Free Trade Union Institute, and Center for International Private Enterprise), the International Foundation for Electoral Systems, and the Center for Democracy.
4. These include Human Rights Watch, Amnesty International, the Lawyers Committee for Human Rights, the International Human Rights Law Group, and the International League for Human Rights.
5. See for example, Thomas Frank, "The Emerging Right to Democratic Governance," *American Journal of International Law* 86 (January 1992): 46–91.

# CHAPTER TWO

# Democracy Promotion
# under Clinton
# (1995)

IN HIS FIRST foreign policy speech of the 1992 presidential campaign, then-Governor Bill Clinton called for "an American foreign policy of engagement for democracy."[1] Throughout the campaign and since becoming president, Clinton has continued to emphasize the democracy promotion theme. He and his advisers have also set out an often confusing mix of other foreign policy themes, ranging from economic security and international engagement to multilateralism and "new global issues." But it is democracy promotion that appears most frequently in their speeches on foreign policy. And it is only democracy promotion that they have attempted to elaborate as a comprehensive policy framework, as when Anthony Lake, the president's national security adviser, declared in 1993 that "the successor to a doctrine of containment must be a strategy of enlargement—enlargement of the world's free community of market democracies."[2]

For the Clinton team, torn between deeply rooted liberal impulses and the intellectual recognition of the need for centrism, democracy promotion is a uniquely appealing theme. On the one hand it is strongly Wilsonian, redolent of the notion of U.S. engagement abroad to "do good." On the other hand, with the end of the Cold War, democracy promotion appears more plausibly to be a pragmatic undertaking that serves U.S. security and economic interests. Clinton officials stock almost every general foreign policy speech with the argument that promoting democracy abroad advances U.S. interests because democracies tend not to go to war with each other, not to produce large numbers of refugees, not to engage in terrorism, to make better economic partners, and so on. Not only does democracy promotion promise to fuse the traditionally disparate strands of morality and realpolitik in U.S. foreign policy, it has great simplicity and sweep. And it implies U.S. global leadership through the inherent assumption that the United States is especially qualified to promote democracy around the world.

Although we are well into the Clinton presidency, indeed already in the early stages of the 1996 campaign, the issue of how the administration has performed with respect to its central stated foreign policy ambition is surprisingly unexamined. Complaints from both sides have certainly been heard. Conservative realists accuse Clinton of overextending U.S. resources for peripheral democracy crusades, citing Haiti. On Clinton's left, idealists excoriate the administration for sacrificing democracy and human rights to economic and security concerns, citing China. Yet more systematic analysis has been lacking. How has the Clinton administration translated its overarching pro-democracy rhetoric into practice? Does democracy promotion play a greater role in the Clinton foreign policy than it did in the Bush foreign policy? Is democracy promotion really the logical successor to containment?

## Comparing Clinton and Bush

During the 1992 campaign Clinton attempted to portray George Bush as weak on democracy promotion and human rights. Clinton attacked Bush repeatedly on China and Haiti, presenting those two cases as emblematic failures of a policy supposedly dominated by hardheartedness and obsolete realpolitik concerns. Clinton and his advisers took this misleading tack out of an eagerness to capture democracy promotion as Clinton's own theme and to underscore the idea that Bush lacked "the vision thing" abroad as well as at home.

It is certainly true that as conservative pragmatists George Bush and James A. Baker III had not in 1989 been inclined to give a high level of attention to democracy promotion abroad. Yet by 1992 they had ended up making it an indisputably important element of their foreign policy. This evolution occurred primarily because Bush's presidency coincided with the peak of the global democratic trend—the fall of the Berlin Wall, the emergence in Russia of at least incipient democracy, an unexpectedly vigorous democratic wave in Africa, substantial democratic gains in some Asian countries, and the further spread of democratization in Latin America. Bush and Baker could not help but be responsive to this trend, which was so favorable to the United States and seemed to define the shape of the emerging post–Cold War era. They lauded "the democratic revolution" constantly and established democracy promotion as one of the three principal elements of their foreign policy, alongside economic concerns and national security. In practice, they balanced democracy promotion against a number of other goals. The emphasis they placed on democracy promotion varied greatly from region to region depending on the overall configuration of U.S. interests and the degree of local movement toward democracy. A brief region-by-region comparison of the role accorded to democracy promotion by Bush and by Clinton illuminates the substantial attention the Bush administration in fact devoted to the issue. It also reveals the basic similarity of the Clinton approach.

In the two regions where democracy has advanced broadly and where the United States has sought to promote an integrative relationship with the Western community of industrialized democracies, namely Eastern Europe and Latin America, promoting democracy has become a central element of U.S. policy. The consolidation of democracy in both regions is seen as essential to a positive security environment, to good political relations with the United States and Western Europe, and to the achievement of free market economic reforms. In Eastern Europe after the fall of the Berlin Wall, the Bush administration, with the urging of the Democrats in Congress, initiated a carrot and stick policy of "democratic differentiation" to encourage movement toward democracy and free market economics. The policy tools included diplomatic praise and criticism, economic and political assistance programs, and the granting or withholding of most-favored-nation (MFN) status and other trade benefits. With respect to Romania, for example, the Bush administration attempted to pressure President Ion Iliescu in a pro-democratic direction by conditioning the renewal of MFN status on the holding of free and fair elections and by funding assistance programs for the Romanian political opposition.

Under Clinton, U.S. policy toward Eastern Europe has maintained the same dual emphasis on democratic development and free market reforms with only some minor changes of emphasis. Somewhat greater attention is now being given to regional security issues, particularly the Partnership for Peace and possible expansion of the North Atlantic Treaty Organization, reflecting the evolution of events in the region. Economic and political development assistance programs have been continued at approximately the same levels and not changed greatly in terms of their content and objectives.

In Latin America, the Bush administration carried forward the transition initiated during the second Reagan administration away from a policy dominated by military-oriented anticommunism to one aimed at promoting democracy and free market economics. Bush articulated the vision of a hemispheric free trade zone, and he saw the consolidation of Latin democracy as helpful, even crucial, to that goal, with the very important exception of Mexico, where he downplayed the democracy issue sharply. Generally, however, Bush officials expressed support for democracy publicly and privately to their Latin American counterparts. They sought to discourage democratic backsliding in the region, denouncing a possible coup in Venezuela in 1992, and exerting some economic and political pressure on President Alberto Fujimori of Peru to return to democratic rule after his 1991 *autogolpe* and against Haiti's military leaders after their ouster of President Jean-Bertrand Aristide in 1991. And they greatly stepped up assistance programs aimed at democracy promotion, with such assistance exceeding $100 million per year in 1991 and 1992.

Clinton has continued the policy of support for democracy in Latin America, with an essentially similar portfolio of tools to serve the policy, the same parallel emphasis on free market reforms, and the same willingness to soft-pedal democracy in selected cases such as Mexico and the Dominican Republic during that country's problematic elections of 1994. If one looks hard, slight differences can be found between Clinton and Bush on the democracy issue in the region—the former showing a marginally more assertive line in Peru, greater emphasis on U.S. military assistance on human rights and democracy, and a shift from top-down to bottom-up forms of political development assistance. Overwhelmingly, however, the place of democracy in U.S. hemispheric policy under Clinton is basically the same as under Bush.

The one exception, of course, is Haiti, where Clinton has achieved a prodemocratic outcome that Bush did not. It does not simply follow, however, that Clinton placed a much higher priority on democracy in Haiti than did Bush. Clinton's Haiti policy was driven as much by naked political fear—the fear of domestic fallout over continued flows of Haitian refugees and of the righteous wrath of the U.S. community that supported President Aristide—as by a principled concern over Haitian democracy. Also, the Bush administration was not indifferent to democracy in Haiti. It was the Bush administration that pushed for the 1990 electoral process that brought Aristide to power. And it was the Bush team that helped stop the first coup attempt against Aristide in early 1991. After the September 1991 coup Bush officials indeed wanted to see democracy in Haiti but did not believe that the return to power of Aristide, whom they saw as fundamentally flawed, would necessarily bring about that result. In any event, the significance of the Clinton administration's achievement in Haiti remains open to doubt. The rest of the world has been less astonished than the Clinton team that the U.S. government is actually able to use military force to impose its political will on a small, powerless neighbor. And although the political situation in postintervention Haiti has been positive to date, the long-term fate of democracy there remains uncertain.

In the two regions of the world where democracy has not been advancing broadly and where the United States has significant economic and security interests not clearly related to democratization, namely, Asia and the Middle East, democracy promotion is not a major element of U.S. policy. In Asia, Bush maintained the long-standing U.S. focus on economic and security concerns, accepting as a given that U.S. interests in both domains required cordial relationships with many of the authoritarian governments of the region. Bush's forgiving response to the 1989 Tiananmen Square crackdown by the Chinese government dramatically demonstrated that view. Yet the Bush team was not indifferent to the rise of democracy that was occurring in some parts of Asia, such as Cambodia, Mongolia, Nepal, South Korea, and Taiwan. Under Bush, the United States provided diplomatic support and implemented democracy assistance programs for Asian countries in political transition.

Having criticized Bush so strenuously during the campaign on human rights in China, Clinton took office laden with the expectation that he would significantly bolster the place of human rights and democracy in U.S. policy toward Asia. Clinton and his advisers asserted a new policy framework for Asia, a "New Pacific Community," that added democracy as a third leg to the traditional economic and security bases of U.S. policy. For a brief time in 1993 it appeared that the administration would pursue a more aggressive human rights policy, not only toward China but also Indonesia. This faded quickly, however, in the face of the powerful countervailing U.S. economic interests and the increasing self-confidence and even self-righteousness of many Asian leaders about the "Asian approach" to development. Clinton's agonized but reasonable decision in May 1994 to renew China's MFN status despite China's lack of progress on human rights signaled the end of any significant departure from the Bush policy on the issue of democracy and human rights in Asia.

In the Middle East, the Bush administration's attention was heavily occupied by the Arab–Israeli peace process and the Persian Gulf War, two matters in which democracy promotion played little role and which necessitated close workings with nondemocratic regimes such as those in Saudi Arabia, Kuwait, and Egypt. Although Bush officials welcomed nascent trends toward political liberalization in Jordan and Yemen, they remained generally wary of democratization in the region due to the possibility that Islamic fundamentalist regimes might emerge there. In this vein, the administration raised no voice of protest when in early 1992 the Algerian military canceled an electoral process that the Islamic Salvation Front appeared likely to win.

The Clinton administration has not altered the low priority accorded to democracy promotion in the Middle East in recognition of the continuing absence of a significant democratic trend in the region and the realities of U.S. economic and security interests. The administration has taken a somewhat less accepting line than did Bush with respect to the Algerian government's hard line toward the Islamic Salvation Front. This slight shift is more of a reaction to the worsening situation in Algeria than a general change in approach to the issue of democratization in the Middle East.

Democracy promotion plays an important role in U.S. policy toward the former Soviet Union. From 1989 up to the breakup of the Soviet Union in 1991, Bush sought a strategic partnership with Soviet president Mikhail Gorbachev. Although based on the underlying belief that Gorbachev's economic and political reform initiatives could and should succeed, this policy in practice consisted more of support for political stability than for democratic change in the Soviet Union. After the breakup of the Soviet Union, however, Bush overcame his initial skepticism about Boris Yeltsin and pursued a strategic partnership with Russia. Bush and his advisers accepted the proposition that only a democratic Russia could be a close partner of the United States and accordingly built democracy promotion into their Russia policy. The actual resources they devoted to support Russia's political and economic reforms were, however, quite modest. With respect to the other states of the former Soviet Union, the Bush administration declared its support for democracy and capitalism as a general matter but focused its attention on security issues, primarily the disposition of the nuclear weapons in Ukraine and Kazakhstan.

Clinton has continued the partnership strategy with respect to U.S.–Russian relations. Even more explicitly than Bush, he has tied the success of such a partnership to the success of Russia's attempt to build a democratic political system and a capitalist economy. In corresponding fashion, Clinton has substantially increased U.S. assistance to Russia.[3] Also more explicitly than Bush, Clinton has equated Yeltsin with democracy in Russia and interpreted the goal of support for democracy in Russia in terms of support for the Yeltsin government. This approach has come under increasing strain as the democratic shortcomings of Yeltsin's rule have become more and more marked. The Clinton team has also maintained the basic policy line established by Bush with respect to the other Soviet successor states. The administration attempts to support democratic and market reforms where they are occurring and has increased U.S. assistance aimed at building democracy in some countries of the region such as Ukraine, Moldova, Kazakhstan, and Kyrgyzstan.

In Africa, the one region of the world where a widespread democratic trend is present but the United States does not have significant economic or security interests, democracy promotion has become a central element of U.S. policy. Unlike in Eastern Europe or Latin America, the Bush administration incorporated democracy promotion into its Africa policy not to help strengthen a broader economic and security relationship but rather as an end in itself, with vaguely humanitarian overtones. The personal involvement of Bush and Baker in the policy, as a result, was much lower than in the other regions. Nonetheless, the administration's actual measures of support for democracy in Africa were significant. The administration reconfigured long-standing U.S. economic assistance relationships in the region to reward those governments undertaking democratic reforms. Each U.S. embassy in Africa was instructed by the State Department to formulate a democracy promotion strategy. The U.S. Agency for International Development (USAID) created a number of major assistance programs to support the many democratic transitions. And in some countries where recalcitrant strongmen resisted the regional democratic trend, such as Kenya and Malawi, the Bush administration exerted substantial diplomatic pressure for democratic change.

Clinton's Africa policy has been largely similar with regard to the role accorded to democracy promotion. The administration seeks to support the ongoing trend toward democracy in many African countries, out of the general belief that democratization will improve the lives of everyday Africans and in the long run lead to greater stability in a conflict-ridden continent. The various Bush initiatives to support the democratic trend in Africa have been continued without significant change and U.S. military training assistance in the region now has an explicit democracy promotion element.

The Clinton team came to power with some partly formed intentions to move U.S. policy to a more active pro-democracy stance in certain African countries where its members felt the Bush administration had not done enough. The opportunities for such change have turned out to be minimal. In Zaire, the Clinton administration has not altered the relatively passive policy line followed by Bush, because of both a lack of high-level interest in Zaire among Clinton officials and the absence of any credible alternative policy approach. In Nigeria, the administration has given somewhat more attention to the reestablishment of elected civilian rule, although the changes in U.S. policy have only been small, evolutionary steps and are largely in response to the 1993 elections and their aftermath. In Angola, the Clinton administration moved initially to improve relations with the Angolan government but soon realized the limitations of such an approach and settled into the same mediator role between the Angolan government and the National Union for the Total Independence of Angola (UNITA) that was developed by the Bush administration.

## Institutionalizing Democracy Promotion

With the singular exception of Haiti, therefore, Clinton has not, relative to Bush, substantially increased the U.S. emphasis on democracy promotion in any country or region. Democracy promotion has not become the central organizing principle of U.S. policy, as Clinton's rhetoric often suggests. The Clinton approach in practice is a moderate, semirealist one in which democracy promotion alternately surfaces and submerges depending on the context. Where U.S. economic and security interests correlate with the advance of democracy and a democratic trend is occurring, U.S. policy incorporates democracy promotion. Where U.S. interests necessitate working relationships with nondemocratic governments and where no democratic trend is evident, U.S. policy largely eschews it.

When pressed to identify differences between the Clinton and Bush policies relating to democracy promotion, Clinton officials, after highlighting the Haiti intervention, tend to point to their administration's efforts to institutionalize democracy promotion in the policy-making process. They speak of this effort as an attempt to embed democracy promotion permanently into the foreign policy machinery. And they argue that it may prove to be a crucial, albeit not very visible, Clinton legacy in foreign policy.

This institutionalization effort was initially related to a policy review directive, known as "PRD 26," that was to help define the place of democracy promotion in the Clinton foreign policy. In 1993 the Clinton team devoted considerable interagency effort to PRD 26 as part of its overall foreign policy review process. A draft was produced but never finalized, apparently out of a lack of high-level interest and of any real pressing need to get it done. In any event, a number of institutional measures have been implemented, including creating deputy assistant secretary of state positions with democracy promotion portfolios in the regional bureaus of the State Department, creating a directorship for democracy promotion on the National Security Council staff, converting the Bureau for Human Rights and Humanitarian Affairs of the State Department into the Bureau for Democracy, Human Rights and Labor, establishing a mid-level interagency working group on democracy, and restructuring the international affairs budget of the executive branch to consolidate and highlight democracy-related activities.

The creation of new positions with explicit democracy promotion portfolios and the reformulation of the human rights bureau at the State Department have not had any identifiable impact on the policy process. And the interagency working group on democracy has established only a minor role for itself as a mechanism for coordinating budgetary matters and sharing information between agencies. These efforts to institutionalize democracy promotion in the policy-making process inevitably run into the general difficulty in the U.S. foreign policy bureaucracy of wresting policy control away from the regional bureaus in favor of "thematic" bureaus. More fundamentally, however, these efforts face the fact that by the time Clinton was elected, democracy promotion issues had already been significantly factored into the U.S. policy process. State Department career officials who were involved in democracy promotion policies during the Bush and Reagan administrations comment in private that the issue is not so much how the new positions and portfolios can gain influence in the policy-making process as whether they have anything new to add to it.

The restructuring of the international affairs budget is also of limited significance. The restructuring groups the many different parts of the international affairs budget under six clearly stated objectives, one of which is "Building Democracy." The restructuring was closely tied to the Clinton administration's proposed rewrite of the foreign assistance act, the "Peace, Prosperity and Democracy Act of 1994." With the Republican takeover of the House and Senate, however, the administration's foreign assistance rewrite died in its tracks. As a result, the budget restructuring process is limited to being essentially a relabeling process rather than a mechanism for changing actual budget priorities.

The Clinton administration has strengthened the place of democracy promotion within U.S. foreign assistance. USAID Administrator Brian Atwood came the agency in 1993 from a democracy promotion organization, the National Democratic Institute for International Affairs. Under his leadership USAID has made democracy promotion one of the four core elements of its overall strategy of promoting sustainable development. Specific measures relating to the upgrading of the role of democracy promotion in U.S. foreign assistance include establishing a Center for Democracy and Governance within the new USAID Bureau for Global Programs, instructing all USAID missions to give increased attention to democracy promotion, and giving greater weight to the democratic status of recipient governments in decisions about allocating assistance.

Although the push in this direction is significant, it represents the bolstering of an ongoing trend rather than the charting of a new course in U.S. foreign assistance. Starting in the mid-1980s, USAID and the U.S. Information Agency increasingly funded programs aimed at democracy promotion. By the end of the Bush years, democracy promotion was an important element of U.S. foreign assistance in every region of the world except the Middle East. Given the overall pressure on the foreign aid budget in 1993 and 1994, the Clinton administration was not able to increase substantially the level of funds devoted to democracy assistance in any region other than the former Soviet Union. Moreover, with USAID itself under heavy attack by the Republicans in Congress and with foreign aid on the chopping block, the long-term significance of the various changes introduced by the Clinton team at USAID is highly uncertain.

## A Notable Consensus

The argument that Clinton has done little different from Bush with respect to promoting democracy abroad should not be taken as a criticism. The gap between Clinton's rhetoric and actual policies in this domain reflects more the excesses of the former than the shortcomings of the latter. The convergence between Clinton and Bush on democracy promotion is a positive sign that a reasonable, bipartisan consensus exists in practice on an important issue in post–Cold War U.S. foreign policy.

There remain some dissenting voices, generally from the realist and idealist ends of the policy debate. Realists, ever determined to eradicate moralism from U.S. foreign policy, have overreacted to Clinton's over-the-top democracy rhetoric and to the singular case of Haiti and call for a scaling back of U.S. concern with democracy abroad.[4] Idealists, angry with Clinton about China and concerned about the rising anti-internationalist sentiments in the Republican Party, proclaim the need for a redoubling of U.S. attention to democracy and human rights abroad.[5] Neither side's urgings are particularly persuasive.

It is not apparent what the United States would gain from doing much less than it is to promote democracy abroad. Where strong U.S. economic or security interests conflict with promoting democracy, such as in Asia and the Middle East, U.S. policy already subordinates democracy quite thoroughly. Abandoning U.S. concern for the successful consolidation of democracy in Eastern Europe and Latin America would undercut significant economic and security interests and represent a remarkable failure to seize a defining historical moment in those regions. Reducing the already modest U.S. efforts to promote democracy in Africa would at best result in some small, short-term savings of money. In Russia a plausible alternative to the current policy does exist—the neo-containment strategy advocated by some U.S. conservatives, in which the United States would deemphasize the goal of partnership, reduce the attachment to Yeltsin, and instead focus on setting tough limits on Russia's external behavior.[6] The debate between advocates of such a neo-containment strategy and proponents of the current approach is not, however, over *whether* democracy in Russia should be a goal of U.S. policy but rather *how* that goal should be attained. The advocates of neo-containment believe that democracy in Russia should be a long-term goal of U.S. policy but that it can come about only if the United States actively limits the assertion of Russian power and influence among its neighbors. They also recommend a hard-line policy toward Russia on the basis that it will help make democracy possible in the other states of the former Soviet Union by ensuring the sovereignty of those states.

At the same time, there is not much case to be made that the United States can or should be doing much more than it currently is to promote democracy abroad. A sudden shift to aggressive, pro-democratic campaigns in countries where democracy promotion is not currently a significant part of U.S. policy, such as Saudi Arabia, Egypt, China, or Indonesia, would be futile and almost certainly counterproductive to overall U.S. interests. Where democracy promotion is already a significant element of U.S. policy, little room exists to increase its role still further. Although many governments in Eastern Europe, Latin America, Africa, and the former Soviet Union appreciate U.S. support for democracy, they do not necessarily want and would not necessarily tolerate a qualitatively higher level of U.S. government involvement in their affairs. Furthermore, the actual levers available to the United States to foster democracy abroad are really quite few. U.S. assistance programs to support democracy could in principle be increased. Dramatic moves in this regard are highly unlikely, however, given the lack of U.S. domestic support for increased foreign assistance and the limited absorptive capacity of many of the institutions that are the targets of such aid.

The conclusion that the Clinton administration has ended up somewhere near the reasonable middle on democracy promotion is important given the heavy criticism to which Clinton's foreign policy has been subjected over the past several years. The criticisms have been so numerous, and often so reflexive, that it is easy to lose track of what the problems actually are. There have certainly been shortcomings in Clinton's foreign policy, shortcomings endlessly chewed over in the critical debates in Washington about Bosnia, Somalia, North Korea, Haiti, and Rwanda. They include the Clinton team's painful uncertainty about the use of force, its overly enthusiastic embrace of multilateralism and humanitarian intervention, and its unchanging habit of pursuing foreign policy by reaction. And the problems are not just the result of some weak advisers, they also lie with Clinton himself—his lack of engagement in international affairs, his habit of raising unrealistic expectations for U.S. action, and his instinct for weak compromises in the face of difficulty. Although they are many, however, the flaws of Clinton's foreign policy do not stem from or even relate substantially to democracy promotion and its place in U.S. policy.

The newly empowered Republicans in Congress, as well as the Republican sharks already circling in the 1996 electoral waters, should bear this point in mind. In their determination to reverse the aspects of Clinton's foreign policy they do not like, they may mistakenly see democracy promotion as a characteristic Clintonian element of U.S. foreign policy. This is an error that the Clinton people themselves have helped foster by having labored to portray democracy promotion as the Democrats' distinctive cause. The Republican critics may incorrectly associate democracy promotion with what they perceive as a misguided muddle of "feel-good" tendencies in the Clinton foreign policy, such as multilateralism and humanitarianism, rather than recognize it as a solidly bipartisan policy component that actually took shape under Republican administrations.

**Persistent Mistakes**

If the Clinton administration is placing a reasonable level of emphasis in practice on promoting democracy abroad, why is there a prevalent sense of unease and uncertainty about the issue in the U.S. policy community? Partly this is due to the tendency described above for Clinton's democracy promotion efforts to suffer from a general association with his various foreign policy shortcomings. But it goes deeper than that. Although a consensus is identifiable on the overall *place* of democracy promotion in U.S. foreign policy, significant problems remain with respect to *how* the U.S. government goes about constructing and implementing democracy promotion policies.

In the first place, pro-democracy rhetoric is badly overused. The Clinton administration, and to a lesser but still significant extent the Bush administration before it, has been addicted to sweeping statements about promoting democracy abroad that simply do not correspond to policy reality. The overexpansive rhetoric not only fails to stir up any noticeable public enthusiasm, it also has distinct negative consequences. The rhetoric leads to high expectations about U.S. policy, which when unfulfilled result in self-inflicted wounds of considerable severity. China is a clear case in point. The Clinton administration bled profusely and publicly over its decision about renewing China's MFN status in 1994. Because it was making policy against the grain of its own earlier rhetoric, the administration ended up appearing to have suffered a defeat, even though it was making a decision that conformed to its actual intentions and wishes.

Furthermore, although the rhetorical emphasis on democracy promotion is intended to cast the United States as a principled actor in the world, it has the contradictory effect of calling attention to its inconsistencies and saddling it with the reputation of hypocrisy. Exceptions speak louder than rules in policy making when the rules are set forth as grandiose moral principles. Few foreigners are much impressed by U.S. insistence on a global mission to help others and in fact tend to be particularly suspicious of any powerful country that claims to act in the name of anything other than its tangible, material interests.

Second, built into U.S. policies of democracy promotion is the mistaken assumption that the United States can without too much effort have a significant influence on the political evolution of other societies. Americans cling to this assumption despite decades of contrary experiences in countries in all parts of the world. It was fueled with respect to democracy promotion by the experience of the 1980s. The U.S. government adopted both rhetorical and sometimes substantive policies of democracy promotion during the years when democracy was making its most noticeable gains around the world. The fact that in most regions U.S. efforts to promote democracy were largely responses to rather than causes of democratic transitions got lost in the excitement. Americans got in the habit in those years of taking far too much credit for the democratic transitions in Latin America, Asia, Africa, and Eastern Europe.

In the past several years the democracy market has cooled considerably. Democratization is deeply troubled in Russia, much slower than expected in Eastern Europe, marked by frightening bumps in Latin America, very mixed in Africa, and often defied in Asia. Just as the United States took too much credit for the rise of democracy in the 1980s, now it takes on itself too much blame for the leveling off or even downward trend. The Clinton administration is almost inevitably held responsible for the direction of events that are only marginally subject to U.S. influence.

Third, a number of habitual mistakes mark the specific tactics and tools the U.S. government employs in attempting to promote democracy abroad. One principal error is the U.S. tendency in a transitional country to equate a particular leader with democracy and to assume that steadfast support for that leader is the best means of promoting democracy. Through such policies the U.S. government often gives too little support to the systemic reforms that are needed for real democratization, alienates other political forces in the society, and holds onto leaders in decline long after they have been discredited domestically.

Related to this "Great Leader" approach to promoting democracy is a pattern of the U.S. government focusing far too much on formal institutions as the essential elements of democratization at the expense of underlying values and processes. U.S. officials will make much of the fact that a new constitution has been promulgated in a transitional country rather than examining how the constitution was arrived at or how much it embodies an actual sociopolitical consensus. They will extol an election with little attention to the more complex realities of actual political participation. They will herald a new parliament while knowing little of the actual relations between the parliament and the citizenry. Supporting democracy too often resembles the application of a preprinted checklist in which the institutional forms of U.S.-style democracy are financed and praised, while the more complex and more important underlying realities of political life are ignored.

U.S. assistance programs aimed at building democracy abroad have made positive contributions in specific sectors in many countries. Although the U.S. organizations involved in such assistance have begun to try to incorporate lessons from experience into the design and implementation of their projects, this general area of assistance often seems stuck at the first slope of the learning curve. Democracy assistance projects too frequently involve giving funds primarily to Americans for the delivery of costly technical assistance ill-suited to local circumstances. The projects rarely seem to build on one another but are instead discrete undertakings with little interrelation or follow-up. They often emphasize high-visibility activities that seem designed less to meet the needs of the recipient countries than to play well in Washington, in particular to satisfy the unrealistic demands of a Congress determined to see an immediate impact for taxpayer dollars spent abroad.

U.S. policy toward Russia since 1991 vividly embodies all of these problems with U.S. democracy promotion policies. The rhetorical line of U.S. policy—the bold emphasis on U.S. commitment to democracy in Russia—created expectations both in Russia and the United States far in excess of the actual weight of the policy. The policy was built on a serious overestimation of the capacity or ability of the United States to affect the evolution of Russian political life. The United States became far too attached to a single leader as the putative key to democracy. The policy has placed excessive weight on formal institutions in Russian political life rather than underlying values and processes. And the U.S. assistance programs in Russia specifically aimed at promoting democracy have fallen into all of the traps outlined above.

**The Successor to Containment?**

Is democracy promotion "the logical successor to containment," the organizing principle for post–Cold War U.S. foreign policy? With its words the Clinton administration has suggested that it is. But with its deeds the administration has confirmed that it is not. Democracy promotion does serve both moral and pragmatic interests for the United States abroad. It does not, however, represent a grand synthesis of idealism and realism that can operate as a controlling framework for U.S. policy. Neither the moral nor the pragmatic element is strong enough.

Americans prize the notion of their country as a uniquely selfless, principled actor in the world. They are unlikely, however, to find "doing good" a sufficient basis for sustained, costly international engagement in the years to come. During the Cold War, Americans were willing to expend large-scale human and financial resources on problems in small, distant countries less because of a broad moral concern for others than because they could be persuaded that those problems were component parts of a larger threat to their country's security. As a moral enterprise, promoting democracy abroad simply does not provide an adequate level of motivational "traction" for an internationalist foreign policy.

The pragmatic side of democracy promotion exists, but it is hardly overwhelming. Clinton and his advisers are inordinately fond of inserting into policy speeches a standardized litany of good things that democracies do—ranging from not going to war with each other to making better trade partners—as testament to the pragmatic nature of the U.S. interest in promoting democracy abroad. Although this litany is appealing and true at a very general level, democracy promotion does not have the necessary pragmatic reach to serve as a general policy framework. The fact remains that in many significant instances U.S. economic and security interests are quite separate from or even in conflict with a U.S. interest in spreading democracy abroad. Moreover, although it is true that democracies tend not to go to war with one another, it does not follow that democracy promotion is a workable basis for U.S. security policy.[7] Democracy promotion is not, for example, a viable response to the security threats currently presented by North Korea, Iraq, and Iran. Similarly, although democracies may make better trade partners, it is not clear that promoting democracy abroad has much to do with ensuring U.S. international competitiveness in the increasingly challenging international economic environment.

Democracy promotion is a necessary and important element of U.S. policy in the post–Cold War period. It is, however, only one of several major elements of U.S. policy. It does not and cannot serve as a controlling framework or central organizing principle.

The deeper message of this analysis is that the search for a "logical successor to containment" is a misleading quest. There is a rising nostalgia these days for the apparent clarity and simplicity of the Cold War anticommunist framework. Without a singular, overarching threat to U.S. security, however, there simply cannot be a singular, overarching U.S. policy framework. Moreover, in their anxiety about the present Americans must be careful not to gild the past. It is easy to forget how often the overly reductionistic nature of the anticommunist framework was misleading—how often the United States misjudged conflicts and other events around the world because it reflexively applied a simplistic political framework at the expense of understanding dominant local factors of nationalism, religion, ethnicity, historical traditions, or regional dynamics. A democracy promotion framework, or any single-issue framework, will lead to the same sort of mistakes.

The United States must realize that the felt need to replace anticommunism with a new, grand organizing principle—particularly one that reduces intricate local realities to simplified contests between good and evil and is based on the global projection of American values—is itself a vestige of the Cold War. Americans should be energized rather than bewildered by the absence of any overarching threat to U.S. security. They should accept that the world is a complex, heterogeneous mass not defined by any single fault line or trend. They should strive to understand political and economic events around the world on their own terms rather than in American terms. If the United States makes such adjustments, Americans will see that any workable framework for U.S. policy in this new era must inevitably be a messy list of cross-cutting issues and competing priorities rather than a gleaming, unified vision. What is lost in elegance and simplicity, however, will be gained back many times in utility.

## Notes

The Carnegie Endowment gratefully acknowledges the permission of MIT Press Journals to reprint this article, which originally appeared in *The Washington Quarterly*, vol. 18, no. 4 (Autumn 1995).

1. Bill Clinton, "A New Covenant for American Security," speech delivered at Georgetown University, Washington, D.C., December 12, 1991.
2. Anthony Lake, "From Containment to Enlargement," speech delivered at Johns Hopkins University, Washington, D.C., September 21, 1993. Reprinted in *Foreign Policy Bulletin* 4 (November–December 1993).
3. Jeremy D. Rosner, "Clinton, Congress, and Assistance to Russia and the NIS," *SAIS Review* 15 (Winter–Spring 1995).
4. David C. Hendrickson, "The Recovery of Internationalism," *Foreign Affairs* 73 (September/October 1994), and "The Democratist Crusade: Intervention, Economic Sanctions, and Engagement," *World Policy Journal* 11 (Winter–Spring 1995).
5. Tony Smith, "In Defense of Intervention," *Foreign Affairs* 73 (November/December 1994); Holly J. Burkhalter, "The 'Costs' of Human Rights," *World Policy Journal* 9 (Spring 1994).
6. Zbigniew Brzezinski, "The Premature Partnership," *Foreign Affairs* 73 (March/April 1994).
7. Thomas Carothers, "The Democracy Nostrum," *World Policy Journal* 11 (Fall 1994); Edward Mansfield and Jack Snyder, "Democratization and War," *Foreign Affairs* 74 (May/June 1995).

# CHAPTER THREE

# The Clinton Record on Democracy Promotion (2000)

MANY FOREIGN POLICY themes have come and gone in the Clinton years, from assertive multilateralism and humanitarian intervention to strategic partnerships and the indispensable nation. One theme, however, has stayed the course. As a presidential candidate in 1992, Bill Clinton made democracy promotion the organizing concept of his proposed foreign policy. Throughout his presidency he and his top advisers have returned to the theme again and again. They have sounded the Wilsonian trumpet on democracy, but also argued that it is rooted in *realpolitik*, that in the post–Cold War world American ideals and interests have fused. In nearly every major foreign policy address they cite a host of ways that the spread of democracy abroad advances "hard" U.S. security and economic interests, from reducing the chances of war to decreasing terrorism.

With the Clinton era nearly over, an assessment of the Clinton record on democracy promotion is due. It is obvious that the policy has not lived up to the expansive rhetoric—policy so rarely does—but the question remains as to the nature of the relationship between words and deeds in this domain. What role has democracy promotion actually played in Clinton's foreign policy? Where has the administration pursued democracy and where has it not? And why? Although the issue may appear as just so much talk to some, it is widely present in U.S. policy. Just in the past six months, for example, the issue has cropped up in many places. In Peru, the administration has clashed sharply with President Alberto Fujimori over his manipulation of the presidential elections.

Administration officials, U.S. legislators, and policy pundits argued earlier this year over how extending permanent normal trading status to China would affect that country's democratic prospects. The election of Vladimir Putin to the Russian presidency prompted some analysts to question whether U.S. democracy promotion efforts had failed in Russia and whether those efforts should be continued. Secretary of State Madeleine Albright declared her desire to see Serbian President Slobodan Milosevic out of power before the end of the year and, in the name of democracy, has upped U.S. support to the Serbian opposition. When President Clinton went to South Asia in the spring, the wisdom of a presidential stopover in Pakistan was debated in terms of whether it would bolster the legitimacy of the military government there and lessen the prospects for a return to civilian rule. In Warsaw in June, more than 80 foreign ministers met at the first "Community of Democracies" meeting, an effort spearheaded by the administration to bolster worldwide acceptance of a democratic norm.

Only by assessing the actual extent to which democracy promotion has played a role in Clinton's policies is it possible to arrive at some judgment of the significance of those efforts and to identify both major accomplishments and missed opportunities. And that undertaking in turn points to the question of how the next administration—whether Democratic or Republican—is likely to take on the issue of democracy promotion, and what approach would be best.

### Semirealism Rediscovered

No simple, black-and-white judgment of the Clinton record on democracy is possible. U.S. policies on democracy vary sharply from region to region, ranging from serious engagement to almost complete disinterest. Moreover, democracy promotion is pursued both as "high policy" and "low policy," and the degree of engagement at one level often does not correspond with that on the other. Furthermore, the Clinton approach has changed over time, in response to political developments in the world and at home.

The uneven nature of the U.S. commitment to fostering democracy abroad is striking. Several regions or countries stand out on the positive side of the ledger. In Latin America, the Clinton administration, largely following the line set out in the Bush administration, has supported ongoing transitions to democracy and market economics in the belief that a democratic, prosperous hemisphere will best serve U.S. security interests. The administration has spoken out clearly and often on the importance of democracy, helped head off coup threats in Guatemala, Paraguay, and Ecuador, sponsored aid programs to shore up shaky transitions, and tried to push the Organization of American States to take an active role in democracy promotion. Yet the democracy component of

U.S. policy in Latin America is hardly seamless. Across most of the 1990s, for example, the United States maintained close ties to President Fujimori, despite his antidemocratic tendencies, because of his cooperative stance on U.S. antinarcotics efforts. Nevertheless, even many Latin Americans long hostile to U.S. involvement in their countries' internal affairs acknowledge that the United States is now, on balance, a pro-democratic force in Latin America.

Similarly, in Eastern Europe, the Clinton policy line, following that set out by the Bush administration, rests on the view that U.S. interests in democracy, market economics, and security work together. Except in former Yugoslavia, where, as discussed below, democracy has often been a secondary concern, the Clinton administration has emphasized democracy at the diplomatic level and continued many aid programs designed to bolster postcommunist transitions to democracy. Although the root motivation behind the decision to expand the North Atlantic Treaty Organization (NATO) into Central Europe remains an item of debate, at some level NATO expansion represents another element of a policy aimed at "locking in" democracy where it has been achieved in Eastern Europe.

The Clinton administration ratcheted up the place of democracy promotion in U.S. policy toward Russia soon after taking office and devoted real attention to the issue across the span of Boris Yeltsin's rule. As in Latin America and Eastern Europe, the guiding concept was the integration of political, economic, and security goals. Democracy promotion in Russia encountered substantial limitations and tensions in practice. Supporting democracy became a policy of supporting Yeltsin, which put the administration in some awkward spots—such as downplaying large-scale Russian human rights violations in the first war in Chechnya, lauding a presidential election in 1996 marked by significant flaws, and alienating various parts of the Russian democratic political spectrum not closely associated with Yeltsin or with favored groups of reformers. Still, the U.S. commitment to bolstering Russian democracy was real and occupied the attention of senior policy makers.

On the other side of the ledger, a number of equally prominent cases stand out in which the Clinton administration has downplayed democracy. It was China that first took the wind out of the sails of Clinton's early billowing rhetoric about democracy promotion. The administration's 1994 decision to delink human rights and trade effectively meant that human rights, and by extension democracy, would stay at the margins of Clinton's China policy. As the administration intensified its push this year to rebuild U.S.–China relations on the basis of commercial engagement, Clinton officials played up the idea that increased U.S. trade and investment in China would be an important force for political liberalization. Although this idea may have some validity in the long term, it is obvious that Clinton's China policy is primarily about economics and that the democracy rationale is very much an add-on.

In Indonesia, the administration maintained the long-standing U.S. friend-ship with President Suharto—reflecting the traditional U.S. view of Suharto as a politically flawed but nonetheless valuable economic and security partner—right up to the last few weeks and even days before his fall in 1998. In Egypt, Saudi Arabia, and other Middle Eastern countries, this administration has pre-served close U.S. ties with autocratic regimes that serve U.S. interests on oil, the Arab–Israeli peace process, and resistance to Islamic fundamentalist groups. In Central Asia and the Caucasus, the tantalizing vision of huge, newly discov-ered oil and gas reserves spurred the administration, at least until the last year or two, to take a soft line toward most of the strongmen regimes, most notably in Kazakhstan and Azerbaijan. In Africa, Clinton officials enthused for a pe-riod in the mid-1990s over the soft authoritarian regimes in Uganda, Rwanda, and Ethiopia, seizing upon the briefly florescent concept of "Africa's new lead-ers" in the hope that they could deliver regional stability and order.

This divided ledger highlights the fact that, despite the many assertions by Clinton and his top foreign policy advisers that America's ideals and interests in the world are now harmonious, serious conflicts of interest still exist. Eco-nomic and security interests of various types, from access to national resources to regional security issues, still collide with U.S. interest in democracy in many places. The core strategic approach of U.S. policy under Clinton remains what it has been for decades, a semirealist balancing of sometimes competing and sometimes complementary interests. Where democracy appears to fit in well with U.S. security and economic interests, the United States promotes democ-racy. Where democracy clashes with other significant interests, it is downplayed or even ignored. And where the United States has few identifiable economic or security interests of any real consequence—as in large parts of Africa, for ex-ample—the United States will give some attention to democracy out of a gen-eral idealistic impulse but usually not commit major financial or human re-sources to the task.

## Institutionalizing Democracy Promotion

A second element of the Clinton record on democracy promotion renders the already highly varied picture more complex: the gradual institutionalization of democracy promotion mechanisms and mindsets within the policy bureaucracy. This is a process that began during the Reagan years, continued under Bush, then accelerated under Clinton. Evidence of the process is found in many places. The Clinton administration created various democracy promotion positions and offices at the State Department and the U.S. Agency for International Development (USAID) and set up several interagency groups to coordinate democracy programs and policies. The administration reorganized the international affairs budget around strategic priorities and made democracy building one of those priorities. U.S. missions abroad are now required to produce an annual performance plan, one component of which is a democracy promotion strategy. Throughout the policy bureaucracy, U.S. officials are much more conversant with, engaged in, and often serious about democracy-related issues than they were ten or even five years ago.

The most substantial element of this process of institutionalization is the large growth in aid for democracy—assistance programs explicitly designed to foster or bolster democratic institutions and processes. The current wave of U.S. democracy aid began under Reagan but multiplied exponentially under Clinton, from around $100 million annually ten years ago to more than $700 million today. In approximately 100 countries around the world, a raft of U.S. government agencies, quasigovernmental organizations (such as the National Endowment for Democracy and the Eurasia Foundation), and nongovernmental organizations (NGOs) operating with public funds are promoting free and fair elections, sponsoring judicial and legislative reform, supporting independent media, encouraging decentralization, underwriting advocacy NGOs, and pursuing other elements of a by now familiar international agenda of democracy aid. The effects of these programs are usually modest and sometimes paltry. They rarely determine political outcomes or fundamentally reshape political systems. Nonetheless, they positively affect the skills and outlook of thousands of political actors in other countries and over the long term contribute to helping democratization advance.

For the most part, the institutionalization of democracy promotion in the policy and aid bureaucracies—what can be considered the "low policy" side of the picture—fits within the "high policy" framework. Where the United States has defined its overall diplomatic line as one that seeks actively to back democracy, these programs help fill out the policy. In Peru this year, for example, the forthright election monitoring carried out by the National Democratic Institute (NDI) and the Carter Center in the run-up to the first round of presidential balloting provided the State Department with a strong basis for taking a tough line on President Fujimori's manipulation of the process. In some cases, however, low policy quietly operates against the main current of high policy. While the U.S. government maintained cordial relations with President Tudjman of Croatia in the mid-1990s, the NDI worked extensively to train those Croatian political parties not linked with Tudjman. When Tudjman died in 1999, the activists and parties that NDI had worked with emerged quickly as major actors on the new political scene. Similar examples could be cited from Indonesia, Kazakhstan, Vietnam, and elsewhere.

## Change Over Time

Still another complicating factor is the fact that Clinton's policies in this realm have shifted over time. Setting aside the pro-democracy rhetorical framework, which has been largely constant, the actual level of attention to democracy has increased somewhat, especially since 1997. In some cases, political develop-ments—sometimes positive, sometimes negative—in other countries have spurred greater U.S. attention to democracy building. After dictators fell in Indonesia and Nigeria, for example, the administration shifted gears to broadly promote democracy in those two countries and now counts them as two (along with Ukraine and Colombia) of four priority countries for democracy promo-tion. Sometimes it is democratic backsliding rather than breakthroughs that prompt a new look. For example, in contrast to a fairly forgiving U.S. approach to democracy in Central Asia in the first half of the 1990s, Secretary of State Madeleine Albright came down hard on the issue during her trip to the region this year. Albright's advisers explain the new tougher line as a result in part of the accumulated backsliding of democracy in the region and the sense that some threshold of political decay had been crossed, especially in the former democratic bright spot, Kyrgyzstan.

In other contexts, a changed security situation has provoked a different line on democracy. During the war in Bosnia, for example, U.S. policy toward Serbia, Croatia, and the rest of former Yugoslavia had little to do with democracy. The administration felt it was necessary to deal cooperatively with Milosevic in Belgrade and Tudjman in Zagreb, dictators though they might be, for the sake of peacemaking goals. After the Kosovo crisis and NATO military action there, however, promoting democracy in Serbia—or at least ousting Milosevic—became something of a priority. And with Tudjman gone, the administration is now openly enthusiastic about democracy building in Croatia (though short of resources for the task).

Personnel changes in Washington as well as political developments abroad have also moved the Clinton administration toward a somewhat greater em-brace of democracy concerns. Secretary of State Albright is the only top offi-cial in either the first or second Clinton administration who has demonstrated a searching, sustained interest in democracy promotion. Albright has had to face some major limitations on her role as secretary of state—a president only inter-mittently engaged in foreign affairs, a cautious national security adviser with the ear of the president, an aggressive Treasury Department with a lock on international economic policy, and a Defense Department determined to control military-related security issues. Moreover, the Kosovo crisis took up most of one full year of her tenure. Nevertheless, she has stayed with the theme and helped connect high and low policy in a pro-democratic direction in various places, such as Peru, Pakistan, Serbia, and Central Asia.

It should be noted that the Republican-controlled Congress has done little to increase the place of democracy building in U.S. policy. With their aversion to or even disdain for international issues, the 1994 House Republicans have been suspicious of any U.S. commitments abroad beyond certain basic security arrangements. They are prone to lump democracy promotion together with the humanitarian interventions they so much dislike and seem at times willfully ignorant of the fact that democracy promotion is not a Clintonian do-gooder invention. Congress's constant cutting of the international affairs budget has inevitably crimped what is possible on democracy promotion. After Indonesia and Nigeria launched potentially historic democratic transitions in 1998, for example, the administration had trouble coming up with funds to support new democracy aid programs in those countries. Only by taking money away from already lightly funded democracy-building activities in other countries was the administration able to create special initiatives in those two important transitions.

## The Balance Sheet

The Clinton administration clearly fell short of its lofty rhetorical aspirations on democracy. It neither fundamentally revised the semirealist framework of U.S. policy nor devoted high-level attention to the topic in a broad, sustained fashion. Democracy concerns have, however, played a supporting but genuine role in U.S. policy toward many countries and merged with U.S. economic and security interests in more places than ever before. The institutionalization of democracy programs and policies within the policy and aid bureaucracies has accelerated under Clinton, and a tendency toward somewhat increased attention to the issue is evident in the last several years.

To assess the significance of Clinton policies in this domain and identify the major accomplishments and shortcomings, it is useful to take a brief look at the overall state of democracy in the world. In the early 1990s, democracy was dramatically on the rise, and facile assumptions about a major U.S. role in that trend were easy to make. The state of the "worldwide democratic trend" is today rather more sobering, leading to less expansive views about the U.S. causal role.

Of the nearly 100 countries that experienced political openings in the 1980s or early 1990s and were counted by exultant democracy promoters as part of democracy's "Third Wave," only a small number have succeeded in consolidating democracy. These are the dozen or so relatively affluent countries of Central Europe, East Asia, and the Southern Cone of Latin America. And only a few new countries have joined the Third Wave since the early 1990s, most notably Indonesia, Nigeria, and Mexico. Most of the transitional countries are still far from liberal democracy. Some of them, such as Belarus, Uzbekistan, Tunisia, and Côte d'Ivoire, have slipped back to outright authoritarianism, raising doubts about whether they should have been considered transitional in the first place. Many of them are stuck awkwardly in a gray zone between democracy and dictatorship, with democratic forms but little real democratic substance. Whole regions have made disappointingly little democratic progress to date in the Third Wave. Central Asia and the Caucasus are dominated by undemocratic strongmen. A small number of African countries are making valiant efforts to preserve political pluralism work, but failed states, new interstate wars, and seemingly unending old civil wars tragically dominate large sections of the continent. The Middle East remains a political backwater, with political liberalization visible only in a few places. Although Latin America seemed a few years ago to be firmly in the democratic camp, a whole subregion—the Andean countries of Venezuela, Colombia, Ecuador, and Peru, as well as Paraguay—is unnervingly close to democratic breakdown.

It is tempting for some commentators simply to ascribe blame or credit for the overall state of democracy in the world to whichever U.S. administration is in power. Democracy on the rise—kudos to the administration! Democracy losing ground—what are those idiots in Washington doing! Certainly at some very general levels—as guarantor of a security framework in many regions and as bedrock of the international economy—the United States helps create the underlying conditions of peace and prosperity in which democracy can flourish. Yet the direct effects of U.S. policies on the success or failure of democracy in most countries are usually fairly limited. The difficulties that have plagued so many of the attempted democratic transitions around the world are for the most part internal factors on which outside actors can have only secondary influence: Such factors include deeply rooted psychological legacies of dictatorial rule, heavily concentrated economic power structures, and debilitatingly weak governmental institutions. And those countries that have managed to consolidate democracy in recent years have drawn primarily on their own resources, innovations, and resilience.

At the same time, it is possible to identify some ways in which U.S. policies and programs have contributed to democratization abroad in the past ten years. To start with, the strong, positive incorporation of democracy as a mutually reinforcing goal alongside U.S. economic and security interests in some places—

primarily Latin America, Eastern Europe, and Russia—has been useful. It has helped firm up the idea in these countries or regions that democracy is the normal, expected outcome; stimulate the creation of multilateral mechanisms to support democracy; and put the weight and prestige of the United States clearly on the side of democracy. This does not ensure democracy, but it is a tangible positive factor widely felt in relevant foreign political circles.

Second, active U.S. diplomatic involvement at some critical political junctures has helped keep democracy intact or increase the possibility of its return. U.S. opposition to threatened coups in Guatemala, Ecuador, Paraguay, and elsewhere in Latin America was not the only factor causing their defeat, but it was significant. U.S. pressure on Fujimori in Peru's presidential elections this year did not stop him from manipulating the process but raised the price he is paying at home and abroad for doing so. U.S. support for Georgian president Eduard Shevardnadze at several key moments helped him hold on to power. The administration's nuanced response to the recent military coup in Pakistan—attempting to blend democracy concerns with a recognition of the profound political problems of the past decade there—has not had decisive effects, but it struck the right note in unusually difficult circumstances.

Third, in dozens of countries, U.S. democracy aid programs have in small but real ways helped successful transitions advance or keep troubled transitions from closing down entirely. Aid efforts have improved the quality of many elections in Africa, Eastern Europe, Latin America, and Asia. They have helped sustain and diversify independent media in numerous countries. Although the Clinton administration's sudden, urgent enthusiasm about civil society and its promotion were overblown, U.S. aid to advocacy NGOs all around the world did stimulate some positive reforms. Similarly, although the administration's "discovery" of rule of law as a means of promoting democracy abroad was laden with simplistic assumptions, the burgeoning world of law-related programs has encouraged some countries to take seriously the need to reform legal and judicial institutions.

Alongside these positive effects are some shortcomings. The administration failed to integrate democracy concerns effectively with economic and security interests in some regions, weakening the credibility of the democracy theme overall. The administration can claim to have arrived at a China policy that successfully combines U.S. economic and security interests. Even if that is true, which is debatable, the path getting there was rocky. For years the administration failed to pursue a consistent, persuasive approach to combining human rights and democracy concerns with economic and security interests. The administration's obvious eagerness for most of its tenure to downplay the deficiencies of strongman rule in Central Asia and the Caucasus reflected a disappointing lapse into old-think about the value of "friendly tyrants." And in the Middle East the administration showed little proclivity to find a way to introduce a policy of real U.S. support for even gradual political reform.

Although the administration acted successfully at some key junctures for democracy, it did not in others. The administration uttered no words of criticism when Egyptian President Hosni Mubarak steamrolled his way through yet another national election in 1996. In Indonesia, the administration missed the chance in 1997–1998 to get out in front on democracy in Suharto's declining months. In the period immediately following the signing of the Dayton accords, Clinton and his top advisers failed to take tough measures—such as pushing for the arrest of top-level Bosnian Serb war criminals—that might have given Bosnian democracy a real chance.

Haiti was the single most visible disappointment of the Clinton administration's democracy promotion efforts, if only because it was initially touted by Clinton officials as the leading edge of the new democracy policy. Haiti was and remains a remarkably difficult place to try to build democracy, due to its catastrophic economic situation and ragged sociopolitical history. But there have also been flaws in the post-1994 U.S. effort there, including an unwillingness to push harder on some of the key political leaders and some second-rate efforts on democracy aid. More generally, the fact that the administration chose one of the least promising countries in the world to be the leading edge of its democracy policy reflects a persistent unwillingness to think strategically rather than idealistically in this domain.

### Looking Ahead

What role will democracy promotion likely play in the foreign policy of the next administration? What role should it play? Governor George Bush and his advisers are emphasizing a return to realism, promising to set America's sights firmly back on the big power issues and to stop what they see as a pattern of dispersing American resources and attention on issues of secondary importance, especially those of a humanitarian nature. Though of course not openly critical of Clinton policies, Vice President Al Gore and his advisers quietly echo elements of the same theme, stressing that the vice president is fully comfortable with geopolitical and military issues, in an implicit contrast to the president.

A certain corrective toward a greater focus on power and geopolitical strategy is natural and desirable given Clinton's shortcomings on this plane. Whichever candidate wins the White House, however, should be careful not to throw democracy promotion unthinkingly into the revisionist hopper. The Bush team in particular should not make the mistake of viewing or characterizing democracy promotion as a Clintonian concern per se. On the rhetorical level, Clinton did try to claim the term as his own. The current emphasis on democracy promotion got its start, however, in the Reagan years, and has demonstrated bipartisan appeal now for almost two decades.

Certainly democracy promotion policies must be built on realistic assumptions about the ability of the United States to affect the political direction of other societies. And the ebullient pro-democracy rhetoric should be scaled back. However, the core idea that democracy promotion is not merely an idealistic enterprise but is often integral to U.S. "hard" interests should be preserved. Slipping back to the view that democracy is merely a nice "add-on" in U.S. policy would be an unfortunate retrogression.

It is likely that the next administration will hew to the well-established policy line in Latin America and Eastern Europe of linking democracy to economic and security goals. Adverse developments in the Andean region—such as continued defiance of democratic norms by President Fujimori in Peru and democratic slippage in Venezuela—may test that policy line early on. A much bigger and less certain question is whether the next administration can settle on policies toward Russia and China that incorporate democracy concerns into the framework of a renewed focus on the larger security issues.

In Russia it is clear that, in this new Putin-led phase of Russian politics, the U.S. government should not try to engage in the same sort of domestic politicking that it did in the Yeltsin era, especially the anointing of favorites and the efforts to influence elections. Yet this does not mean returning to some "billiard ball" model of the past, which some Bush advisers seem at times to propose, in which only Russia's international behavior matters to the United States. The next administration will engage the Russian government actively on a host of security issues and might be able to maintain a constructive security dialogue even if Russia slides toward authoritarianism. But U.S. security interests will be facilitated and much improved over the long run if democracy succeeds in Russia. And the United States can still play a positive, albeit modest role in that process, by consistently articulating the belief and expectation that Russia will continue on a democratic path, speaking out forcefully if the Russian government takes openly antidemocratic actions, and expanding U.S. support for the wide-ranging but precarious universe of NGOs that are broadening sociopolitical participation in Russia.

Similarly, U.S.–China relations in this decade will be dominated by economic and security issues, however Chinese politics evolve. But as with Russia, U.S. security concerns will be ameliorated if China moves toward liberalization, pluralism, and, eventually, democracy. And though U.S. influence on that process is limited, democracy promotion should nonetheless be viewed as part of, and even integral to, the overall approach. Increased U.S. trade with and investment in China may be a force for positive political change over the long term, but there is nothing automatic about it. U.S. businesses pushing for permanent normal trade relations with China have argued that they will serve as models and leaders in China on the rule of law, transparency, accountability, and corporate social responsibility. The next administration should hold them to account on these grounds, and establish some specific advisory consultative mechanisms for doing so. The next administration must also renew and broaden U.S. human rights policy toward China, going well beyond pressure on individual dissident cases to systematic, high-level attention to religious rights, labor rights, freedom of speech, and freedom of association.

Elsewhere, in such places as Central Asia, the Caucasus, and the Middle East, the next administration should limit as much as possible the cases where it keeps democracy completely off the table for the sake of other interests. This means taking seriously even small differences between autocratic regimes that are at least attempting limited reforms and those that are completely set in their ways. Everywhere the next president must be ready to respond boldly to critical political junctures abroad—whether it is the unexpected weakening of a dictator or the threatened breakdown of a democracy—and to assume that its responses in such situations will reverberate widely. Finally the institutionalization of democracy promotion in the policy and aid bureaucracies should be continued. It is easy for those persons primarily focused on large-scale geopolitical issues to brush aside democracy aid and other such efforts as marginal. Such a view, however, ignores the fact that democratization often begins as the result of accumulated attitudinal change in publics and policy elites, change that the "low policy" methods can actually foster over time.

In short, it is well past the time to be debating the role of democracy promotion in U.S. foreign policy in simplistic realist versus idealist terms. The traditional boundaries of hard and soft U.S. interests are much less clear than before, and democracy concerns are to some extent present in U.S. policy in most countries in the world. The challenges at hand now are understanding when democratic change is likely to occur, how it will affect the full range of U.S. interests, and whether and how the United States can make a difference in trying to advance it. It is difficult to balance a sober view of the often limited ability of the United States to foster democratic change abroad with a genuine acceptance of the often integral nature of democracy in other countries to America's national interest. But achieving such a balance is the key to effective policy in this critical domain.

## Other Writings on Democracy Promotion Under Clinton

Brinkley, Douglas. "Democratic Enlargement: The Clinton Doctrine," *Foreign Policy* 106 (Spring 1997): 111–27.

Carothers, Thomas. *Aiding Democracy Abroad: The Learning Curve*. Washington, D.C.: Carnegie Endowment for International Peace, 1999.

Carothers, Thomas. "Democracy Promotion Under Clinton," *The Washington Quarterly* 18(4) (Autumn 1995): 13–28.

Cox, Michael, G. John Ikenberry, and Takashi Inoguchi, eds. *American Democracy Promotion: Impulses, Strategies, and Impacts*. Oxford, U.K.: Oxford University Press, 2000.

Dalpino, Catharin E. *Anchoring Third Wave Democracies: Prospects and Problems for U.S. Policy*. Washington, D.C.: The Institute for the Study of Diplomacy, Georgetown University, 1998.

Diamond, Larry. *Promoting Democracy in the 1990s: Actors and Instruments, Issues and Imperatives*. Washington, D.C.: Carnegie Commission on Preventing Deadly Conflict, 1995.

Hendrickson, David C. "The Democratist Crusade: Intervention, Economics Sanctions and Engagement," *World Policy Journal* 11 (Winter 1994/1995): 18–30.

Henry, Clement M. "Promoting Democracy: USAID, at Sea or off to Cyberspace?" *Middle East Policy* 5(1)(1997): 178–90.

Hook, Steven W. "'Building Democracy' Through Foreign Aid: The Limitations of United States Political Conditionalities, 1992–96," *Democratization* 5(3) (Autumn 1998): 156–80.

Kagan, Robert. "Democracy and Double Standards," *Commentary* 104(2) (August 1997): 19–26.

Ottaway, Marina, and Theresa Chung. "Debating Democracy Assistance: Toward a New Paradigm," *Journal of Democracy* 10(4) (October 1999): 99–113.

Von Hippel, Karin. *Democracy by Force: US Military Intervention in the Post–Cold War World*. Cambridge, U.K.: Cambridge University Press, 2000.

Wiarda, Howard J. *Cracks in the Consensus: Debating the Democracy Agenda in U.S. Foreign Policy*. The Washington Papers, vol. 172. Westport, Conn.: Praeger Publishers, 1997.

Zakaria, Fareed. "The Rise of Illiberal Democracy," *Foreign Affairs* 76(6) (November/December 1997): 22–43.

## Note

Originally published as Carnegie Working Paper 16 (September 2000).

# CHAPTER FOUR

# Ousting Foreign Strongmen: Lessons from Serbia (2001)

DURING HIS FINAL YEAR in power, Yugoslav leader Slobodan Milosevic found himself contending not only with rising social discontent and political opposition, but with a remarkably extensive set of Western aid initiatives aimed at speeding his ouster. When he did fall—after losing to Vojislav Kostunica in the first-round elections on September 24, 2000, then denying those results, and finally giving way in the face of enormous popular protests on October 5—Washington policy makers and aid officials celebrated. Milosevic's departure was only one step in what will inevitably be a drawn-out, difficult process of democratization in Yugoslavia. Nevertheless, it was a major breakthrough, opening the door to genuine change at all levels.

The apparent success of what Michael Dobbs recently described in the *Washington Post* as "an extraordinary U.S. effort to unseat a foreign power" raises important questions. First, was the U.S. and European aid campaign actually a key factor in Milosevic's downfall? Second, although democracy assistance is usually marginal to overall political outcomes, here it appears to have been more than that. Why? And finally, as we look forward, can the experience of democracy aid in Yugoslavia be transferred to other settings—that is, do the United States and its European allies now have a proven method for ousting strongmen leaders they dislike?

**Promoting an "Electoral Revolution"**

In the several years prior to the 1999 NATO military campaign against Yugoslavia, the U.S. government viewed Slobodan Milosevic as a pernicious political figure who was nevertheless necessary to maintaining the structure of peace in Bosnia created by the Dayton Accords. The United States funded some democracy programs for Yugoslavia in those years, but they were only small-scale. Coming out of the NATO campaign, however, Washington and other Western capitals reached a clear conclusion: it was time for Milosevic to go. Western governments asserted a policy of pressure for political change in Yugoslavia made up of three components: economic sanctions; diplomatic isolation (including the indictment of Milosevic by the International Criminal Tribunal for the former Yugoslavia); and, most actively, significant amounts of aid to promote what U.S. democracy promoters liked to call "an electoral revolution."

The aid strategy was rooted in the belief that a political transition in Yugoslavia was more likely to occur through elections than through a popular revolt. This strategy built on previous election-oriented campaigns against strongmen in the region, notably Vladimir Meciar in Slovakia and Franjo Tudjman in Croatia, though it had deeper roots, back to at least the U.S. and European democracy aid barrage against Augusto Pinochet in Chile in the late 1980s. In the months following the end of NATO military action against Yugoslavia, Western governments launched or expanded an interconnected set of aid initiatives designed to (1) bolster the credibility of the next national elections (through parallel vote counts and domestic election observing), (2) strengthen opposition political parties, (3) foster public belief in the desirability and possibility of political change, and (4) support a massive get-out-the-vote campaign. Parts of this strategy were formulated as nonpartisan civil society–building while others were explicitly partisan, especially the work with parties. Overall, the central objectives of the strategy were clear—to defeat Milosevic in credible national elections and simultaneously build core institutions and processes for a long-term process of democratization.

To implement this strategy, Western aid flowed to four arenas: opposition parties, the civic advocacy sector, independent media, and opposition-controlled municipalities. From mid-1999 through late 2000, the main opposition coalitions (first the Alliance for Change and then the Democratic Opposition of Serbia, or DOS) received direct material aid and huge doses of training and advice from the U.S. Democratic and Republican party institutes. The U.S. institutes trained more than 5,000 opposition party activists in campaign methods and more than 10,000 in election monitoring. The party aid reached every major area of Serbia and ran the gamut of issues from mobilizing volunteer networks to developing effective campaign messages. Representatives of the U.S. party institutes regularly counseled opposition party leaders, drawing on extensive U.S.-financed polling to calibrate campaign strategy.

Hundreds of Serbian civic education organizations, NGO advocacy groups, student groups, labor unions, community associations, policy institutes, and other civic associations received Western funding. These groups strove to build citizens' awareness of the need for and possibility of democratic change and to motivate them to act, through voting and other forms of civil engagement. Western aid also underwrote much of the independent media in the country, helping ensure the expansion of an enterprising network of independent local radio and television stations and the survival of many independent magazines and newspapers. The independent media played a major role in challenging Milosevic's efforts to control public information. Finally, municipalities that were under opposition political control received special aid packages for infrastructure, education, and other services. This aid aimed to show Yugoslavs the material benefits an opposition victory at the national level could bring to the whole country.

When in July 2000 Milosevic called for elections, the aid campaign moved into high gear. Donors rushed in money to support a massive get-out-the-vote campaign, carefully targeted to reach those voters most likely to oppose Milosevic. Aid and advice to the DOS stepped up, and funding for civic groups and media organizations supported the intensification of their public awareness campaigns and other work.

The U.S. government, through the U.S. Agency for International Development (USAID) and the State Department, was the largest funder of this aid campaign. But the government was only one of many actors. Also involved were the National Endowment for Democracy and its four core grantees (the two party institutes as well as the American Center for International Labor Solidarity and the Center for International Private Enterprise), Freedom House, the German Marshall Fund of the United States, the International Research and Exchanges Board, the Institute for Democracy in Eastern Europe, the Open Society Institute, the Charles Stewart Mott Foundation, and others. In a striking example of the increased blurring of lines in international affairs between different types of actors, public and private funds flowed together, complementing each other and sometimes intermingling. Altogether, U.S. public and private groups spent approximately $40 million from mid-1999 to late 2000 on democracy programs for Serbia.

Though it is a common conceit in Washington to view these undertakings as a largely American effort, Western Europe and Canada were also very much part of the picture. The aid agencies and foreign ministries of Britain, the Netherlands, Sweden, Canada, Norway, Finland, Germany, Italy, and the European Union contributed significantly, especially on NGO support and aid to the opposition-controlled municipalities. Some European private foundations also took part, in some cases drawing on years of presence and experience in the region. The European aid probably totaled close to or a little less than the U.S. aid.

## Whose Victory?

After Kostunica's victory and Milosevic's exit from power, it was hard for U.S. policy makers and democracy promoters not to feel that, as some said in private, "we did it!" Secretary of State Madeleine Albright had insisted in early 2000 on the necessity of political change in Yugoslavia; months later, Milosevic was out. Rarely does foreign policy seem to bring such clear-cut results. Yet if we look at the broader picture, especially giving attention to the Yugoslav political context and the views of key Serbian political and civic actors, the need for a more balanced assignment of credit is evident.

The defeat of Milosevic in the September 2000 elections must be understood as the culmination of a more than decade-long struggle by Serbian opposition politicians and civic activists to challenge the hold of Milosevic and the Socialist Party of Serbia. Ever since Yugoslavia started to open up politically in the second half of the 1980s but then failed to keep pace with most of the rest of Eastern Europe, opposition to Milosevic had grown.

What U.S. democracy promoters have been holding out as key accomplishments of their work generally entailed strengthening features of Yugoslav political life that already existed. U.S. democracy promoters, for example, have made much of their efforts to persuade Serbian political leaders to unify, describing the U.S.-financed polls as critical information that opened Serbs' eyes to the importance of unity. In fact, however, the need for opposition unity had been a driving theme of Serbian politics throughout the 1990s, with constant efforts to form coalitions—sometimes successful, sometimes not. The unity achieved for the 2000 elections was certainly positive, but it was neither total (the long-standing division between the two largest opposition parties was never overcome) nor much broader than the accords achieved in some previous elections. Similarly, U.S. aid representatives glowingly cite their own success in helping the opposition parties take seriously the task of monitoring the elections and fighting against the falsification of results. Yet in the local elections four years earlier, prior to any extensive U.S. aid to the parties, the opposition and some civic groups uncovered Milosevic's attempted manipulation of the results and successfully overturned it in the streets.

The same pattern holds true in the NGO and media sectors. Western NGO aid certainly helped multiply the number of Serbian NGOs. Yet the most innovative, influential groups, such as the Otpor (Resistance) movement and the G-17 Plus organization, were clearly not developed from any U.S. or European mold but were the creations of remarkably talented Serbian activists. They benefited from aid but were not products of it. Likewise, Western media support definitely helped independent media groups get through hard times. But it was the credibility and experience of scores of Serbian journalists working in media outlets they had created themselves, often long before Western aid was available, that made the sector so important.

In short, it was the ideas, persistence, courage, and actions of Serbian politicians, civic activists, and ordinary citizens that brought down Milosevic. U.S. and European support made real contributions in broadening and deepening that opposition, but the aid campaign was a facilitator of change, not the engine of it. Other elements of the anti-Milosevic policy carried some weight, but were neither determinative nor always consistent in effect. Economic sanctions, for instance, added to Serbs' sense of isolation from Europe, increasing some people's desire to turn against Milosevic. However, the sanctions also fed a sense of victimization by the West, encouraging some Serbs to keep supporting Milosevic as their defender against a hostile outside world. The indictment of Milosevic at the Hague tribunal and the diplomatic branding of him as a rogue dictator had similarly divided effects. The NATO bombing campaign against Yugoslavia in 1999 was primarily about protecting Kosovar Albanians, but Milosevic's defeat there certainly contributed to his political decline. That defeat came late in a decade, however, in which Milosevic had been only inconsistently stymied by the West in his aggressions against neighboring areas, actions that often boosted his domestic standing, at least in the short run.

### Distinguishing Features

Even if the extensive U.S. and European democracy aid campaign did not determine the political outcome in Yugoslavia, it was a well-conceived, well-executed effort of genuine consequence. It is important to extract from the record of experience some of the features that gave the campaign greater weight than democracy aid typically has. Seven elements stand out:

- *The aid effort was large.* Often the United States pronounces the lofty goal of aiding democracy in another country, but then commits laughably few resources to the task. Here, not only did public and private U.S. funders spend roughly $40 million in a little over a year, but the various European actors probably spent a similar amount. On a per capita basis, the $40 million of U.S. aid would translate into more than $1 billion in the United States. Adjusting for the fact that dollars have much greater purchasing power in Yugoslavia than in the United States, the comparable amount is even greater. Clearly, if an outside group had spent one billion dollars to influence last year's U.S. elections in favor of one side, it could well have had major impact.

- *The democracy aid campaign was a sustained effort.* The lion's share of the aid came in the last year of Milosevic's rule. But the high-octane strategy of "electoral revolution" was built on foundations that had been laid before. Critically important relationships forged throughout the decade between Western aid providers and Serbian political parties, NGOs, and media made possible the rapid, decisive action in 2000. Although the aid effort of 1999–2000 was indeed fast-moving, the notion that it was an in-and-out blitzkrieg is simply wrong.

- *The aid was decentralized.* Too often democracy aid is concentrated in the capital of the recipient society, going primarily to a limited range of elite organizations and only secondarily trickling out to other parts of the country. A distinctive feature of all four components of the aid campaign in Yugoslavia was that support was distributed all over the country, with a focus on networks of locally oriented organizations and with no special emphasis on Belgrade.

- *Much of the aid went directly into the recipient society.* Milosevic made it impossible for most U.S. and European democracy promoters to get into the country in 1999–2000, presumably believing he was making their work more difficult. The actual effect of this ban, however, was otherwise. Aid groups adapted to adversity, developing flexible mechanisms, from offshore bank accounts to informal couriers, to get aid into the country. Unable to send in the usual expatriate consultants and experts, aid groups devoted a larger-than-usual share of their funds to precisely targeted small grants that went directly to local groups.

- *Aid and diplomacy reinforced each other.* U.S. democracy aid sometimes floats out by itself in a country, unsupported by or even in tension with the U.S. diplomatic line. This was the case in Indonesia in the first half of the 1990s, where small-scale efforts by USAID to nurture independent civic groups were mere dots in a deeper U.S. policy of supporting President Suharto; and it is currently the case in Egypt, one of the largest recipients of U.S. democracy aid in the world. In Yugoslavia, although there were certainly disagreements at times between diplomats and democracy promoters about specific methods, the core objectives of U.S. aid and diplomacy were the same.

- *U.S. and European aid worked from the same script.* West European governments varied in how hard they were willing to push on Milosevic and the types of aid they were willing to give. But on the essential point of seeking Milosevic's ouster, they were largely united with the United States. As a result, U.S. and European aid cumulated rather than competed, and Yugoslavs received a strong, unified message about the degree to which Milosevic's continued rule was isolating their country.

- *Aid coordination was better than usual.* When numerous democracy promotion groups rush into a country at a critical transition juncture, aid programs are often poorly coordinated, resulting in duplication, conflicting messages, and unclear priorities. In Yugoslavia, a strong sense of common purpose among the many different aid groups, as well as the adverse conditions for administering aid, prompted aid representatives to take more active steps than usual to share information with each other and create mechanisms for coordination.

### Beyond Yugoslavia?

Flush with the apparent success of the effort to oust Milosevic, U.S. policy makers and commentators are asking whether and where that success can be repeated. Especially when it is viewed, as it often is, as the third in a series of "electoral revolutions" in the region, after Slovakia and Croatia (though Croatian strongman Franjo Tudjman himself played a useful role in his fall from power by dying on the job), the Yugoslav experience appears to represent the consolidation of a proven method. Possible next targets are beginning to multiply. Belarus appears to some democracy promoters as a natural next step given that President Aleksandr Lukashenko, popularly elected in 1994, has decayed into a harsh tyrant. Opposition parties and independent NGOs are struggling against his authoritarian methods. With national elections in Belarus scheduled for later this year, Western aid groups are increasing democracy-building assistance there, consciously modeling their efforts on the Yugoslav case.

The stark descent of Robert Mugabe's rule in Zimbabwe into virulent authoritarianism has also provoked some U.S. and European democracy promoters to step up efforts there to aid civil society, promote more credible safeguards for future elections, and move toward a more openly oppositional approach. President Mugabe has already responded with measures to protect himself against a foreign financed ouster campaign, calling for legislation to ban foreign aid to political parties.

Bush administration officials and members of Congress are debating whether more aid to Iraqi opposition groups and a tougher diplomatic line could send Saddam Hussein packing as well. The approach there would primarily be a military-oriented overthrow campaign with covert military aid at the core of the U.S. effort. Nevertheless, U.S. support for the Iraqi opposition has already included a democracy aid component, managed by the State Department, aimed at strengthening civil society and opposition groups.

In considering the possibility of new campaigns to oust foreign strongmen, U.S. and European officials must keep the central lesson from Serbia in mind: even when a democracy aid campaign is extensive and sophisticated, it is at most a facilitator of locally rooted forces for political change, not the creator of them. Also, the seven characteristics listed above that helped make the aid for Serbia effective are difficult to reproduce, for various reasons, including the unavailability in most cases of large amounts of funds, the challenge of sustaining aid over time, the tendency toward centralization and bureaucratization of aid, and the frequent divergences between the United States and Europe or even just among the differing parts of the U.S. policy bureaucracy.

Moreover, it must be remembered that certain features of the recipient society also contributed to the success of the aid effort in Yugoslavia. Though Slobodan Milosevic pursued thuggish policies outside Serbia's borders, within the narrower confines of Serbian domestic politics he was not an out-and-out dictator. He was a semiauthoritarian leader who permitted some real political space for opposition parties, independent NGOs, and media. He pressured, harassed, and disadvantaged those groups to varying degrees, but they operated openly and actively. As a result, credible local partners existed for Western groups to support. The task of assistance was not introducing democratic values and methods for the first time, but strengthening those people and groups who were already practicing them.

Related to this, elections were already well established as a genuine mechanism of political competition in Yugoslavia well before the 1999–2000 campaign. Milosevic had certainly cheated and bullied his way through past elections, but some of them, such as the 1992 contest between Milan Panic and Milosevic as well as the 1996 local elections, were serious affairs in which opposition groups competed hard and, in the latter case, successfully fought to uphold its victories. Thus, while promoting an "electoral revolution" in Yugoslavia was an ambitious strategy, a critical part of the important groundwork on elections was already in place.

More broadly, though Serbs could not draw on much significant pre-1990 history of democracy in their political struggles of the 1990s, Yugoslavia was nonetheless a country with some tradition of the rule of law, civil society, and political pluralism, as well as relatively high levels of education and equality. These characteristics are not absolute preconditions for democratization—but they do help. And although they did not prevent the violent collapse of Yugoslavia in the first half of the 1990s, they nonetheless facilitated the work of democracy promoters in Serbia later in the decade.

In short, the hope of quickly multiplying "electoral revolutions" around the world must be viewed with considerable caution. It will be a significant challenge to mount aid campaigns outside of Eastern Europe that share critical features that helped make the efforts in Yugoslavia, as well as Slovakia and Croatia, effective. And many societies in the former Soviet Union, Middle East, Africa, and Asia lack the attributes that made those three countries fertile ground for such processes of change. This does not mean that leaders such as Lukashenko in Belarus, Mugabe in Zimbabwe, Moi in Kenya, or the generals in Burma will never fall, or that the United States should not even try to foster change in countries where strongmen rule. But it must do so with a clear focus on existing lessons for making such aid effective and the inevitably long-term and uncertain prospects for success.

**Note**

Originally published as Carnegie Policy Brief 5 (May 2001).

# Promoting Democracy and Fighting Terror (2003)

## Split Personality

WHEN GEORGE W. BUSH TOOK OFFICE two years ago, few observers expected that promoting democracy around the world would become a major issue in his presidency. During the 2000 presidential campaign Bush and his advisers had made it clear that they favored great-power realism over idealistic notions such as nation building or democracy promotion. And as expected, the incoming Bush team quickly busied itself with casting aside many policies closely associated with President Bill Clinton. Some analysts feared democracy promotion would also get the ax. But September 11 fundamentally altered this picture. Whether, where, and how the United States should promote democracy around the world have become central questions in U.S. policy debates with regard to a host of countries including Egypt, Iran, Iraq, Kyrgyzstan, Pakistan, Russia, Saudi Arabia, Uzbekistan, and many others.

Although the war on terrorism has greatly raised the profile of democracy as a policy matter, it has hardly clarified the issue. The United States faces two contradictory imperatives: on the one hand, the fight against Al Qaeda tempts Washington to put aside its democratic scruples and seek closer ties with autocracies throughout the Middle East and Asia. On the other hand, U.S. officials and policy experts have increasingly come to believe that it is precisely the lack of democracy in many of these countries that helps breed Islamic extremism.

Resolving this tension will be no easy task. So far, Bush and his foreign policy team have shown an incipient, albeit unsurprising, case of split personality: "Bush the realist" actively cultivates warm relations with "friendly tyrants" in many parts of the world, while "Bush the neo-Reaganite" makes ringing calls for a vigorous new democracy campaign in the Middle East. How the administration resolves this uncomfortable dualism is central not only to the future of the war on terrorism but also to the shape and character of Bush's foreign policy as a whole.

## Friends in Low Places

It is on and around the front lines of the campaign against Al Qaeda that the tensions between America's pressing new security concerns and its democracy interests are most strongly felt. The most glaring case is Pakistan. The cold shoulder that Washington turned toward General Pervez Musharraf after he seized power in 1999 has been replaced by a bear hug. In recognition of the Pakistani leader's critical supporting role in the war on terrorism, the Bush administration has showered Musharraf with praise and attention, waived various economic sanctions, assembled a handsome aid package that exceeded $600 million in 2002, and restarted U.S.–Pakistan military cooperation.

Bush officials insist that they combine their embrace with frequent private messages to Musharraf about the importance of returning to democracy. But during the past year the Pakistani president has steadily consolidated his authoritarian grip, a process punctuated by a clumsy referendum last spring and a sweeping series of antidemocratic constitutional amendments in the summer. Bush and his aides have reacted only halfheartedly to this process, publicly repeating tepid calls for democracy but exerting no real pressure.

This soft line is a mistake and should be revised, yet the complexities of the situation must also be acknowledged. Pakistan's cooperation in the campaign against Al Qaeda is not a nice extra—it is vital. In addition, a return to democracy in Pakistan is not simply a matter of getting an authoritarian leader to step aside. The two main civilian political parties have failed the country several times and during the 1990s discredited themselves in many Pakistanis' eyes with patterns of corruption, ineffectiveness, and authoritarian behavior. Democratization will require a profound, multifaceted process of change in which Pakistan's military will have to not only give up formal leadership of the country but pull out of politics altogether. Meanwhile, the civilian politicians will have to remake themselves thoroughly and dedicate themselves to rebuilding public confidence in the political system. Rather than erring on the side of deference to Musharraf, Washington should articulate such a long-term vision for Pakistan and pressure all relevant actors there to work toward it.

Central Asia, meanwhile, presents a mosaic of dilemmas relating to the tradeoff between democracy and security in U.S. foreign policy. The U.S. need for military bases and other forms of security cooperation in the region has moved Washington much closer to the autocratic leaders of Uzbekistan, Kazakhstan, and Kyrgyzstan. Even Saparmurat Niyazov, the totalitarian megalomaniac running Turkmenistan, received a friendly visit from Defense Secretary Donald Rumsfeld in April 2002. At the same time, U.S. officials are pushing for reform in the region, emphasizing to their local counterparts that this is a once-in-a-lifetime opportunity for the region's states to obtain significant outside support for the full set of economic, political, and social reforms necessary to join the modern world.

Surprisingly, it is in Uzbekistan, one of the region's harshest dictatorships, where this dual approach may pay at least modest dividends. President Islam Karimov has undoubtedly received a boost at home from the new diplomatic attention, economic aid, and military partnership with the United States. Yet for the first time since Uzbekistan became independent, U.S. officials are also meeting regularly with a wide range of Uzbek officials and conveying strongly worded messages about the need for change. And there are signs of nascent political and economic reforms, albeit small, tentative ones. Karimov is still very much a dictator with little understanding of or interest in either democracy or market economics. But he also seems to realize that some positive moves are necessary to ensure his own political future and that the increased external support post–September 11 is a real opportunity.

Unfortunately, in Kazakhstan the U.S. approach appears less promising. President Nursultan Nazarbayev displays no interest in meeting the United States even partway. Instead, he is using the new context to tighten his dictatorial hold on the country and is openly spurning U.S. reform efforts. Given Kazakhstan's sizable oil and gas reserves, and Nazarbayev's cooperation on both security and economic measures, he appears to have calculated correctly that the Bush administration is unlikely to step up its mild pressure for reform. If the United States is serious about trying to steer Kazakhstan away from potentially disastrous authoritarian decay, however, Washington will have to become more forceful.

Kyrgyzstan is a more ambiguous but still discouraging case. President Askar Akayev is less dictatorial than Karimov or Nazarbayev but has also slid toward authoritarianism in recent years. The Bush administration has made some effort to steer him away from this unfortunate path. But it has not taken full advantage of the Kyrgyz elite's obvious eagerness for a close security relationship with the United States to push hard on key issues such as freeing political prisoners or curbing corruption.

Running throughout all of the new U.S. security relationships in South and Central Asia is an institutional divide that weakens the administration's ability to balance security and democracy. The State Department has shown some real commitment to raising human rights and democracy issues with these countries. The Pentagon, however, often focuses more on the immediate goal of securing military access or cooperation and less on the politics of the relevant host government. Given the importance that foreign leaders place on the U.S. military, they may sometimes assume that friendly words from the Pentagon mean they can ignore other messages they are receiving. Ensuring a consistent U.S. front on democracy and human rights, therefore, is a prerequisite for a coherent approach.

Afghanistan is perhaps the most telling example of this challenge. The initial post–September 11 action by the United States in that country was of course not a downgrading of democracy concerns but a sudden step forward, through the ouster of the fundamentalist Taliban regime. But the conduct of U.S. military operations there has since undermined the administration's promises of a lasting, deep commitment to democratic reconstruction. The Pentagon initially relied on Afghan warlords as proxy fighters against Al Qaeda, arming them and thus helping them consolidate their regional power. This assistance helped entrench the centrifugal politics that threaten Afghanistan's weak new government. Ironically, the strategy seems also to have been a partial military miscalculation, leading to the escape of a significant number of Al Qaeda fighters at Tora Bora.

At the same time, administration opposition to the use of either U.S. or UN peacekeeping troops outside of Kabul, and significant shortfalls in the delivery of promised aid, make it impossible for the Karzai government to guarantee security, gain meaningful control beyond the capital, or achieve legitimacy by delivering peace to its citizens. Ethnic rivalries, the opium trade, and newly empowered local strongmen make a return to state failure and civil war a very real possibility. Despite the insistence of many U.S. officials in the immediate aftermath of September 11 on the connection between failed states and vital U.S. security interests, the Bush team's aversion to nation building has not really changed.

No easy solutions to Afghanistan's profound political problems are in sight. At a minimum, however, the administration must strengthen its commitment to making reconstruction work. This means not only delivering more fully on aid, but exerting real pressure on regional power brokers to accept the Kabul government's authority and working harder to establish an Afghan national army. No matter how pressing are the other fronts of the war against Al Qaeda (such as the increasingly worrisome situation in northern Pakistan), the United

States must fulfill the responsibilities for reconstruction that came with its invasion of Afghanistan.

## Ripple Effects

The tensions posed by the war on terrorism for U.S. support of democracy abroad have quickly spread out beyond the immediate front lines. Southeast Asia is one affected region. Indonesia has become an important theater in the U.S. antiterrorist campaign, because of U.S. fears that Al Qaeda leaders are taking refuge there and that the country's numerous Islamist groups are connecting with extremist networks. The White House continues to support Indonesia's shaky, somewhat democratic government. But in a setback on human rights policy, the administration has proposed restarting aid to the Indonesian military. That aid was progressively reduced during the 1990s in response to the Indonesian forces' atrocious human rights record and was finally terminated in 1999, when Indonesian troops participated in massacres in East Timor. Administration officials have downplayed this decision to renew military aid, stressing that most of the proposed $50 million package is directed at the police rather than the military. But the willingness of the U.S. government to enter into a partnership with a security force that just a few years ago was involved in a horrendous campaign of slaughter and destruction against civilians sends a powerful negative message throughout the region and beyond. Some officials argue that the new training programs will give U.S. military personnel a chance to instruct their Indonesian counterparts in human rights. But U.S. officials repeatedly made the same argument in defense of these programs in previous decades, right up to when the Indonesian military committed the human rights abuses that sank the relationship.

Malaysia's leader, Prime Minister Mahathir Mohamad, is another beneficiary of a changed U.S. foreign policy. Mahathir has made himself useful to Washington by arresting Islamic militants, sharing intelligence, and cooperating in other ways with an antiterrorist campaign that neatly dovetails with his authoritarian domestic agenda. And in response, Washington's previous critical stance toward the Malaysian leader—highlighted in Vice President Al Gore's much-publicized call for reforms during his visit to Kuala Lumpur in 1998—has been reversed. Top U.S. officials now laud Mahathir as "a force for regional stability" and "a model of economic development that has demonstrated tolerance," and President Bush praised him at an amicable joint press conference after Mahathir's visit to the White House in May 2002.

An emphasis on democracy and human rights is also in question in U.S. policy toward Russia and China. Russia's new role as a U.S. ally in the war on terrorism has progressed less smoothly than some initially hoped, with significant continuing differences over Iraq, Iran, Georgia, and other places. Nevertheless, President Bush regards President Vladimir Putin very favorably and has not pressed the Russian leader about his shortcomings on democracy and human rights, such as in Chechnya or with regard to maintaining a free press. Somewhat similarly, the Chinese government has been able to leverage the new security context to solidify a much friendlier U.S.–China relationship than seemed likely in the early months of 2001, when the Bush administration appeared to view China as threat number one.

In both cases, however, the change is more of degree than kind. Bush's surprisingly personal and warm embrace of Putin started before September 11, with Bush getting "a sense of [Putin's] soul" during their meeting in Slovenia in June 2001. And at no time prior to September 11, whether under Bush or Clinton before him, was the Russian government subjected to any significant U.S. government criticism for Chechnya or any of its other democratic flaws. With respect to China, it is true that September 11 did block movement toward a new hard-line policy from Washington that some administration hawks may have wanted. But the current relatively positive state of relations, with mild U.S. pressure on human rights greatly outweighed by an ample, mutually beneficial economic relationship, is not especially different from the overall pattern of the past decade or more.

One can look even further afield and identify possible slippage in U.S. democracy policies resulting from the war on terrorism, such as insufficient attention to the growing crisis of democracy in South America or inadequate pressure on oil-rich Nigeria's flailing president, Olusegun Obasanjo, to turn around his increasingly poor governance of Africa's most populous nation. Ironically, and also sadly, however, the greatest source of negative ripple effects has come from the administration's pursuit of the war on terrorism at home. The heightened terrorist threat has inevitably put pressure on U.S. civil liberties. But the administration failed to strike the right balance early on, unnecessarily abridging or abusing rights through the large-scale detention of immigrants, closed deportation hearings, and the declaration of some U.S. citizens as "enemy combatants" with no right to counsel or even to contest the designation. The Justice Department's harsh approach sent a powerful negative signal around the world, emboldening governments as diverse as those of Belarus, Cuba, and India to curtail domestic liberties, supposedly in aid of their own struggles against terrorism. In the United States, an independent judiciary and powerful Congress ensure that the appropriate balance between security and rights is gradually being achieved. In many countries, however, the rule of law is weak and copycat restrictions on rights resound much more harmfully.

## Reagan Reborn?

Whereas "Bush the realist" holds sway on most fronts in the war on terrorism, a neo-Reaganite Bush may be emerging in the Middle East. In the initial period after September 11, the administration turned to its traditional autocratic allies in the Arab world, especially Egypt and Saudi Arabia, for help against Al Qaeda. This move did not sacrifice any U.S. commitment to democracy; for decades, the United States had already suppressed any such concerns in the region, valuing autocratic stability for the sake of various economic and security interests. Over the course of the last year, however, a growing chorus of voices within and around the administration has begun questioning the value of America's "friendly tyrants" in the Middle East. These individuals highlight the fact that whereas the autocratic allies once seemed to be effective bulwarks against Islamic extremism, the national origins of the September 11 attackers make clear that these nations are in fact breeders, and in the case of Saudi Arabia, financiers, of extremism. Invoking what they believe to be the true spirit of President Ronald Reagan's foreign policy, they call for a change toward promoting freedom in U.S. Middle East policy. The core idea of the new approach is to undercut the roots of Islamic extremism by getting serious about promoting democracy in the Arab world, not just in a slow, gradual way, but with fervor and force.

President Bush is clearly attracted by this idea. Last summer his declarations on the Middle East shifted noticeably in tone and content, setting out a vision of democratic change there. According to this vision, the United States will first promote democracy in the Palestinian territories by linking U.S. support for a Palestinian state with the achievement of new, more democratic Palestinian leadership. Second, the United States will effect regime change in Iraq and help transform that country into a democracy. The establishment of two successful models of Arab democracy will have a powerful demonstration effect, "inspiring reforms throughout the Muslim world," as Bush declared at the United Nations in September. As the policies toward Iraq and Palestine unfold, the administration may also step up pressure on recalcitrant autocratic allies and give greater support to those Arab states undertaking at least some political reforms, such as some of the smaller Persian Gulf states. The decision last August to postpone a possible aid increase to Egypt as a response to the Egyptian government's continued persecution of human rights activist Saad Eddin Ibrahim was a small step in this direction.

It is not yet clear how sharply Bush will shift U.S. Middle East policy toward promoting democracy. Certainly it is time to change the long-standing practice of reflexively relying on and actually bolstering autocracy in the Arab world. But the expansive vision of a sudden, U.S.-led democratization of the Middle East rests on questionable assumptions. To start with, the appealing idea that by toppling Saddam Hussein the United States can transform Iraq into a democratic model for the region is dangerously misleading. The United States can certainly oust the Iraqi leader and install a less repressive and more pro-Western regime. This would not be the same, however, as creating democracy in Iraq.

The experience of other countries where in recent decades the United States has forcibly removed dictatorial regimes—Grenada, Panama, Haiti, and most recently Afghanistan—indicates that postinvasion political life usually takes on the approximate character of the political life that existed in the country before the ousted regime came to power. After the 1982 U.S. military intervention in Grenada, for example, that country was able to recover the tradition of moderate pluralism it had enjoyed before the 1979 takeover by Maurice Bishop and his gang. Haiti, after the 1994 U.S. invasion, has unfortunately slipped back into many of the pathologies that marked its political life before the military junta took over in 1991. Iraqi politics prior to Saddam Hussein were violent, divisive, and oppressive. And the underlying conditions in Iraq—not just the lack of significant previous experience with pluralism but also sharp ethnic and religious differences and an oil-dependent economy—will inevitably make democratization there very slow and difficult. Even under the most optimistic scenarios, the United States would have to commit itself to a massive, expensive, demanding, and long-lasting reconstruction effort. The administration's inadequate commitment to Afghanistan's reconstruction undercuts assurances by administration officials that they will stay the course in a post-Saddam Iraq.

Furthermore, the notion that regime change in Iraq, combined with democratic progress in the Palestinian territories, would produce domino democratization around the region is far-fetched. A U.S. invasion of Iraq would likely trigger a surge in the already prevalent anti-Americanism in the Middle East, strengthening the hand of hard-line Islamist groups and provoking many Arab governments to tighten their grip, rather than experiment more boldly with political liberalization. Throughout the region, the underlying economic, political, and social conditions are unfavorable for a wave of democratic breakthroughs. This does not mean the Arab world will never democratize. But it does mean that democracy will be decades in the making and entail a great deal of uncertainty, reversal, and turmoil. The United States can and should actively support such democratic change through an expanded, sharpened set of democracy aid programs and real pressure and support for reforms. But as experience in other parts of the world has repeatedly demonstrated, the future of the region will be determined primarily by its own inhabitants.

Aggressive democracy promotion in the Arab world is a new article of faith among neoconservatives inside and outside the administration. However, it combines both the strengths and the dangers typical of neo-Reaganite policy as applied to any region. Perhaps the most important strength is the high importance attached to the president's using his bully pulpit to articulate a democratic vision and to attach his personal prestige to the democracy-building endeavor.

But two dangers are also manifest. One is the instrumentalization of pro-democracy policies—wrapping security goals in the language of democracy promotion and then confusing democracy promotion with the search for particular political outcomes that enhance those security goals. This was often a problem with the Reagan administration's attempts to spread democracy in the 1980s. To take just one example, for the presidential elections in El Salvador in 1984, the Reagan administration labored mightily to establish the technical structures necessary for a credible election. The administration then covertly funneled large amounts of money to the campaign of its preferred candidate, José Napoleón Duarte, to make sure he won the race. This same tension between democracy as an end versus a means has surfaced in the administration's press for democracy in the Palestinian territories. Bush has urged Palestinians to reform, especially through elections, yet at the same time administration officials have made clear that certain outcomes, such as the reelection of Yasir Arafat, are unacceptable to the United States. A postinvasion process of installing a new "democratic" regime in Iraq would likely exhibit similar contradictions between stated principle and political reality.

The administration demonstrated worrisome signs of the same tendency last April during the short-lived coup against Venezuela's problematic populist president, Hugo Chávez. Washington appeared willing or even eager to accept a coup against the leader of an oil-rich state who is despised by many in the U.S. government for his anti-American posturing and dubious economic and political policies. But given that it came in a region that has started to work together to oppose coups, and that other regional governments condemned Chávez's ouster, the administration's approach undermined the United States' credibility as a supporter of democracy. If democracy promotion is reduced to an instrumental strategy for producing political outcomes favorable to U.S. interests, the value and legitimacy of the concept will be lost.

The second danger is overestimating America's ability to export democracy. U.S. neoconservatives habitually overstate the effect of America's role in the global wave of democratic openings that occurred in the 1980s and early 1990s. For example, they often argue that the Reagan administration brought democracy to Latin America through its forceful anticommunism in the 1980s.

Yet the most significant democratization that occurred in Argentina, Brazil, and various other parts of South America took place in the early 1980s, when Reagan was still trying to embrace the fading right-wing dictators that Jimmy Carter had shunned on human rights grounds. Excessive optimism about U.S. ability to remake the Middle East, a region far from ripe for a wave of democratization, is therefore a recipe for trouble—especially given the administration's proven disinclination to commit itself deeply to the nation building that inevitably follows serious political disruption.

## A Fine Balance

The clashing imperatives of the war on terrorism with respect to U.S. democracy promotion have led to a split presidential personality and contradictory policies—decreasing interest in democracy in some countries and suddenly increasing interest in one region, the Middle East. The decreases are widespread and probably still multiplying, given the expanding character of the antiterrorism campaign. Yet they are not fatal to the overall role of the United States as a force for democracy in the world. Some of them are relatively minor modifications of policies that for years imperfectly fused already conflicting security and political concerns. And in at least some countries where it has decided warmer relations with autocrats are necessary, the Bush administration is trying to balance new security ties with proreform pressures.

More broadly, in many countries outside the direct ambit of the war on terrorism, the Bush administration is trying to bolster fledgling democratic governments and pressure nondemocratic leaders for change, as have the past several U.S. administrations. Sometimes diplomatic pressure is used, as with Belarus, Zimbabwe, and Burma. In other cases, Washington relies on less visible means such as economic and political support as well as extensive democracy aid programs, as with many countries in sub-Saharan Africa, southeastern Europe, the former Soviet Union, Central America, and elsewhere. Quietly and steadily during the last 20 years, democracy promotion has become institutionalized in the U.S. foreign policy and foreign aid bureaucracies. Although not an automatically overriding priority, it is almost always one part of the foreign policy picture. Partly to address "the roots of terrorism," moreover, the administration has also proposed a very large new aid fund, the $5 billion Millennium Challenge Account. By signaling that good governance should be a core criterion for disbursing aid from this fund, President Bush has positioned it as a potentially major tool for bolstering democracies in the developing world.

Although the new tradeoffs prompted by the war on terrorism are unfortunate, and in some cases overdone, the fact that U.S. democracy concerns are limited by security needs is hardly a shocking new problem. Democracy promotion has indeed become gradually entrenched in U.S. policy, but both during and after the Cold War it has been limited and often greatly weakened by other U.S. interests. President Clinton made liberal use of pro-democracy rhetoric and did support democracy in many places, but throughout his presidency, U.S. security and economic interests—whether in China, Egypt, Jordan, Kazakhstan, Saudi Arabia, Vietnam, or various other countries—frequently trumped an interest in democracy. The same was true in the George H.W. Bush administration and certainly also under Ronald Reagan, whose outspoken support for freedom in the communist world was accompanied by close U.S. relations with various authoritarian regimes useful to the United States, such as those led by Suharto in Indonesia, Mobutu Sese Seko in Zaire, the generals of Nigeria, and the Institutional Revolutionary Party of Mexico.

George W. Bush is thus scarcely the first U.S. president to evidence a split personality on democracy promotion. But the suddenness and prominence of his condition, as a result of the war on terrorism, makes it especially costly. It is simply hard for most Arabs, or many other people around the world, to take seriously the president's eloquent vision of a democratic Middle East when he or his top aides casually brush away the authoritarian maneuverings of Musharraf in Pakistan, offer warm words of support for Nazarbayev in Kazakhstan, or praise Mahathir in Malaysia. The war on terrorism has laid bare the deeper fault line that has lurked below the surface of George W. Bush's foreign policy from the day he took office—the struggle between the realist philosophy of his father and the competing pull of neo-Reaganism.

There is no magic solution to this division, which is rooted in a decades-old struggle for the foreign policy soul of the Republican Party and will undoubtedly persist in various forms throughout this administration and beyond. For an effective democracy-promotion strategy, however, the Bush team must labor harder to limit the tradeoffs caused by the new security imperatives and also not go overboard with the grandiose idea of trying to unleash a democratic tsunami in the Middle East. This means, for example, engaging more deeply in Pakistan to urge military leaders and civilian politicians to work toward a common vision of democratic renovation, adding teeth to the reform messages being delivered to Central Asia's autocrats, ensuring that the Pentagon reinforces proreform messages to new U.S. security partners, not cutting Putin slack on his democratic deficits, going easy on the praise for newly friendly tyrants, more effectively balancing civil rights and security at home, and openly criticizing other governments that abuse the U.S. example. In the Middle East, it means developing a serious, well-funded effort to promote democracy that reflects the difficult political realities of the region but does not fall back on an underlying acceptance of only cosmetic changes. This will entail exerting sustained pressure on autocratic Arab allies to take concrete steps to open up political space and undertake real institutional reforms, bolstering democracy aid programs in the region, and finding ways to engage moderate Islamist groups and encourage Arab states to bring them into political reform processes.

Such an approach is defined by incremental gains, long-term commitment, and willingness to keep the post–September 11 security imperatives in perspective. As such it has neither the hard-edged appeal of old-style realism nor the tantalizing promise of the neoconservative visions. Yet in the long run it is the best way to ensure that the war on terrorism complements rather than contradicts worldwide democracy and that the strengthening of democracy abroad is a fundamental element of U.S. foreign policy in the years ahead.

## Note

The Carnegie Endowment gratefully acknowledges the permission of the Council on Foreign Relations to reprint this article, which originally appeared in *Foreign Affairs*, vol. 82, no. 1 (January/February 2003).

# CHAPTER SIX

# Democracy Promotion: Explaining the Bush Administration's Position (2003)

## The Core of U.S. Foreign Policy

### BY PAULA J. DOBRIANSKY

*Paula J. Dobriansky is Undersecretary of State for Global Affairs.*

THOMAS CAROTHERS' *FOREIGN AFFAIRS* ARTICLE "Promoting Democracy and Fighting Terror" (January/February 2003) critiques the Bush administration's democracy promotion record and offers some broad recommendations on how best to integrate human rights causes into American foreign policy. The author's long-term involvement in democracy-related activities and his passion about this subject are commendable, but both his analysis and his policy prescriptions are unpersuasive.

Carothers alleges that, driven by imperatives related to the war on terrorism, the administration has come to cooperate with a number of authoritarian regimes and turned a blind eye to various antidemocratic practices carried out by these newfound allies. This claim is incorrect. The administration's September 2002 National Security Strategy, which lays out our post–September 11 strategic vision, prominently features democracy promotion. The strategy describes it as a core part of our overall national security doctrine and commits us to help other countries realize their full potential:

> In pursuit of our goals, our first imperative is to clarify what we stand for: the United States must defend liberty and justice because these principles are right and true for all people everywhere. . . . America must stand firmly for the nonnegotiable demands of human dignity: the rule of law; limits on the absolute power of the state; free speech; freedom of worship; equal justice; respect for women; religious and ethnic tolerance; and respect for private property.

It is also a matter of record that this administration, whenever it encounters evidence of serious human rights violations or antidemocratic practices in specific countries, has raised a voice of opposition to such violations and sought to address these problems. This is certainly the case with such countries as Pakistan, Indonesia, and Malaysia, as well as Russia, Uzbekistan, and China. In general, we do this irrespective of the identity of the offender and, when circumstances merit it, criticize even some of our close allies. We manifest our concerns through a variety of channels, including diplomatic dialogue, both public and private, and the State Department's reports on human rights, international religious freedom, and trafficking in persons.

Bilateral efforts aside, a great deal of our multilateral diplomacy, including American engagement at the United Nations and the Organization of American States, is shaped by the imperatives of human rights and democracy promotion. Although greatly distressed by the selection of Libya to chair the UN Human Rights Commission, the United States intends to remain a driving force at the commission and will challenge this forum to fulfill its mandate to uphold international standards on human rights. We have also worked hand in hand with other democracies to strengthen the Community of Democracies (CD). I led the American delegation to last November's CD meeting in Seoul, where delegates adopted an ambitious plan of action with many specific initiatives designed to enable emerging democracies from different parts of the world to share "best practices" and help each other.

For the Bush administration, democracy promotion is not just a "made in the U.S." venture, but a goal shared with many other countries. We also seek to broaden our partnerships with local and global nongovernmental organizations and international organizations, so that we can work together on democracy promotion, advancement of human rights, and humanitarian relief. In fact, the National Endowment for Democracy, Freedom House, and other organizations have played pivotal roles in the development of a democratic culture and the strengthening of civil society.

Ironically, many of the world's countries, including some of our allies, often chide us not for failing to do enough in the democracy arena, but for trying to do too much, for elevating democratic imperatives above those of trade and diplomatic politesse. Yet we remain committed to doing what is right. President George W. Bush observed in his June 1, 2002, West Point speech, "Some worry that it is somehow undiplomatic or impolite to speak the language of right or wrong. I disagree. Different circumstances require different methods, but not different moralities." When appropriate, we go beyond words and subject persistent human rights violators to economic sanctions and other forms of pressure. I cannot think of any other country that has been as willing as the United States has to use both soft and hard power to promote democracy.

To be sure, some have argued that we should do even more, and specifically that we should withhold military and intelligence cooperation from certain of our allies whose human rights records leave much to be desired. As they see it, we improperly allow realpolitik considerations to trump the human rights imperatives. But this argument is myopic. No responsible U.S. decision-maker can allow our foreign policy to be driven by a single imperative, no matter how important. Thus, our policy toward a given country or region is shaped by a variety of considerations, including security concerns, economic issues, and human rights imperatives. The most difficult task of our statecraft is to strike the right balance among these imperatives and arrive at the policy mix that best advances an entire set of our values and interests. Invariably, it is a nuanced and balanced approach that produces the best results. And invariably, this administration has struck the right balance. For example, in the post–September 11 environment, as we began to engage a number of Central Asian governments whose help we needed to prosecute the war against Al Qaeda and the Taliban, we simultaneously intensified our efforts to improve the human rights situation in these countries. By cooperating on intelligence and security issues, we have actually enhanced our leverage on democracy-related matters. Although a great deal more needs to be done, we believe that this integrated approach is working.

Any effort to juxtapose or contrast our efforts to win the war against terrorism and our democracy-promotion strategy is conceptually flawed. Pan-national terrorist groups (such as Al Qaeda) and rogue regimes (such as that of the Taliban or of Saddam Hussein) pose grave threats to democratic systems, as do the xenophobic, intolerant ideologies that they espouse. Accordingly, fighting against these forces is both in our national security interest and a key ingredient of democracy promotion. And democracy promotion is the best antidote to terrorism. Significantly, the Seoul Plan of Action, adopted at the 2002 CD meeting, contains a series of actions that democracies can take to counter emerging threats through the promotion of democracy.

Carothers also criticizes what he terms an "instrumentalization" of our democracy promotion. In essence, he complains that, for example, the administration's efforts to promote democracy in a post-Saddam Iraq and, more generally, to advance democracy across the Arab world are somehow tainted because we have other reasons for our actions—for example, removing the threat that Saddam's arsenal of weapons of mass destruction and his long-standing defiance of the international community pose to the world. Democracy promotion, it seems, should not only trump all other foreign policy imperatives; it should always be the one and only policy driver. This, of course, would immunize human rights offenders and despots who also present security threats—not an outcome that anyone who cares about human rights causes should welcome. More generally, the fact that we are advancing policies that simultaneously promote democracy over the long haul and mitigate the security threats that we face in the near term underscores the extent to which human rights causes have become integrated into our foreign policy. In a very real sense, this is American statecraft at its best.

Despite the enormous demands of the war against terrorism, this administration has found time for and evidenced keen interest in launching several major new democracy-promotion initiatives. Although human rights and democracy causes have a long bipartisan pedigree, it has been the Bush administration that has reordered the country's approach to development assistance so as to reward and encourage "good governance" through a pathbreaking initiative: the Millennium Challenge Account (MCA). In 2003 alone, the administration has requested $1.3 billion for the MCA, which means 15 percent of our foreign assistance will be dedicated to good governance, investment in people, and economic development. In addition to changing our own policy, the leadership and commitment President Bush displayed at the March 2002 Monterrey summit on financing development have convinced many of our allies, international lending and aid-delivery institutions, and the United Nations to change the ways in which they do business.

The administration has also launched a high-level initiative to improve political, economic, and cultural participation by women and combat discrimination against them. This effort began in Afghanistan, where the Taliban regime practiced what amounted to gender apartheid, and grew into a broad, sustained campaign focused on those governments that deprive women of political and economic opportunity. This strategy is spearheaded by the Office of International Women's Issues at the State Department and has featured participation by the president and the first lady, Secretary of State Colin Powell, presidential adviser Karen Hughes, and numerous other senior administration officials. Our overarching goal is to improve women's access to education and health and ensure that nowhere in the world are women treated as second-class citizens, unable to work, vote, or realize their dreams. We have also launched a Middle East Partnership Initiative that seeks to support political, economic, and educational reform in that region.

Overall, the promotion of democracy is a key foreign policy goal of the Bush administration. This sentiment is reflected in all of our international endeavors and is animated by a mixture of both idealistic and pragmatic impulses. We seek to foster a global society of nations, in which freedom and democracy reign and human aspirations are fully realized.

# *Carothers Replies*

I am frankly astonished that Undersecretary of State Paula Dobriansky attempts to refute the central thesis of my article: that the war on terrorism has impelled the Bush administration to seek friendlier relations with authoritarian regimes in many parts of the world for the sake of their cooperation on security matters. It is simply a fact that since the terrorist attacks of September 11, 2001, the Bush administration has sought closer ties and enhanced security cooperation with a host of authoritarian or semi-authoritarian regimes—in Algeria, Bahrain, China, Egypt, Jordan, Kazakhstan, Kuwait, Malaysia, Pakistan, Qatar, Uzbekistan, Yemen, and even Syria.

Dobriansky claims that the administration always strikes the right balance between democracy and security, and that whenever the administration has encountered antidemocratic practices on the part of its security partners, it has raised a voice of opposition. As I highlighted in my article, in some cases, such as Uzbekistan, the administration has indeed tried to leaven its new security embrace with urgings to do better on human rights and democracy. Even in such situations, however, the overall message of the new relationships—with their friendly, public words of praise during high-level visits, their heightened security cooperation, and, often, their enlarged aid packages—is one of support for undemocratic regimes. Moreover, unfortunately, in some cases the administration has not voiced any substantial objection to overtly antidemocratic practices.

For example, the renewed U.S.–Pakistan relationship developed precisely in a period when President Pervez Musharraf was carrying out a series of antidemocratic actions, including rewriting key parts of the Pakistani constitution to ensure his continued rule. President Bush has repeatedly avoided making any criticisms of these measures. At a press conference last August, he made America's priorities with Pakistan crystal clear when, in response to a direct question about Musharraf's manhandling of the constitution, he said the following: "My reaction about President Musharraf, he's still tight with us on the war against terror, and that's what I appreciate." About the Pakistani leader's abridgment of human rights and democracy, Bush could manage only a tepid statement: "To the extent that our friends promote democracy, it's important. We will continue to work with our friends and allies to promote democracy."

The point of my article was not to excoriate the Bush administration for struggling with the tension between the war on terrorism and democracy promotion. Rather, it was to discuss the problem openly and clearly and to identify where and how the tension can be better mitigated.

Dobriansky's insistence that there is no tension, and her relentless portrait of the United States as a country uniquely devoted to democracy promotion, is part of a pattern of rhetorical overkill by administration officials that weakens rather than strengthens this country's credibility in the eyes of others. People around the world are quite capable of seeing that the United States has close, even intimate relations with many undemocratic regimes for the sake of American security and economic interests, and that, like many other countries, the United States struggles very imperfectly to balance its ideals with the realist imperatives it faces. A more honest acknowledgment of this reality and a considerable toning down of self-congratulatory statements about the United States' unparalleled altruism on the world stage would be a big boost in the long run to a more credible pro-democracy policy.

## Note

The Carnegie Endowment gratefully acknowledges the permission of the Council on Foreign Relations to reprint this article, which originally appeared in *Foreign Affairs*, vol. 82, no. 3 (May/June 2003).

# Core Elements
# of Democracy Aid

THREE OF THE BIGGEST enthusiasms in the democracy aid world have been election observing, civil society promotion, and rule-of-law development. Probably no other element of the democracy aid repertoire has achieved the visibility and public recognition of election observing; indeed it is as close as democracy aid gets to having an archetypical activity. At nearly every important election in the developing and postcommunist worlds since the late 1980s, hundreds and sometimes thousands of international observers have been present. Domestic observers, usually funded and trained by U.S. or other international democracy groups, have become increasingly active as well.

Election observing plays a valuable role in many cases. But as I took part in various observer missions and studied others in the 1990s, I became aware that the competence, objectivity, and basic utility of election observers should not be automatically assumed, as it often seems to be by journalists and others eager to get a quick assessment of an important foreign election. In the first essay in this section, "The Rise of Election Monitoring: The Observers Observed," I turn a critical eye on election observing, seeking to highlight some of its shortcomings and areas for improvement.

No enthusiasm hit the world of democracy aid harder than what might be called the civil society craze in the 1990s. *Civil society* went from being a relatively arcane term primarily invoked in the Eastern European context to a global catch phrase. Aid programs to support civil society—a term that was rather narrowly interpreted by most aid groups to mean Western-style advocacy or service nongovernmental organizations (NGOs)—mushroomed, helping produce large new NGO sectors in many countries struggling to become democratic. Although I am generally favorable to the idea of "bottom-up" approaches to democracy promotion, I grew concerned in the second half of the 1990s that the civil society concept was being badly overused as well as misused, and that far too high expectations had been invested in civil society programs. In a 1999 "Think Again" article in *Foreign Policy*, included here as the second piece in this section, I addressed the use and misuse of the civil society concept. On the occasion of the tenth anniversary of the fall of the Berlin Wall, I was asked to give a speech to a gathering of civil society aid providers. In that speech, which was later published in *East European Constitutional Review* and is the third selection in this section, I reviewed the record of Western civil society to the postcommunist world.

The rule of law has followed hard on the heels of civil society as a fashionable concept in the democracy promotion arena. Like civil society, the rule of law is a tremendously appealing concept for democracy promoters, as well as developmentalists. It appears to lie at the core of both political and economic development. It has a supra-ideological quality with attraction to both the right (which reads into it law and order, as well as property rights) and to the left (which interprets the term as being related to human rights and citizen empowerment). And the rule of law relates directly to many of the key issues arising in societies attempting democratic transitions, such as crime and corruption. Rule-of-law aid has multiplied quickly to the point where it is a field of its own, overlapping but not contiguous with the domains of both democracy promotion and socioeconomic development assistance. In "The Rule of Law Revival," written in 1998, I offer an explanation for the dramatic rise of attention to rule-of-law development and an analytic framework for trying to promote it. In the last essay in this section, "Promoting the Rule of Law Abroad: The Problem of Knowledge," I argue that despite the many rule-of-law programs now under way, we actually know troublingly little about what we are doing in this domain.

# CHAPTER SEVEN

# The Rise of Election Monitoring:
# The Observers Observed
# (1997)

THE SCENARIO BY NOW is familiar. Elections are announced in a politically transitional country of importance to the international community, elections that look as if they will be pivotal to the country's democratic prospects. Several months before the vote, the first foreign observers arrive, a few people from the United States or Western Europe who settle in to monitor the electoral process from start to finish. Around the same time, a small team of Western technical advisors sets up shop in the country to assist the national election commission with its task of administering the elections. After the electoral process gets under way, with candidates registering and the campaign starting, several preelectoral survey missions arrive from abroad. These teams assess the political climate, the administrative preparations, and the early campaign period. They then issue reports—which are much debated in the country under scrutiny—calling attention to deficiencies in the process and exhorting the political authorities to take remedial steps.

The campaign intensifies, and more foreign observers join the early arrivals. As the administrative preparations advance, foreign technical assistance to the election commission also expands. A week before the elections, the international observation effort moves into high gear. Delegations of foreign observers arrive daily, a stream that becomes a flood late in the week as hundreds or thousands of observers descend on the country. They fill the hotels and restaurants in the capital, as well as the schedules of the election commissioners and the major candidates. The day before the vote, the observers fan out around the country, overwhelming the local airlines, renting every four-wheel-drive vehicle available, and hiring every plausible interpreter in sight.

Election day finally arrives. The observers rise early and travel in small groups from polling station to polling station, posing questions to poll workers and watching people vote. The day is long, but eventually the polls close and the vote counting begins. Most of the foreign observers stay for a few hours at polling stations to watch the laborious ballot-counting process get under way before they go to bed or head back to the capital. A few hardy souls in the observer ranks stay up all night to watch the counting.

The next morning, though the results are not yet in, the larger observer delegations hold press conferences in hotels in the capital, each racing to be the first to go public with its assessment. Their initial statements released (and often already reported on local television), many of the foreign observers leave that afternoon, jostling for seats on long-overbooked flights out. Within a day or two, most are gone, already back at home sharing their experiences with friends and co-workers. A few stay on, usually those who arrived months before, to monitor the eventual release of the official results and the disposition of claims by the losing parties of electoral wrongdoing. Weeks or even months later, the major observer groups release their final reports, although the election is by then old news.

This scenario could be Nicaragua, Bosnia, or Russia in 1996, South Africa a few years back, or any of the other recent high-profile cases of countries attempting transitions to democracy. International election observation has mushroomed in the past 15 years, paralleling the global spread of democratization.[1] Not all transitional elections receive the kind of intense scrutiny described above, but international observers are now present at most elections that appear significant for a country's democratic development. Election observation is the best-established, most visible, and often best-funded type of democracy-related assistance. The United States is a major source of election observers, who are sent by groups specializing in democracy promotion such as the Carter Center, the National Democratic Institute for International Affairs, and the International Republican Institute as well as by myriad other nongovernmental organizations with interests in particular regions or countries.[2] Countless observer delegations also originate in Europe, sponsored by the European Union, the Council of Europe, European governments, parliamentary groups, political parties, and many other European associations and organizations. A number of international organizations have also gotten into the act, including the United Nations, the Organization of American States (OAS), the Organization for Security and Cooperation in Europe (OSCE), and the Organization of African Unity.

All this activity has clearly had positive effects on many elections and represents an important evolutionary step by the international community in promoting the principle of democracy around the world. At the same time, however, there lurks the troubling sense that election-observation efforts often involve as much show as substance. It is difficult to get close to a major international election-observation effort without feeling that something is amiss in the zoo-like atmosphere on election day, and that many of the observers are motivated as much by vanity and a tourist's taste for the exotic as by a serious commitment to supporting democracy abroad. Furthermore, government officials, journalists, and others have made a habit of misunderstanding and misusing election-observation efforts in ways that end up deforming the observation efforts themselves. It is time, therefore, to step back and take stock of this now ubiquitous but still relatively unexamined feature of contemporary international affairs.

## Positive Contributions

A basic function of international election observation is detecting—and, if possible, deterring—electoral fraud. Election observers have indeed helped draw attention to fraud in many countries. Two prominent such cases occurred in the 1980s in the Philippines and Panama. U.S. observers cried foul, to great effect, when President Ferdinand Marcos of the Philippines tried to steal the 1986 "snap" election and when General Manuel Antonio Noriega did the same for his chosen candidate in Panama in 1989. More recently, international observers usefully highlighted substantial problems with the 1996 presidential election in Armenia and parliamentary elections in Albania, as well as with Haiti's local and parliamentary elections of 1995 and the Dominican Republic's parliamentary elections of 1994.

Election observers not only publicize electoral fraud but sometimes help prevent it. Out of fear of being caught by foreign observers, political authorities may abandon plans to rig elections. Of course, few foreign officials would readily acknowledge having had such plans, making it hard to measure precisely the deterrent effect of electoral observation. Yet that effect should not be underestimated. In reality, the ability of many observer missions to detect fraud, beyond blatant ballot-stuffing, is weak. Very well designed observation efforts mounted by experienced organizations (with extensive preelection coverage, close coordination with domestic monitors, and a parallel vote count) do have a chance of catching the subtler forms of wrongdoing, such as manipulation of voter-registration lists, strategic ballot-tampering, and small but significant distortions in vote tabulation.[3] But the numerous teams of inexperienced observers who stay for only a short time around election day are unlikely to see beyond the obvious. Yet government officials planning elections in transitional countries often overestimate the ability of foreign observers to detect fraud, at least the first time they deal with them. Thus the deterrent effect of foreign observers can be substantial.

In addition to detecting and deterring fraud, election observation, if properly structured, can help hold together shaky electoral processes in transitional countries. The sustained engagement of international groups can encourage a wary citizenry to take the electoral process seriously and participate in it. The involvement of international observers may also convince skeptical opposition politicians that competing in the elections is preferable to engaging in civil disobedience or violence. Last year in the Dominican Republic, for example, politicians opposed to President Joaquín Balaguer were steered away from boycotting or otherwise disrupting the national elections, largely by the assurance that credible international observers would monitor the process. Observers can help keep an electoral process on track when an entrenched leader loses the election and then balks at giving up power. The presence of international observers at the 1990 Nicaraguan elections, for example, helped bring about President Daniel Ortega's acceptance of the results.[4]

More generally, international election observation has contributed greatly to the dissemination and strengthening of basic standards of election administration. For more than ten years, observers have stressed to election officials, politicians, and others in countries attempting democratic transitions that, for elections to gain international credibility, certain procedures must be followed: ballots must be counted at the polling stations and the results for each station posted at the site; measures must be taken to ensure that voters cast only one ballot; voter-registration lists must be posted in public areas before election day; poll workers must be trained; local political-party observers and domestic monitoring groups must be allowed to monitor the process; and so forth. In combination with extensive technical assistance to help election commissions effect such reforms, these efforts have led to significant improvements in the quality of many elections. They have also established a much broader recognition of a set of "best practices" concerning the administration of elections.

Election observation not only helps propagate standards for the conduct of elections, it advances the principle that holding genuinely competitive elections on a regular basis is an international norm. The right of people in every society to express their will through "periodic and genuine elections" is enshrined in the Universal Declaration of Human Rights (Article 21.3) and other basic international human rights instruments.[5] The right to elections was overlooked by most human rights advocates throughout the 1970s and 1980s. The political relativism of many in the human rights movement led to a disinclination to emphasize a right that seemed tied to a particular kind of political system. Moreover, in a period when numerous dictatorships were inflicting horrendous violence on their citizens, human rights advocates naturally focused on more basic rights issues like torture and political murder.

With the recent increase in democratic transitions (or at least attempted transitions) in many parts of the world and with the end of the Cold War, the idea that elections are a political right rather than merely a political option has gained considerable ground internationally.[6] By sending out more and more delegations to monitor elections in politically transitional countries, the established Western democracies have reinforced the basic idea that holding elections is something that civilized countries do. Like all internationally established political and civil rights, the right to elections is still often breached, but it is increasingly acknowledged as an important principle.

**Amateurs at Work**

Although international election observation has developed considerably over the past decade and has helped improve elections in many countries, it is not a cure-all. Flawed or even fraudulent elections still occur frequently despite the presence of international observers. The massive involvement of foreign observers in the Nicaraguan presidential and parliamentary elections of October 1996, for example, failed to prevent numerous technical flaws in the voting process, a highly politicized and inefficient election commission, and an extremely slow and problematic vote-counting process.[7] The extensive international support for the Bosnian elections of September 1996 was insufficient to ensure that they were free and fair. Observers noted—but could not forestall—the significant problems surrounding the Albanian parliamentary elections and the Armenian presidential elections of 1996.

In part this reflects the inevitable limitations of observing. Foreign observers cannot force profoundly polarized political factions to cooperate with one another. They cannot counter the deeply antidemocratic instincts of a strongman intent on holding on to power. And they cannot guarantee that the international community or individual nations will back up findings of electoral fraud with any punitive action. More generally, the continuation of problems with elections in many countries indicates that, despite significant evolution in recent years, international election observation still has a number of shortcomings.

To begin with, election observation has attracted too many groups, many of whom do amateurish work. For example, more than 80 different foreign groups observed the 1996 elections in Nicaragua.[8] There is a small core of organizations with a serious commitment to high-quality election observation and assistance, including the two U.S. political-party institutes, the Carter Center, the International Foundation for Election Systems, the Democracy Promotion Unit of the OAS, the UN Electoral Assistance Unit, and the Office for Democratic Institutions and Human Rights of the OSCE. Many of the rest are "dabblers" who come in for high-profile elections with short-term, poorly prepared delegations. They obtain little information of any value. Their observers often behave in embarrassingly unprofessional, patronizing ways. They deluge election commissions with requests for briefings during the most critical period of administrative preparations. And they usually make hasty postelection statements that divert attention from the more important reports issued by the organizations with more experience and a longer-term presence. European parliamentary and political-party groups seem particularly inclined toward this sort of "electoral tourism," although the United States makes its own contributions, with a variety of nongovernmental groups that seem motivated to observe foreign elections—particularly in Latin America—by political curiosity or a desire to express solidarity. Like any high-growth industry, election observation has become hindered by an excess of supply.

Another problem is the disproportionate attention that observers tend to give to election day itself, which is actually just one part of a long process that also includes the passage of the election law, the registration of parties and candidates, the preparation of voter lists, media coverage of competing parties during the campaign, campaign financing, the adjudication of complaints lodged against the election commission, and so on. The more professional observer organizations have modified their programs over time to give more attention to such elements, although they still tend to devote too great a share of their resources to the balloting process. The less experienced organizations devote almost all of their attention to election-day events, undermining the efforts of more professional groups to promote a more balanced approach.

An overemphasis on election day often leads observers to produce overly favorable assessments of the electoral process. In many cases the mechanical aspect of the voting is reasonably fair, but the preelection period is plagued by numerous problems, such as obstacles to the registration of certain candidates, unequal access to the media, and the governing party's use of state resources to finance its campaign. Such problems have become increasingly common in the past few years. Although blatant electoral fraud still occurs, efforts by entrenched leaders to manipulate electoral processes to their advantage have become more subtle as such leaders have been socialized into the new world of global democracy and internationally observed elections. The distortions now usually occur during the run-up to the election rather than on voting day itself. Short-term observers focused on election-day events miss this story altogether. Even the groups that monitor the entire process tend to base their postelection statements primarily on election-day events. They often begin by praising the authorities and the citizenry for the relative orderliness of the elections and only touch briefly on the many problems observed during the preelection period, such as a biased election commission, a lack of any serious civic-education efforts, grossly unfair campaign coverage on state television, or blatantly unequal resources.

The Russian presidential election of June 1996 exemplified this pattern. In general, the dozens of observer groups that collectively fielded well over a thousand foreign observers on election day issued ringing endorsements of the process, highlighting the lack of apparent fraud or widespread administrative problems with the voting. The fact that Boris Yeltsin's campaign almost certainly used significant state resources for its own purposes, benefited greatly from biased coverage on state television, paid journalists to write favorable stories, and used various other stratagems to ensure Yeltsin's victory received relatively little attention from the foreign observers.[9] This is not to say that the Russian elections were illegitimate, or not valuable to both Russia and the West. Yet the picture of the elections presented by the international observation effort was neither particularly revealing nor accurate.

A broader shortcoming of most observation efforts is that they give little attention to the deeper political functions and contexts of elections. An implicit assumption of most observers is that elections are perforce a good thing. Yet the experience of the past several years shows that elections in countries attempting democratic transitions are sometimes problematic. Elections may fail as a capstone of a conflict-resolution effort and trigger a return to civil conflict, as occurred in Angola in 1992 and Burundi in 1993. They may be a means of legitimating the power of an entrenched undemocratic leader who is able to make elections turn out in his favor without using too much fraud, as in Kazakhstan in 1995 or Gabon in 1993. Or elections may be part of a longer-term struggle for power that has little to do with democratic practices and outcomes, as in Pakistan in recent years.

In such situations, reporting on the technical conditions of the elections without confronting their deeper political function tells a dangerously incomplete story and risks legitimating undemocratic political processes. International election observation can thus end up feeding the broader tendency of the United States and other Western countries to push elections almost reflexively as a short-term solution to political problems of all sorts in countries racked with chronic instability, civil conflict, and other woes.

## Elusive Standards

In addition to these methodological shortcomings, international election observation faces problems related to the standards it applies. It is widely believed in the international community that elections can be judged according to a clear standard of "free and fair." Indeed, what journalists, policy makers, politicians, and others usually expect from election observers after important transitional elections is a simple answer to a basic question: "So, were they free and fair?" Paradoxically, the more experienced and professional an observer organization is, the more hesitant it will be to provide a clear-cut answer.

As mentioned above, the growth of international election observation during the past ten years has done much to spread the idea of a set of "best practices" or specific criteria for electoral competition. Yet in many cases it is still difficult to render an overall judgment about whether a particular election is free and fair. If an election meets all or nearly all the criteria, it is clearly free and fair; if it violates nearly all of them, it is clearly not free and fair. Many elections in politically transitional countries, however, fall somewhere in between. There is no set answer to the question of how many specific shortcomings must be observed, and how serious they must be, before an election can be called "*not* free and fair." For example, what are we to make of an election that was fairly well organized on election day but featured problems with the registration of candidates and unequal access to the media, as well as occasional but serious incidents of harassment of opposition parties? Can such an election be judged free and fair? What about an election with a relatively open, equitable campaign but with major administrative disorganization in a few parts of the country on election day and evidence of manipulation of the vote counting in one major region?

There are no simple answers to such questions. The idea that there exists an unambiguous standard of free and fair that permits definitive judgments about profoundly complex transitional elections is an unhelpful illusion. As Jørgen Elklit and Palle Svensson conclude, "The phrase 'free and fair' cannot denote compliance with a fixed, universal standard of electoral competition: No such standard exists, and the complexity of the electoral process makes the notion of any simple formula unrealistic."[10]

The more seasoned election-observation organizations have come to understand this by dint of experience. They may refer to obviously problem-free elections as free and fair or to blatantly fraudulent elections as not free and fair. For many transitional elections, however, they avoid those magic words, instead describing the positive and negative aspects of the process and leaving it to others to draw conclusions. Or they stick with more basic, and obviously subjective, judgments such as whether an election reflected the overall will of the people. The less experienced observer groups, less aware of the complexities of the free and fair standard, are more likely to offer the sound bite that journalists and others seek. In the process they hinder the efforts of more professional groups to present an accurate picture of elections that may have been sensitive, ambiguous, and complex.

A related problem is that international observers are often too easy on electoral wrongdoing. To be sure, they condemn blatantly fraudulent elections. Yet they frequently go relatively lightly on elections that, while not obviously fraudulent, nonetheless have significant flaws. This results in part from observers' tendency to overemphasize election-day events at the expense of other elements of the process. There are other reasons as well. In elections in countries with little history of democracy, particularly in Africa and the former Soviet Union, foreign observers sometimes take the attitude, "Well, what can you expect?" The notion that it is important to offer at least some encouragement to societies that are struggling with the basics leads them to downplay serious problems.

Some groups find it difficult to criticize governments that have extended the courtesy of opening their doors to the observers. Intergovernmental organizations like the United Nations, the OSCE, and the OAS are understandably reluctant to direct harsh criticism at member states, although in the past several years the OSCE and the OAS have begun to overcome this tendency and to speak out forthrightly against electoral abuses. Observer organizations are sometimes involved in other assistance programs in the countries whose elections they are observing. Coming down hard on a flawed election can mean being shut out of that country altogether, a consideration that can weigh against observers' taking a tough stance. After the National Democratic Institute issued a critical statement on the 1992 presidential elections in Cameroon, for example, the Cameroonian government made clear its disinclination to allow the group to do further work in the country.

Local political realities can also inhibit observers from expressing critical views of an election. Elections are sometimes held in an environment of great civil tension and potential conflict. A sharp condemnation by foreign observers of a flawed election could precipitate serious violence or political instability. Observers inevitably seek to avoid this outcome, even if it means soft-pedaling their findings.

**Partiality and Other Problems**

If international observers are often too lenient, they are also not always impartial. The image of objectivity that election observers cultivate is sometimes undeserved. Observers can and do pursue partisan political agendas, to the detriment of their work. Among U.S. observer groups, such divisions were often obvious during the Cold War: Many ideological clashes occurred over accounts of elections in El Salvador and Nicaragua during the 1980s. The end of the Cold War has not eliminated this tendency. With regard to the June 1995 legislative and local elections in Haiti, it was hardly surprising that the official U.S. observer delegation, representing an administration intent on proving that its policy of establishing democracy in Haiti had been a success, reached a favorable conclusion about the elections, whereas the International Republican Institute, affiliated with a political party harshly critical of the Clinton administration's policy toward Haiti, found much to condemn in the process.[11]

Partisanship among international election observers is by no means limited to U.S. groups. The findings of observer missions sponsored by European political parties or the party internationals—such as the Socialist International or the Liberal International—sometimes seem to reflect party allegiances, particularly in Eastern Europe and Latin America, where certain parties are linked in various ways to European counterparts. In the disputed Albanian parliamentary elections of May 1996, for example, OSCE observers publicly split over their assessment of the elections, at least in part along ideological lines. The faction taking the more critical line consisted primarily of representatives of a Norwegian left-of-center party whose participation in the observer effort was facilitated by the Socialist International in cooperation with the Albanian socialists, who were the principal aggrieved party in the elections.

A final shortcoming of international election observation is its underemphasis on domestic election monitors. Domestic election monitoring in transitional countries, which consists of efforts by nonpartisan civic groups as well as local political parties, has gained considerable ground in recent years. There are still cases in which international observers are clearly needed, such as first-time elections in highly polarized societies emerging from civil conflict. Yet domestic monitors can largely fulfill the need for observation in many transitional situations. They have played a significant role in elections in many countries, including Chile, South Africa, Nicaragua, Peru, the Dominican Republic, Romania, Bulgaria, Benin, Paraguay, Mexico, Panama, Bangladesh, Zambia, and the Philippines.[12]

Domestic election monitors, if properly organized and prepared, have important advantages over foreign observers. They can much more easily turn out in very large numbers, usually in the thousands. They know the political culture, the language, and the territory in question and consequently are capable of seeing many things that short-term foreign observers cannot. As citizens, they embody the crucial idea that the society in question should take primary responsibility for improving its own political processes. Domestic monitoring often involves the establishment and development of substantial local organizations that stay in place after the elections are over, using their newly honed skills for civic education and other pro-democratic undertakings, in sharp contrast to the "here today, gone tomorrow" nature of foreign observers. And domestic monitors can deliver much more "bang for the buck" than can foreign groups, given that their travel, accommodation, and other logistical costs are much lower.

Despite these significant strengths of domestic monitors, most international observer groups have done relatively little to support them. International observer organizations do sometimes work cooperatively with domestic groups where such groups already exist, but most have not invested substantial resources in supporting the formation, training, and development of local monitors. A major exception is the National Democratic Institute, which has a notable record of fostering domestic observation efforts in a number of countries and has done much to establish nonpartisan domestic monitoring as an accepted part of the international electoral scene.

This pattern of neglect in part reflects international observer groups' lingering fear that domestic monitors will prove incompetent and too caught up in local political affairs to be impartial. Clearly, this approach fails to acknowledge the frequent problems of amateurism and partiality among international groups themselves. It also ignores the many recent examples—of which Nicaragua is just one—of elections in which domestic observers have proved themselves capable of highly professional, nonpartisan work. There is another, equally important, reason for the neglect of domestic observation: Many international groups prefer to send out their own high-profile, exciting missions around the world rather than engage in the unglamorous and painstaking work of helping local groups to do the work themselves.

**Looking Ahead**

The recent wave of international election observation has probably crested but has not yet run its course. In Latin America, the first region where election observation became widespread, the need for international observers is diminishing as more and more countries regularize their electoral practices. International observers will, however, still have a role to play in a few countries in the region over the next several years, most notably Mexico and a few Caribbean and Central American states. Similarly, the hour for large-scale foreign observer missions in Central and Eastern Europe has passed, with the important exceptions of Albania, Bulgaria, and parts of the former Yugoslavia. In Asia, the utility of further election observation will depend largely on whether political openings occur in some of the region's currently nondemocratic countries, such as Burma, China, Indonesia, and Vietnam. With so many elections going awry in the former Soviet Union and sub-Saharan Africa, it appears that observers are still much needed in those regions. And if the Middle East ever decides to get serious about political liberalization, foreign observers will undoubtedly expand their activities (to date limited) in that region.

Given that international election observation will continue for some time, it is worth considering how it can be improved. In general, the evolution away from short-term, in-and-out missions to longer-term, more comprehensive efforts should continue. In parallel fashion, observers must continue to strive for professionalism and adherence to high standards. They should work to counteract the pressures that lead observers to be too lenient in their assessments; take much greater pains to be impartial; and become warier of facile invocation of the often-misused free and fair standard. Observer groups must pay closer attention to the political setting of the elections that they observe, being careful not to perpetuate the flawed notion that early elections are desirable in every case. Finally, international observer organizations must devote more of their resources to building up domestic monitoring groups and pressing for the acceptance of such groups by the international community.

The single most obvious solution to many of the problems of international election observation is a reduction in the number of international observation groups. Bluntly stated, the amateurs need to leave the field to the professionals. Bringing this about will not be easy given that there is not—nor should there be—a central body that decides who will observe each election. Donor agencies can help by resisting the temptation to over-fund observation efforts for prominent elections. It is not clear, for example, why the U.S. government had to fund five separate U.S. observer missions to the 1996 Nicaraguan elections, in addition to the official U.S. delegation. Governments should resist the temptation to send symbolic observer teams to prominent transitional elections. Having twelve separate official European delegations (averaging five members each) in Nicaragua for the 1996 presidential election was an example of unnecessary observer clutter, especially given the presence of a large European Union delegation and more than 20 other European delegations made up of European parliamentarians, local politicians, and political activists. Some attrition may occur in the ranks of the foreign observers as the number of exciting breakthrough elections in such popular places as Chile, Poland, and South Africa declines relative to more ambiguous, problem-ridden elections in less fashionable places like Azerbaijan, Sierra Leone, and Pakistan. The current effort by the Stockholm-based International Institute for Democracy and Electoral Assistance to establish a code of conduct for election observers may help to solidify basic professional standards for international election observation.[13]

Election-observation groups and their funders must take primary responsibility for improving election observation. Yet change can and should come from other sources as well. Government officials and members of the media frequently misunderstand and misuse election observers. Because they are among the most important consumers of the work of election observers, their mistaken approaches end up deforming the overall enterprise.

In important transitional elections, officials of governments with strong diplomatic ties to the country in question are often committed to helping ensure that the elections go reasonably smoothly. These governments frequently send observer delegations in the hope of producing an independent stamp of approval for the electoral process. Not surprisingly, these officials become alarmed if the observers uncover problems. Embassy officers of the interested governments respond to such situations by trying to "massage" the postelection statements of observer groups. They often attempt to persuade observers to tone down their criticisms and put the elections in what embassy officers like to call a "broader perspective"—in other words, concluding that they were, in effect, "not that bad considering the country's atrocious history." Such reeducation efforts start with the briefings that embassy officers give to observers when they arrive in the country and then take the form of insistent phone calls and emotional meetings in the often frenetic morning hours on the day after the election, when observers are finalizing their postelection statements. The less experienced groups are sometimes greatly influenced by such efforts. The more professional groups have learned to maintain a certain degree of independence. Yet given that the major observer groups are usually operating with government funds and relying to some extent on the services provided by their local embassy, such efforts are never completely ineffectual.

Another common—and equally problematic—idea entertained by government officials is that their country should send observers to a particular election in order to "show the flag." This assigns to observers the hollow and essentially inappropriate role of simply affirming their government's support for the electoral process in question. It detracts from the idea that the observers' mission is to uphold international standards rather than to advance bilateral policy interests. It leads to the sending of observers to elections where they are not needed. More generally, it works against the more discriminating use of the relatively scarce resources available for election assistance.

Not only do government officials sometimes misuse observers, they also often misunderstand their capabilities and methods. Journalists are also guilty on this score. Officials concerned about a possibly shaky electoral process in another country tend to overestimate the beneficial effects of observers. Often, they seem to envisage squads of objective, tough-minded outsiders descending on the local scene, nipping fraud in the bud and providing a certificate of good health, much like a team of incorruptible customs inspectors going through a shipment of dubious foreign meat. Journalists will report that international observers have blessed an election in some conflict-ridden foreign land, with little understanding of what those observers could actually accomplish, along with a naive assumption that observers can always be trusted.

Like election observers themselves, many government officials and journalists evaluating elections in transitional countries devote too much attention to voting day and too little to the rest of the electoral process. Journalists often behave the same way as inexperienced observers, flying in a few days before crucial elections, having a look around on voting day, then issuing proclamations the day after. The questions that officials and journalists pose to observer groups too often focus on whether the voting was calm and orderly, and whether ballot-stuffing or other obvious fraud was observed. They also attach too much importance to the concept of free and fair as a sharp dividing line. Both groups display a strong need to boil down the complexities of transitional elections into simple "either-or" judgments. And they try to force this need onto election observers. Finally, officials and journalists tend to give short shrift to the work of domestic monitor. They are often unfamiliar with the operation of such efforts and inclined to believe that domestic groups' conclusions will be biased. They want the word from the foreign observer, not the locals; they thus reinforce the tendency of many international organizations to give inadequate support to domestic monitoring programs.

Election observation will continue to be an important part of international politics for at least the next five to ten years. Its capacity to detect and deter fraud, and to reinforce shaky electoral processes, will be put to many hard tests in regions such as the former Soviet Union, Africa, and Asia. Election-observation groups must push themselves to further the professionalization of election observation that has begun to occur, and their efforts in this area must be supported by donors. At the same time, consumers of the work of observers, particularly government officials and journalists, must aim to improve their own understanding of the observers' roles. If these goals are faithfully pursued, election observation will continue to mature, and its already significant contributions to the spread of democracy around the world will increase.

### Notes

The Carnegie Endowment gratefully acknowledges the permission of the Johns Hopkins University Press to reprint this article, which originally appeared in the *Journal of Democracy*, vol. 8, no. 3 (July 1997).

1. For a broader historical perspective on international election observation, see David Padilla and Elizabeth Houppert, "International Election Observing: Enhancing the Principle of Free and Fair Elections," *Emory International Law Review* 7 (Spring 1991): 73–132.

2. The Washington-based International Foundation for Election Systems is a major actor in elections in politically transitional countries but concentrates more on technical assistance to election administrators than on election observation.

3. On parallel vote counts, see Larry Garber and Glenn Cowan, "The Virtues of Parallel Vote Tabulations," *Journal of Democracy* 4 (April 1993): 95–107.

4. On the broader issue of the role of international actors in keeping shaky political transitions on track, see Jennifer McCoy, "Mediating Democracy: A New Role for International Actors," in David Bruce, ed., *Security in a New World Order* (Atlanta: Georgia State University Press, 1992), pp. 129–40.

5. See Padilla and Houppert, "International Election Observing," 80–5.

6. See Thomas Franck, "The Emerging Right to Democratic Governance," *American Journal of International Law* 86 (January 1992): 46–91.

7. See Jennifer L. McCoy and Shelley A. McConnell, "Nicaragua: Beyond the Revolution," *Current History* 96 (February 1997): 75–80.

8. Data on the Nicaraguan election observation were provided by the International Institute for Democracy and Electoral Assistance (Stockholm).

9. On Yeltsin's campaign methods, see Lee Hockstader, "Yeltsin Paying Top Ruble for Positive News Coverage," *Washington Post*, 30 June 1996, p. AI; and European Institute for the Media, "Media and the Russian Presidential Elections" (Dusseldorf: 4 July 1996).

10. Jørgen Elklit and Palle Svensson, "What Makes Elections Free and Fair?" p. 43 below. On the free and fair standard see also Guy S. Goodwin-Gill, *Free and Fair Elections: International Law and Practice* (Geneva: Inter-Parliamentary Union, 1994); and Gregory H. Fox, "Multinational Election Monitoring: Advancing International Law on the High Wire," *Fordham International Law Journal* 18 (May 1995): 1658–7.

11. U.S. Agency for International Development Administrator Brian Atwood, who led the official U.S. observer delegation, described the 1995 Haitian elections as "a very significant breakthrough for democracy." By contrast, on the same day, the International Republican Institute criticized "the nationwide breakdown of the electoral process" in Haiti. State Department Briefing, 27 June 1995; International Republican Institute, "Haiti Election Alert," 27 June 1995.

12. For an analysis of domestic observation efforts, see Neil Nevitte and Santiago A. Canton, "The Role of Domestic Observers" *Journal of Democracy*, 8 (July 1987): 47–61.

13. International Institute for Democracy and Electoral Assistance, "Draft Code of Conduct for the Ethical and Professional Discharge of Election Observation Activities" (Stockholm, 1996).

# CHAPTER EIGHT

# Civil Society:
# Think Again
# (1999)

## The Concept of Civil Society Is a Recent Invention

ENLIGHTENMENT NEEDED. The term *civil society* can be traced through the works of Cicero and other Romans to the ancient Greek philosophers, although in classical usage civil society was equated with the state. The modern idea of civil society emerged in the Scottish and Continental Enlightenment of the late eighteenth century. A host of political theorists, from Thomas Paine to Georg Hegel, developed the notion of civil society as a domain parallel to but separate from the state—a realm where citizens associate according to their own interests and wishes. This new thinking reflected changing economic realities: the rise of private property, market competition, and the bourgeoisie. It also grew out of the mounting popular demand for liberty, as manifested in the American and French revolutions.

The term fell into disuse in the mid-nineteenth century as political philosophers turned their attention to the social and political consequences of the industrial revolution. It bounced back into fashion after World War II through the writings of the Marxist theorist Antonio Gramsci, who revived the term to portray civil society as a special nucleus of independent political activity, a crucial sphere of struggle against tyranny. Although Gramsci was concerned about dictatorships of the right, his books were influential in the 1970s and 1980s with persons fighting against dictatorships of all political stripes in Eastern Europe and Latin America. Czech, Hungarian, and Polish activists also wrapped themselves in the banner of civil society, endowing it with a heroic quality when the Berlin Wall fell.

Suddenly, in the 1990s, civil society became a mantra for everyone from presidents to political scientists. The global trend toward democracy opened up space for civil society in formerly dictatorial countries around the world. In the United States and Western Europe, public fatigue with tired party systems sparked interest in civil society as a means of social renewal. Especially in the developing world, privatization and other market reforms offered civil society the chance to step in as governments retracted their reach. And the information revolution provided new tools for forging connections and empowering citizens. Civil society became a key element of the post–Cold War zeitgeist.

### NGOs Are the Heart of Civil Society

**Not really.** At the core of much of the current enthusiasm about civil society is a fascination with nongovernmental organizations (NGOs), especially advocacy groups devoted to public interest causes–the environment, human rights, women's issues, election monitoring, anticorruption, and other "good things." Such groups have been multiplying exponentially in recent years, particularly in countries undertaking democratic transitions. Nevertheless, it is a mistake to equate civil society with NGOs. Properly understood, civil society is a broader concept, encompassing all the organizations and associations that exist outside of the state (including political parties) and the market. It includes the gamut of organizations that political scientists traditionally label interest groups—not just advocacy NGOs but also labor unions, professional associations (such as those of doctors and lawyers), chambers of commerce, ethnic associations, and others. It also incorporates the many other associations that exist for purposes other than advancing specific social or political agendas, such as religious organizations, student groups, cultural organizations (from choral societies to birdwatching clubs), sports clubs, and informal community groups.

Nongovernmental organizations do play important, growing roles in developed and developing countries. They shape policy by exerting pressure on governments and by furnishing technical expertise to policy makers. They foster citizen participation and civic education. They provide leadership training for young people who want to engage in civic life but are uninterested in working through political parties. In many countries, however, NGOs are outweighed by more traditional parts of civil society. Religious organizations, labor unions, and other groups often have a genuine base in the population and secure domestic sources of funding, features that advocacy groups usually lack, especially the scores of new NGOs in democratizing countries. The burgeoning

NGO sectors in such countries are often dominated by elite-run groups that have only tenuous ties to the citizens on whose behalf they claim to act, and they depend on international funders for budgets they cannot nourish from domestic sources.

## Civil Society Is Warm and Fuzzy

**That depends on whether you like snuggling up to the Russian mafia and militia groups from Montana as well as to your local parent-teacher association.** They are part of civil society too. Extrapolating from the courageous role of civic groups that fought communism in Eastern Europe, some civil society enthusiasts have propagated the misleading notion that civil society consists only of noble causes and earnest, well-intentioned actors. Yet civil society everywhere is a bewildering array of the good, the bad, and the outright bizarre. A random walk through Web pages on the Internet helps convey a sense of that diversity. Recognizing that people in any society associate and work together to advance nefarious as well as worthy ends is critical to demystifying the concept of civil society. As commentator David Rieff wrote recently in connection with Bosnia, "[Former Bosnian Serb leader Radovan] Karadzic represented the aspirations of ordinary Serbs in that extraordinary time all too faithfully, and could rightfully lay just as great a claim to being an exemplar of civil society as Vaclav Havel." If one limits civil society to those actors who pursue high-minded aims, the concept becomes, as Rieff notes, "a theological notion, not a political or sociological one."

The idea that civil society inherently represents the public good is wrong in two other ways as well. Although many civic activists may feel they speak for the public good, the public interest is a highly contested domain. Clean air is a public good, but so are low energy costs. The same could be said of free trade versus job security at home or free speech versus libel protection. Single-issue NGOs, such as the National Rifle Association and some environmental groups, are intensely, even myopically, focused on their own agendas; they are not interested in balancing different visions of the public good. Struggles over the public interest are not between civil society on the one hand and bad guys on the other but within civil society itself.

Moreover, civil society is very much concerned with private economic interests. Nonprofit groups, from tenants' organizations to labor unions, work zealously to advance the immediate economic interests of their members. Some civil society groups may stand for "higher"—that is, nonmaterial—principles and values, but much of civil society is preoccupied with the pursuit of private and frequently parochial and grubby ends.

## A Strong Civil Society Ensures Democracy

**Tempting thought.** An active, diverse civil society often does play a valuable role in helping advance democracy. It can discipline the state, ensure that citizens' interests are taken seriously, and foster greater civic and political participation. Moreover, scholars such as Harvard political scientist Robert Putnam— whose influential 1995 article, "Bowling Alone: America's Declining Social Capital," chronicled an apparent decline in U.S. community-oriented associations—have argued forcefully that a weak civil society leads to a lack of "civic engagement" and "social trust." But other evidence suggests that a strong civil society can actually reflect dangerous political weaknesses. In a 1997 article that some have nicknamed "Bowling With Hitler," Princeton professor Sheri Berman presented a sobering analysis of the role of civil society in Weimar Germany. In the 1920s and 1930s, Germany was unusually rich in associational life, with many people belonging to the sorts of professional and cultural organizations that are thought to be mainstays of pro-democratic civil society. Berman argues, however, that not only did Germany's vibrant civil society fail to solidify democracy and liberal values, it subverted them. Weak political institutions were unable to respond to the demands placed on them by the many citizens' organizations, leading the latter to shift their allegiance to nationalist, populist groups and eventually to the Nazi Party. In the end, the density of civil society facilitated the Nazis' rapid creation of a dynamic political machine.

Even in established democracies with strong political institutions, however, there are reasons to doubt the simplistic idea that when it comes to civil society, "the more the better." As early as the 1960s, some scholars warned that the proliferation of interest groups in mature democracies could choke the workings of representative institutions and systematically distort policy outcomes in favor of the rich and well connected or, more simply, the better organized. In the 1990s, warnings about "demosclerosis" have intensified as advocacy and lobbying organizations continue to multiply.

## Democracy Ensures a Strong Civil Society

**No guarantees here either.** Japan has been a stable democracy for half a century but continues to have a relatively weak civil society, particularly in terms of independent civic groups working on the kinds of issues that activists in the United States and Europe hold dear, such as the environment, consumer protection, human rights, and women's issues. In France, one of the mother countries of Westen liberal democracy, civil society takes a distant back seat to a powerful state. Spain, the exemplar of recent democratic transitions, is relatively weak in associational life. Political parties and elections are what ensure a pluralism of political choices; they can certainly operate in a country with only lightly developed civic associations. Some American political analysts criticize Japan, France, Spain, and other countries where civic participation is low, arguing that these states are at best stunted democracies because they lack what Americans believe is an optimal level of citizen engagement. Many Japanese, French, and Spanish people, however, contend that their systems better accord with their own traditions concerning the relationship of the individual to the state and allow their governments to make more rational, less fettered allocations of public goods. Obviously, the argument that a democracy is not a real democracy unless it has American-style civil society is not only wrong but dangerous. A strong belief in civil society should not fuel an intolerant attitude toward different kinds of democracies.

## Civil Society Is Crucial for Economic Success

**It's not so simple.** As part of their "all good things go together" approach, enthusiasts hold out civil society as a guarantee not only of political virtue but also of economic success. An active, strong civil society, they say, can give useful input on economic policy issues, facilitate the growth of private enterprise, and help ensure that the state does not suffocate the economy. In practice, however, the connection between economic growth and civil society is not so straightforward.

Compare two cases. South Korea's economic miracle was built on the back of a repressed civil society, especially a besieged labor sector. Only in the 1980s, when the military regime felt it could afford to loosen up, was civil society given space to flourish. Unions, student groups, and religious organizations took full advantage of the opportunity and pressed bravely and effectively for democratization. Heroic as they were, these groups cannot be given credit for one of the fastest growing economies to emerge in the last 50 years. By contrast, Bangladesh is rich in civil society, with thousands of NGOs, advocacy groups, and social service organizations operating at the national and local levels. Yet this wealth of NGOs, by no means a new phenomenon in Bangladesh, has not translated into wealth for the people. Bangladesh remains one of the poorest countries in the world, with an annual per capita income of less than $350.

A well-developed civil society can be a natural partner to a successful market economy. When citizens reach a comfortable standard of living, they have more time, education, and resources to support and take part in associational life. And many sectors of civil society can reinforce economic development by encouraging sound governmental policies and by increasing the flow of knowledge and information within a society. As with the relationship between civil society and democracy, however, it is important not to assume any iron laws of causality. The path to economic success is not necessarily paved with civil society, and a strong civil society can co-exist with a relatively weak economy (and vice versa). What's more, too much or the wrong type of civil society can be economically harmful. Some economists believe, for example, that Latin American labor unions, a mainstay of the region's civil society, have been one of the largest obstacles to Latin America's economic growth and stability.

## Real Civil Society Doesn't Take Money from the Government

**Oh, really?** When civil society groups wage a campaign for freedom in a dictatorship, a key element of their political bona fides is complete independence, financial and otherwise, from the government. In democratic and democratizing countries, however, the rules are different. Many civil society groups receive government funding. In parts of Western Europe, government support for civil society is widespread, including among groups that take on the government, such as human rights and environmental organizations. Even in the United States, governmental funding of civil society is much more extensive than many people realize. A major comparative study of nonprofit sectors, sponsored by Johns Hopkins University, found that "Government is thus almost twice as significant a source of income for American nonprofit organizations as is private giving, despite the presence there of numerous large foundations and corporate giving programs."

## The Rise of Civil Society Means the Decline of the State

**Definitely not.** The rise of civil society induces some to see a nearly state-free future in which tentative, minimalistic states hang back while powerful nongovernmental groups impose a new, virtuous civic order. This vision is a mirage. Civil society groups can be much more effective in shaping state policy if the state has coherent powers for setting and enforcing policy. Good nongovernmental advocacy work will actually tend to strengthen, not weaken state capacity. A clear example is U.S. environmental policy. Vigorous civic activism on environmental issues has helped prompt the creation of governmental environmental agencies, laws, and enforcement mechanisms. Nothing cripples civil society development like a weak, lethargic state. In Eastern Europe, civil society has come much further since 1989 in the countries where governments have proved relatively capable and competent, such as Poland and Hungary, and it has been retarded where states have wallowed in inefficiency and incompetence such as Romania, and for parts of the decade, Bulgaria.

Outside of dictatorial contexts, states can play a valuable role in developing a healthy civil society. They can do so by establishing clear, workable regulatory frameworks for the nongovernmental sector, enacting tax incentives for funding of nonprofit groups, adopting transparent procedures, and pursuing partnerships with NGOs. Civil society can and should challenge, irritate, and even, at times, antagonize the state. But civil society and the state need each other and, in the best of worlds, they develop in tandem, not at each other's expense.

## Civil Society Has Gone Global

**Not quite.** The recent success of the International Campaign to Ban Landmines, in which a coalition of NGOs (together with some governments, in particular Canada's) took on the United States and other powerful states, sparked tremendous interest in the idea of transnational civil society. Activists, scholars, journalists, and others began talking up the phenomenon of advocacy across borders. Global civil society appears a natural extension of the trend toward greater civil society within countries. At last count, more than 5,000 transnational NGOs—NGOs based in one country that regularly carry out activities in others—had been identified.

The phenomenon is significant. A confluence of factors—the lowering of political barriers after the end of the Cold War, new information and communications technologies, lowered transportation costs, and the spread of democracy—has created a fertile ground for nongovernmental groups to widen their reach and form multicountry links, networks, and coalitions.

Some caution is nonetheless in order. In the first place, transnational civil society is not as new as it sounds. The Roman Catholic Church, to name just one example, is a transnational civil society group that has had major international impact for many centuries. Second, most of the new transnational civil society actors are Western groups projecting themselves into developing and transitional societies. They may sometimes work in partnership with groups from those countries, but the agendas and values they pursue are usually their own. Transnational civil society is thus "global" but very much part of the same projection of Western political and economic power that civil society activists decry in other venues. Third, like civil society within borders, civil society across borders has its dark side. Hate groups are now hooking up with like-minded extremists in other time zones, feeding off each other's ugly passions. Organized crime is a transnational venture par excellence, exemplifying the most advanced forms of flexible, creative international organization and operation.

In short, transnational civil society is much like domestic civil society in its essentials. It has been around for a long time but is now growing quickly, both feeding and being fed by globalization. It carries the potential to reshape the world in important ways, but one must not oversell its strength or idealize its intentions. Whether local or global, civil society realism should not be a contradiction in terms.

**Note**

Originally published in *Foreign Policy* (Winter 1999–2000).

# CHAPTER NINE

# Western Civil Society Aid to Eastern Europe and the Former Soviet Union (1999)

I HAVE BEEN ASKED to offer some reflections on Western aid for civil society development in Eastern Europe and the former Soviet Union, to look back on the past ten years, to consider the challenges of the next decade, and also to place the aid in the context of developments in the region.

I do this as someone who is in between the categories of donor and recipient. I have worked on some democracy-related aid projects in Eastern Europe and the former Soviet Union. But my main involvement with the subject has been in studying the burgeoning world of aid for the promotion of democracy, of which civil society assistance is a critical part. I have sought to take an independent look at this field in an effort to understand its strengths and weaknesses, how it is evolving, and how it might be improved.

Any anniversary occasion, but especially the tenth anniversary of the fall of the Berlin Wall, presents the temptation to make rather grand statements and indulge in deep but probably not very lasting philosophizing. I have already heard various speeches and read articles occasioned by this especially important anniversary and have taken note of the serious dangers in such efforts—the danger of self-congratulation, the reverse danger of excessive gloom, and, above all, the danger of restating a stock set of platitudes and clichés.

I will attempt to avoid those temptations and dangers and will address the topic at hand in fairly plain terms. I begin with a bit of context, in a straightforward, almost clinical fashion, about the experience in the region during the past ten years and the Western role in this experience.

**War and Conflict**

Assessing the state of the postcommunist world, as it is often still known, is an enormous topic, one that could and, in fact, has consumed huge amounts of attention and inquiry. Here, I outline a few facts and trends, focusing initially on two essential issues—first, war and conflict and, second, the health of the many attempted transitions to democracy and capitalism.

Concerning war and conflict, we should remember that expectations about the possibility of armed conflict in Eastern Europe and the former Soviet Union were very uncertain when the Berlin Wall fell and, two years later, when the Soviet Union broke up. There were some alarming predictions of a wave of wars and ethnic-related violence. But the truth is, most of us had little idea what to expect.

Six major armed conflicts occurred in the 1990s. Two of these were in the former Yugoslavia—the war in and over Bosnia in the first half of the 1990s, with the related fighting between Serbia and Croatia, in which approximately 200,000 people died, and the war in Kosovo in 1999, where perhaps 10,000 died. In the former Soviet Union, there was the first Chechen war of the mid-1990s, with around 70,000 deaths; the ongoing second Chechen war, with as-yet-uncounted thousands of deaths; the civil war in Tajikistan in the first half of the 1990s, where 50,000 people died; and the conflict over Nagorno-Karabakh of the same years, where approximately 20,000 died. In addition, several smaller conflicts occurred—the Albanian civil war of 1997, the fighting involving Georgia and South Ossetia, the Moldovan conflict of 1992, and the fighting in Kyrgyzstan in 1990.

Alongside this sobering list is some good news, some "dogs that did not bark." Several relationships between different nationalities or ethnicities that appeared to have the potential for conflict remained within reasonable bounds, such as the Romanian–Hungarian conflict in Transylvania, the Czechs and Slovaks, the Kazakhs and Russians, the Latvians and Russians, and others.

The wars that did occur were primarily about borders and territory and about flawed politicians' use of war as a means of self-aggrandizement or self-promotion. Issues of ethnicity and nationality were often present, and ethnic tactics of the most vivid and horrible type were exploited. But the wars have not been a wave of ethnic conflict but rather a settling of borders and of territorial prerogatives. War is undoubtedly not at an end in the region. Given the problematic conditions of political life in many countries and the continuation of these conditions in what are still new states and new borders in Central Asia, southern Russia, the Caucasus, and the Balkans, more armed conflicts will probably erupt in the years ahead.

## The State of Transitions

The state of the many attempted transitions to democracy and capitalism is also a vast subject. Here, I can note only some of the basic trends, leaving untouched deeper questions about the texture of life and the complex cultural, moral, and personal experiences of transition. These are subjects for writers, artists, and philosophers. The many transitions in Eastern Europe and the former Soviet Union fall into three general groups. Seven countries, mostly with relatively small populations, have made substantial progress on both democratization and economic transitions. These are the Czech Republic, Hungary, Poland, the Baltic states, and Slovenia. Nine are doing badly on both fronts and have authoritarian or semi-authoritarian governments and statist economies. These include all of the Central Asian countries (except Kyrgyzstan), Armenia, Azerbaijan, Belarus, and two countries in the former Yugoslavia—Serbia and Croatia. The largest category of countries, with eleven members, are those hovering uneasily between success and failure. Some are stuck in a halfway state between democracy and dictatorship and between statism and market economics; others are drifting backward; and a few are creeping ahead. This is a broad category that spans more positive cases, such as Bulgaria, Slovakia, Macedonia, and Romania, and more negative ones, such as Ukraine and Albania, as well as Russia, Moldova, Kyrgyzstan, Georgia, and Bosnia.

Simplistic though they are, these categories show that 20 of the 27 countries in Eastern Europe and the former Soviet Union are either in a transitional gray zone or are not doing well at all. For many people in these 20 countries, the basic conditions of life have worsened significantly in the past ten years. In the former Soviet Union, for example, the GDP per capita has declined more than 40 percent since 1991. The GDP per capita in Russia proper, one of the richer countries of the former Soviet Union, is now well below that of Mexico, a country commonly associated with classic Third World poverty.

I will not attempt, here, to advance any explanations for the troubling state of these transitions but will set forth several conclusions about the process of transition. First, we have learned that economic and political reforms stand or fall together. At the start of the 1990s, some observers harbored the view that only strongman rule would succeed in making painful market reforms work. Others postulated that economic reforms would have to lead political reforms or vice versa. The experience on the ground has been clear—economic and political reforms reinforce each other and rarely proceed separately. This does not mean that every aspect of democratization and market reforms are complementary or that tensions of the dual transitions do not frequently arise. Yet, on the whole, countries move forward on both fronts or stay behind on both fronts.

Second, both economic and political reforms are not naturally forward-moving processes. In the excitement of the early 1990s, many people both outside and inside Eastern Europe and the former Soviet Union thought that once launched, transition processes would unfold naturally, with their own internal logic and momentum. People imagined that transition would be akin to placing a boat in a rapidly moving river and then simply steering it along. It turns out that reforms can and often do get captured or blocked at every step of the way. And the capture or blockage is not only the work of the losers in the transition processes but, just as often, of the winners. Those who gain from one phase of reforms frequently seek to freeze the process in place so they can milk the benefits of whatever position they have attained. The occurrence of this phenomenon in the economic sphere has been ably identified by Joel Hellman in his influential article "Winners Take All: The Politics of Partial Reform in Postcommunist Transitions" (*World Politics* 50, January 1998).

Third, no alternative political or economic ideology has arisen to challenge democracy or market capitalism. Although democratization and market reforms are failing in many former communist countries, they are not being trumped by some other positive alternative vision. There has not emerged, for example, a coherent model of a go-slow, protected, partial-transition approach. As transitions fade or fail, they produce no new alternatives but rather end up in banal dictatorships and the bleakest of corrupted statist economies.

Fourth, elections are very limited as tools to break up concentrated power. Basically, those countries where the old power structures were genuinely overturned in 1989 or 1991 are advancing democratically, and their elections are largely meaningful. Where power structures stayed in place and only changed their labels or public faces, elections, though regularly held, are not proving very meaningful. They are manipulated by the power holders and are merely exercises relegitimizing entrenched political forces rather than allowing citizens to choose their government. In short, elections are good for distributing power that has been broken up previously; they are not good for breaking up existing power structures.

Fifth, the experience of transition has been so varied and the countries of Eastern Europe and the former Soviet Union have had such disparate experiences that the very concept of postcommunism is now almost useless. To say that Poland and Turkmenistan are both postcommunist states says very little. It is time to bury the concept of postcommunism. There is no postcommunist region or world; there is Central Europe, southeastern Europe, the Baltic region, Central Asia, the Caucasus, Russia, and a few other subregions, all better understood for their particularities rather than their commonalties.

## The Western Role

The other part of the context of Western aid for civil society in Eastern Europe and the former Soviet Union is the overall Western role of which this aid is but one part. As with the transitions in these regions, this is a broad-ranging subject. I will be even briefer than in my treatment of the above issues, limiting myself to noting the many dimensions of the Western role. These dimensions include the following:

- The diplomatic role—the high level of government-to-government interaction between the American and West European governments, on the one hand, and the governments of the countries in Eastern Europe and the former Soviet Union, on the other, on virtually every major economic, political, security, and social issue of concern;
- The military role—which includes the expansion of the North Atlantic Treaty Organization (NATO) into Eastern Europe, the involvement of U.S. and West European military forces in the former Yugoslavia, and the continuing U.S. military stance and security relationship vis-à-vis Russia;
- The economic role—an increasing amount of Western trade with and investment in Eastern Europe and the former Soviet Union, as well as the uneven but significant spread of Western economic principles and practices;
- The institutional role—above all, the prospect of accession into the European Union for some East European and Baltic states but also the increased presence of the Council of Europe, the Organization for Security and Cooperation in Europe (OSCE), and various other multilateral institutions;
- The cultural role—from Western television, movies, music, and consumerism to scholarly exchanges and educational links;
- The symbolic role—the often intangible but nonetheless extremely important influence of the West by way of example; the West as the state of "normalcy" to which many Eastern European and some former Soviet republics aspire;
- And finally, the role of aid—the influence of the economic, political, social, and humanitarian aid that flowed into Eastern Europe and the former Soviet Union in the 1990s. I list aid last, not because it is the least important but to emphasize that it is just one element of a tremendously complex overall relationship.

Western aid to Eastern Europe and the former Soviet Union was on the order of $50 billion to $100 billion in the 1990s, depending on what one counts as aid and how one measures it. This is obviously a large amount of money but in per capita terms amounts to roughly $100 to $200 per person over the decade, or $10 to $20 per person per year. This is similar to Western aid to many parts of the developing world and is not an especially intensive effort when compared, for example, with the surge of U.S. aid to Central America in the 1980s, when, in the cause of combating the spread of leftist governments, the Reagan administration committed more than $100 per person per year in some countries.

I do not have space, here, to characterize the West's overall post-1989 role in Eastern Europe and the former Soviet Union in any searching or detailed way. The West generally has been a tremendously important influence in Eastern Europe, particularly in defining the basic endpoints to which transitions are directed but of only moderate importance in most of the former Soviet Union. The fact that it is generally a positive influence does not, however, remove a sense of flatness or disappointment about the Western role among many in the two regions. After the bubble of excitement around the fall of the Berlin Wall, the West never really seized the historical moment. Western societies were quick to move on with their own preoccupations and pastimes and to expect former communist countries to either get into line or go away. This was felt as a chilly reception, at least among some East Europeans. For them, it was akin to a person, who after trudging through a cold, dark forest for years, finally makes it to the grand, safe house they have been seeking as refuge. They knock at the door and are met by a blasé host who greets them perfunctorily then turns immediately back to working on a computer in another room, leaving the exhausted guest wondering whether they can come in and whether they are really welcome at all.

I cannot leave the issue of the West's role without noting that there have been at least two major failures. One was the failure of the United States and the major European powers, in the early 1990s, to seize the moment of the breakup of the Soviet Union and make a grand gesture toward Russia—to commit a dramatic quantity of resources to help Russia with its transition, and to set Western–Russian relations on a genuinely new footing. This failure may eventually be seen as one of the greatest lost opportunities of the second half of the twentieth century. The second failure was the entire unfortunate story of Western policy toward the former Yugoslavia, and in particular Bosnia, in the first half of the 1990s.

### Discovering Aid

With a decade of aid to Eastern Europe and the former Soviet Union under the bridge, we now take the fact of Western aid to these regions for granted. It is difficult to remember how strange and even exotic the mere idea of Western aid to these regions was, just a decade ago. During the 1980s, there had been Western aid to Solidarity in Poland and to dissident groups in some of the other communist countries. These were generally limited, specialized initiatives. Suddenly, with the fall of the Berlin Wall and the breakup of the former Soviet Union, the ground shifted rapidly, and Western aid agencies were opening offices in Moscow and Kiev and undertaking other previously unimaginable ventures.

The Soviet Union and the countries of Eastern Europe had not only been sealed politically from the West, they had been aid providers themselves. Aid programs sponsored by Romania, East Germany, the former Soviet Union, and other communist countries were common in parts of Africa, the Middle East, and Asia. The sudden status of these societies in the 1990s as recipients of Western aid was thus a profound reversal of their self-image as aid givers.

As Western aid providers rushed into the unfamiliar territory of Eastern Europe and the former Soviet Union at the start of the 1990s—I am referring, here, primarily to the major public providers of Western aid rather than to private Western foundations—they tended to follow one of two approaches, neither of which proved to be an effective strategy over time.

One approach was to view the provision of aid as a continuation of the ideological battles of the Cold War period. It entailed using aid to try to promote anticommunist groups and anticommunist individuals, as well as to exclude anyone with a politically tainted past, in pursuit of the idea that transition was equivalent to a process in which the "good guys" would push the "bad guys" completely off the political stage.

This ideological approach was appealing at first; it gave aid providers a compass in societies where they had seldom traveled. Although it led aid providers to support a number of worthwhile groups and initiatives, it did not, on the whole, wear well over time as an aid strategy. The idea of a clean line between the good guys and the bad guys often proved illusory or highly subjective. Although some people stood as clear examples of each category, many individuals did not fall so easily into either category and were not especially interested in having outsiders make moralistic judgments about their pasts. In a number of states, former communists reintegrated themselves into the new pluralistic political life, gaining public support and playing by the rules. In these countries, the transition process turned out to be about not pushing certain persons off the political stage, and those outsiders who insisted on continuing to act in that fashion were seen as divisive intruders. More generally, the populations of many former communist countries quickly lost interest in ideological positioning or posturing by politicians. They looked for competency and performance in the economic and political domains and were apathetic toward, or even suspicious of, those who continued to insist on a right of place based on intrinsic ideological virtue.

The other approach or set of instincts that aid providers, especially official aid providers, applied initially to their work was the entire methodology of aid they had evolved from decades of development cooperation in the Third World—the bureaucratic structures, the strategies, the attitudes, and even the actual personnel of traditional foreign aid programs. This was understandable, given that Western aid agencies were suddenly asked to set up programs in countries where they had never worked before and were asked to do so in a great rush. Inevitably, they drew on the methods they already knew. The essence of this approach is the external project method. This is the traditional foreign-aid approach in which an external donor organization runs all aspects of the work, largely using its own staff or expatriate consultants—from assessing the needs of the recipient country and designing the aid projects to meet those needs, to implementing the projects (with a subsidiary role for local "partners"), and later evaluating the outcome of the aid. It is a method derived from decades of working in very poor, underdeveloped countries, in which the available local human resources are thin, where the aid itself has established well-worn (largely unhealthy) patterns of dependency, and where donors have accumulated considerable expertise about the countries in which they are working.

These Third World aid patterns, themselves already subject to considerable criticism in aid circles, translated poorly to former Second World countries. Educational levels were often as high as in First World donor countries, radically altering the human-resources issue; recipient cultures were not habituated to the ways of aid donors who were accustomed to trampling, fairly unimpeded, over the sovereignty of their local partners; and donors had little if any on-the-ground experience in the countries in question.

Over time, most aid providers improved on these two initial, problematic strategies. They deemphasized ideological litmus tests and instead began to concentrate on rewarding good performance and pragmatism. They slowly began to recognize the differences between Third World and Second World patterns of underdevelopment and to develop more-genuine partnerships with local counterparts and to eschew the simplistic importation of Western models. In the economic, social, and political realms, Western aid has come to play a useful, though rarely determinative, role. Although official aid has frequently sought to produce large-scale institutional effects, its most important achievements have been the opportunities for education and growth it has offered to thousands of individuals throughout Eastern Europe and the former Soviet Union.

Although Western aid generally plays a positive role, official aid is, after ten years, at something of an impasse: where it works, that is, where governments and major institutions make good use of it, it is not essential; Where it is really needed, in the many countries failing in their economic and political transitions, it does not work well because the main recipients are rarely committed to genuine reform. In this context, aid to promote civil society is of critical importance. In the early years of the decade, most observers regarded civil society aid as a quick-acting dose of support to expand the envelope of freedom in the initial hump of the transition from communism. The assumption was that as the countries of Eastern Europe and the former Soviet Union "normalized," the more traditional forms of top-down aid would take over in importance and help move them toward the institutional consolidation of democracy and market economics. But with transitions moving slowly in most countries and running into many obstacles, civil society aid is now seen as something much more than just an initial boost. Many aid providers have come to see civil society development as the key to unblocking stagnant or failing transitions over the long term.

In the political domain, civil society development is deemed crucial to stimulating the public pressure and participation necessary to force poorly functioning state institutions to become more responsive and accountable. In the social and economic domains, a more diverse and active civil society is now held out as necessary to cushion the effects of restructuring, to ensure public understanding and support for market reforms, to prevent privatization from lapsing into cronyism, to connect newly empowered local governments to citizens, and to create many of the other components necessary to the transition to market economics. In short, Western aid for civil society development in Eastern Europe and the former Soviet Union was originally conceived and portrayed as the key to an initial democratic breakthrough. It has assumed a much wider, more lasting role, as a critical tool in overcoming the many entrenched obstacles to the consolidation of democracy and the achievement of economic success.

## Stages of Growth

Looking at civil society aid in practice, we can see that it passed through two stages in the 1990s and now is at the threshold of a third phase. The first phase was the short, heady, idealistic time of the early 1990s. Western private foundations and the few official aid agencies that had been involved in civil society aid made their initial contacts with new, independent civic groups and civic activists in Eastern Europe and the former Soviet Union. Time seemed to be of the essence, and small amounts of support to the right groups promised to make a great difference. During this period, the providers of civil society aid focused on the newly emergent groups devoted to public-interest advocacy—such as human rights groups, environmental organizations, election-monitoring groups, and civic-education associations—as well as to new, independent media, especially independent newspapers and journals. The idea was to help nurture those persons and groups fighting to assert the new freedoms, to support a core of nonpartisan but politically committed proponents of a civil society that would, in turn, serve as an incubator of democracy.

The second phase, which unfolded in the mid-1990s and continued through the rest of the decade, involved a broadening of civil society aid. Aid providers still interpreted promoting the development of civil society in terms of supporting nongovernmental organizations (NGOs), but the range of NGOs and of NGO aid was expanded considerably. Aid began to go to a wider circle of groups than those in the initial wave—beyond the politically oriented advocacy groups to service-delivery NGOs, working in children's welfare, public health, tenants' rights, and many other fields. Aid providers began to support centers for NGO training and development as NGO sectors grew rapidly, comprising thousands of organizations of all sizes.

As NGO sectors mushroomed in the recipient countries, providers of civil society aid began to confront a number of issues and problems with civil society aid and to accumulate a set of lessons that emerged from studies, reports, and conferences about NGO assistance. These lessons are now commonly held out as a set of "best practices" for aid donors and have rapidly taken on the quality of conventional wisdom. In this view, providers of civil society aid are urged to: (1) go beyond providing aid to the same circle of familiar faces in the capital cities and to disseminate aid to smaller, less Westernized groups in smaller cities and rural areas; (2) help establish mechanisms and incentives inducing the well-established NGOs (which donors initially favored) to provide training to the less well established groups; (3) help NGOs develop their core organizational capacities, especially financial management and human-resources management, rather than just providing support for project activities; (4) focus on sustainability by helping NGOs diversify their donor support, develop local sources of funding, and build local habits of corporate philanthropy; (5) support work to ameliorate the enabling environment for NGOs, such as the basic legal framework for NGOs and government officials' understanding of the nature and purpose of NGOs; (6) encourage advocacy NGOs to develop more-direct ties to the citizens on whose behalf they act; (7) not assume that public-interest advocacy groups have a real social base or are inevitably representative just because of the nature of the issues they pursue; (8) encourage NGOs to develop productive partnerships, when possible, with central and local governments, moving away from the idea that advocacy NGOs must naturally take a completely independent, or even antagonistic, stance toward their governments; and (9) foster greater donor coordination to avoid duplicate funding and contradictory strategies and to promote greater funding synergies.

These lessons now have the feel of well-worn conventional wisdom, at least among habitués of the many conferences on civil society aid in recent years. They did not have this quality five years ago; they had to be identified one by one, in response to shortcomings on the ground and the desire to do better. The fact that they have attained the status of conventional wisdom does not mean they are consistently followed in practice by most aid providers. Like most so-called best practices in the aid world, they remain aspirations for many donors.

This second phase of civil society aid—the expansion of NGO assistance—has peaked, and a third phase may now be starting. The context of this third phase has several features: that most of the postcommunist transitions launched in the early 1990s are in a gray zone or are clearly failing; that Western aid for civil society is shrinking, as U.S. Agency for International Development (USAID), the European Union, the Soros foundations, and other major sources of aid in the 1990s are pulling out of some countries or shifting priorities; and that within the countries of the region, the initial surge of interest and enthusiasm for NGOs has plateaued. The possible shape that this third phase of civil society assistance may take is as yet unclear. The task, now, is to identify the core challenges that lie ahead. I would like to set forth briefly some thoughts on what some of those challenges might be.

## Future Challenges

A critical challenge that providers of civil society aid must face is that of relating the promotion of civil society values to political-party development. Throughout most of Eastern Europe and the former Soviet Union, and for that matter in most politically transitional countries, political parties are a disaster. They are personalistic vehicles that are poorly organized and operated. They attract mediocre people and have especially weak appeal to young people. Their funding bases are often narrow and corrupt. They have no stable constituency and poor relations with the constituencies they do have.

For years, providers of civil society aid have encouraged their NGO recipients to steer clear of political parties and to cultivate both the ideal and the practice of nonpartisan civic engagement. There have been good reasons for this approach, but it is now necessary for persons concerned with civil society development to give attention to political-party development. Simply stated, parties are being left behind by NGOs.

Quite a few NGOs are well-run, relatively well-financed organizations, with highly capable staff working next to parties that are badly run, badly financed, and badly staffed. This is an unhealthy situation; for democracy to work, these countries need a talented, dynamic political class to operate alongside a talented, dynamic civic sector. It is time to think about ways to connect the promotion of civil society and political parties. This does not mean that providers of civil society aid should directly assist political parties or push for direct ties between civil society groups and political parties.

But it does mean not ignoring the political-party domain and not assuming that Western political parties are the only organizations that should play a role in political-party work. One example of an area for possible program development is party funding. Providers of civil society aid have given extensive attention to the question of funding for civil society organizations. They could expand their conferences, legal studies, training exercises, and other efforts in this domain to take on the critical issue of how parties should be funded, in order to interest civil society in this issue (rather than leaving it in the hands of the political parties themselves) and to see if insights from the civil society sector could be relevant.

A second challenge, which is related to the first, is how to go beyond promoting NGOs to promoting civil society itself. Providers of civil society aid have been focused on helping NGOs, for various reasons, including their appeal as "clean" technocratic groups full of Westernized, young staff members who are willing to operate according to the rules and practices that fit the bureaucratic demands of Western funders. But aid providers have gone from favoring NGOs as recipients of aid to equating NGOs with civil society itself and assuming that the growth curve of NGO proliferation is a good measure of civil society development. A fully developed civil society in an established democracy has many more types of organizations than just advocacy NGOs and service NGOs. Civil society includes professional associations, religious organizations, unions, educational institutions, cultural organizations, sports groups, hobby clubs, ethnic associations, community groups, farmers' associations, business associations, and many others. Such organizations, in their variety, may play many roles beyond what is offered in the reductionist idea of civil society as a zone of public-interest advocacy and self-help service provision. It is time for donors to rethink the privileged place that NGOs have had in their civil society portfolios, to study more carefully the sorts of roles and functions that other types of civil society organizations play, and to broaden their assistance approach.

Third, providers of civil society aid need to come to terms with the challenge of trying to foster civil society development in semi-authoritarian countries. A significant number of those former communist countries where democratic transitions are fading or failing have ended up with regimes most accurately characterized as sem-iauthoritarian. These are countries that are partly open and partly closed. The regimes have adopted the institutional forms of democracy, including regular elections, yet they manipulate the political process and the degree of political liberty sufficiently to ensure that their basic hold on power is not threatened. They are trying to carry out a political balancing act: allowing enough democracy to gain international legitimacy and to relieve domestic political pressure, but keeping hold of the levers of political power to a sufficient degree to maintain their power indefinitely. They typically permit some space for civil society to organize and operate and permit foreign donors to provide support. Yet while donors can keep some NGOs alive, it is not clear whether those groups have any realistic chance of changing the basic power structures.

Donors hope that the gradual development of civic ideas and practices will build the long-term base for democracy but this is an approach based more on hope than experience. Providers of civil society aid need to give greater attention to the phenomenon of semi-authoritarianism, in order to understand its political dynamics and to develop their thinking about what kinds of civil society development are most likely to be productive in such contexts.

A fourth challenge is the former Soviet Union. To a great extent, Western providers of civil society assistance have treated their work in the former Soviet Union as an extension of their efforts in Eastern Europe. In the former Soviet Union they have used the ideas and models about civil society and mechanisms of civil society aid that were developed in Eastern Europe. It has become clear, however, that the challenges of political and economic development are qualitatively different, and harder, in most of the former Soviet Union than in most of Eastern Europe. The reasons for the differences are fairly evident— most of the former Soviet republics face the challenge of forming national states for the first time; there is a deeper, harsher legacy of communism in the former Soviet Union compared with most of Eastern Europe; the distance from Western traditions and influences is greater, and so forth. But, in the first half of the 1990s, the dominant idea of "postcommunist transitions" led aid providers to think that transitions in the former Soviet republics were similar to those in Eastern Europe.

Western supporters of civil society must push themselves to commit the energy and resources that match the daunting challenge of bolstering civil society in the former Soviet Union. They should view the trend toward reducing civil society aid to Eastern Europe as an opportunity to increase it proportionally to the former Soviet Union, rather than to view the downward trend in

Eastern Europe as a signal that there will be more declines further to the east. It is obviously hard to make a second big push for aid after the initial effort of the early 1990s, but this is much needed for the former Soviet Union, a region in serious trouble.

Finally, a further challenge is the former Yugoslavia. The settlements of the conflicts in Bosnia and Kosovo are tentative at best and will require extensive Western involvement if they are to hold. The recently introduced idea of a Western-funded stability pact for southeastern Europe is an appealing concept but will require a high degree of effort and commitment by many Western governments and private organizations if it is to take on some weight. Renewed civil society development will have to be one element on the long-term path toward stability in the former Yugoslavia. And extensive, innovative aid for civil society will need to be an integral part of any stability pact.

### Staying to Learn

When Western aid providers rushed out to Eastern Europe and the former Soviet Union in the immediate aftermath of the fall of the Berlin Wall and the breakup of the former Soviet Union, they were infused with the idea that they were going to teach. Yet when they arrived they discovered not only how little they knew about the transformations under way but also that the learning was going to be more mutual than they had anticipated. As they worked, they ended up relearning things they had known intellectually but had not experienced firsthand for years, if ever. These were simple but profound things, like the importance of the individual over institutions, the nature of courage and patience in the face of adversity, and the fact that real integrity has no price. In short, civil society aid turned out to be a process of learning on both sides, a process that is still deepening as the years pass. My summation of ten years of Western civil society aid to Eastern Europe and the former Soviet Union thus boils down to a rather modest conclusion: They went to teach; they stayed to learn; they are learning still.

### Note

This speech was delivered at the annual meeting of Grantmakers East, in Berlin, on November 5, 1999.

The Carnegie Endowment gratefully acknowledges the permission of the *East European Constitutional Review* to reprint this article, which originally appeared in the *East European Constitutional Review*, vol. 8, no. 4 (Fall 1999).

# CHAPTER TEN

# The Rule of Law Revival
# (1998)

ONE CANNOT GET through a foreign policy debate these days without someone proposing the rule of law as a solution to the world's troubles. How can
U.S. policy on China cut through the conundrum of balancing human rights
against economic interests? Promoting the rule of law, some observers argue,
advances both principles and profits. What will it take for Russia to move beyond Wild West capitalism to more orderly market economics? Developing the
rule of law, many insist, is the key. How can Mexico negotiate its treacherous
economic, political, and social transitions? Inside and outside Mexico, many
answer: establish once and for all the rule of law. Indeed, whether it is Bosnia,
Rwanda, Haiti, or elsewhere, the cure is the rule of law, of course.

The concept is suddenly everywhere—a venerable part of Western political
philosophy enjoying a new run as a rising imperative of the era of globalization. Unquestionably, it is important to life in peaceful, free, and prosperous
societies. Yet its sudden elevation as a panacea for the ills of countries in transition from dictatorships or statist economies should make both patients and
prescribers wary. The rule of law promises to move countries past the first,
relatively easy phase of political and economic liberalization to a deeper level
of reform. But that promise is proving difficult to fulfill. A multitude of countries in Asia, the former Soviet Union, Eastern Europe, Latin America, sub-
Saharan Africa, and the Middle East are engaged in a wide range of rule of law
reform initiatives. Rewriting constitutions, laws, and regulations is the easy
part. Far-reaching institutional reform, also necessary, is arduous and slow.

Judges, lawyers, and bureaucrats must be retrained, and fixtures like court systems, police forces, and prisons must be restructured. Citizens must be brought into the process if conceptions of law and justice are to be truly transformed.

The primary obstacles to such reform are not technical or financial, but political and human. Rule of law reform will succeed only if it gets at the fundamental problem of leaders who refuse to be ruled by the law. Respect for the law will not easily take root in systems rife with corruption and cynicism, since entrenched elites cede their traditional impunity and vested interests only under great pressure. Even the new generation of politicians arising out of the political transitions of recent years are reluctant to support reforms that create competing centers of authority beyond their control.

Western nations and private donors have poured hundreds of millions of dollars into rule of law reform, but outside aid is no substitute for the will to reform, which must come from within. Countries in transition to democracy must first want to reform and must then be thorough and patient in their legal makeovers. Meanwhile, donors must learn to spend their reform dollars where they will do the most good—and expect few miracles and little leverage in return.

## Legal Bedrock

The rule of law can be defined as a system in which the laws are public knowledge, are clear in meaning, and apply equally to everyone. They enshrine and uphold the political and civil liberties that have gained status as universal human rights over the last half-century. In particular, anyone accused of a crime has the right to a fair, prompt hearing and is presumed innocent until proved guilty. The central institutions of the legal system, including courts, prosecutors, and police, are reasonably fair, competent, and efficient. Judges are impartial and independent, not subject to political influence or manipulation. Perhaps most important, the government is embedded in a comprehensive legal framework, its officials accept that the law will be applied to their own conduct, and the government seeks to be law-abiding.

The relationship between the rule of law and liberal democracy is profound. The rule of law makes possible individual rights, which are at the core of democracy. A government's respect for the sovereign authority of the people and a constitution depends on its acceptance of law. Democracy includes institutions and processes that, although beyond the immediate domain of the legal system, are rooted in it. Basic elements of a modern market economy such as property rights and contracts are founded on the law and require competent third-party enforcement. Without the rule of law, major economic institutions such as corporations, banks, and labor unions would not function, and the government's many involvements in the economy—regulatory mechanisms, tax systems, customs structures, monetary policy, and the like—would be unfair, inefficient, and opaque.

The rule of law can be conceived broadly or narrowly. Some American jurists invest it with attributes specific to their own system, such as trial by jury, a constitution that is rarely amended, an expansive view of defendants' rights, and a sharp separation of powers. This alienates those from other societies who enjoy the rule of law but do not happen to follow the American approach in its many unusual particulars. Some Asian politicians focus on the regular, efficient application of law but do not stress the necessity of government subordination to it. In their view, the law exists not to limit the state but to serve its power. More accurately characterized as rule by law rather than rule of law, this narrow conception is built into what has become known as Asian-style democracy.

### Transition Trauma

The rule of law is scarcely a new idea. It is receiving so much attention now because of its centrality to both democracy and the market economy in an era marked by a wave of transitions to both. Western observers say that enhancing the rule of law will allow states to move beyond the first stage of political and economic reform to consolidate both democracy and market economics.

Since the early 1980s dozens of countries in different regions have experienced political openings, held reasonably free and fair elections, and established the basic institutions of democracy. Some, however, particularly in Latin America and parts of the former Soviet Union, Eastern Europe, and Asia, are struggling with poorly performing institutions, citizens' low regard for governments, and the challenge of going beyond mere democratic processes to genuinely democratic values and practices. Other countries, in sub-Saharan Africa, Central Asia, and elsewhere, are not just stagnating but slipping backward as newly elected leaders fall into old authoritarian habits. For states grappling with democratic consolidation, fortifying usually weak rule of law appears to be a way of pushing patronage-ridden government institutions to better performance, reining in elected but still only haphazardly law-abiding politicians, and curbing the continued violation of human rights that has characterized many new democracies. For backsliding systems, strengthening the rule of law seems an appealing bulwark against creeping authoritarianism and the ever-present threat of a sabotage of constitutional order.

Many attempted economic transitions are at a similar dip in the road. Reform-oriented governments that have made it through the initial phase of economic liberalization and fiscal stabilization are now pausing before the second, deeper transitional phase, licking their political wounds and hoping for patience on the part of often unpersuaded citizens. As Moisés Naím has pointed out, the first phase of market reform turns on large-scale policy decisions by a small band of top officials. The second phase involves building institutions, such as tax agencies, customs services, and antitrust agencies, and the general amelioration of governance. Strengthening the rule of law is integral to this phase.

The challenges of the second phase are felt not only in Latin America and the former communist states, but also in Asian countries that have made considerable economic progress without the benefit of a strong rule of law. As Asia's recent financial woes highlight, if countries such as Indonesia, Thailand, and Malaysia are to move beyond their impressive first generation of economic progress, they will require better bank regulation and greater government accountability. More generally, economic globalization is feeding the rule of law imperative by putting pressure on governments to offer the stability, transparency, and accountability that international investors demand.

Shoring up the rule of law also helps temper two severe problems—corruption and crime—that are common to many transitional countries, embittering citizens and clouding reform efforts. Debate continues over whether corruption in government has actually increased in transitional societies or whether greater openness, especially in the media, has merely exposed what was already there. Skyrocketing street crime and civil violence are another unfortunate hallmark of many democratizing societies, from Russia to South Africa to Guatemala. Crime erodes public support for democracy and hurts the economy by scaring off foreign investors and interfering with the flow of ideas, goods, and people. Reform-oriented governments around the world are now adding crime and corruption reduction to their agenda for deepening reform. Rule of law development is an obvious place to begin.

For these reasons—political, economic, and social—Western policy makers and commentators have seized on the rule of law as an elixir for countries in transition. It promises to remove all the chief obstacles on the path to democracy and market economics. Its universal quality adds to its appeal. Despite the close ties of the rule of law to democracy and capitalism, it stands apart as a nonideological, even technical, solution. In many countries, people still argue over the appropriateness of various models of democracy or capitalism. But hardly anyone these days will admit to being against the idea of law.

**The Reform Menu**

Although its wonderworking abilities have been exaggerated, the desirability of the rule of law is clear. The question is where to start. The usual way of categorizing rule of law reforms is by subject matter—commercial law, criminal law, administrative law, and the like. An alternate method focuses on the depth of reform, with three basic categories. Type one reform concentrates on the laws themselves: revising laws or whole codes to weed out antiquated provisions. Often the economic domain is the focus, with the drafting or redrafting of laws on bankruptcy, corporate governance, taxation, intellectual property, and financial markets. Another focus is criminal law, including expanding the protection of basic rights in criminal procedure codes, modifying criminal statutes to cover new problems such as money laundering and electronic-transfer fraud, and revising the regulation of police.

Type two reform is the strengthening of law-related institutions, usually to make them more competent, efficient, and accountable. Training and salaries for judges and court staff are increased, and the dissemination of judicial decisions improved. Reform efforts target the police, prosecutors, public defenders, and prisons. Efforts to toughen ethics codes and professional standards for lawyers, revitalize legal education, broaden access to courts, and establish alternative dispute resolution mechanisms figure in many reform packages. Other common reforms include strengthening legislatures, tax administrations, and local governments.

Type three reforms aim at the deeper goal of increasing government's compliance with law. A key step is achieving genuine judicial independence. Some of the above measures foster this goal, especially better salaries and revised selection procedures for judges. But the most crucial changes lie elsewhere. Above all, government officials must refrain from interfering with judicial decision making and accept the judiciary as an independent authority. They must give up the habit of placing themselves above the law. Institutional reforms can help by clarifying regulations, making public service more of a meritocracy, and mandating transparency and other means of increasing accountability. The success of type three reform, however, depends less on technical or institutional measures than on enlightened leadership and sweeping changes in the values and attitudes of those in power. Although much of the impetus must come from the top, nonstate activities such as citizen-driven human rights and anticorruption campaigns can do much to help.

## The Global Picture

Probably the most active region for rule of law reform has been Eastern Europe. Since 1989, most Eastern European societies have taken significant steps to de-Sovietize and broadly reform their legal systems. They have rewritten constitutions and laws and initiated key changes in their legal institutions. Many government officials have begun accepting the law's authority and respecting judicial independence. The Czech Republic, for example, has made major progress on judicial independence, and Hungary has recently launched a comprehensive judicial reform package. Thorough institutional reforms, however, are taking longer than many hoped, and some countries are falling short. The leaders of Croatia and Serbia continue to trample basic rights, and Slovak government institutions show contempt for the Constitutional Court's rulings. Nonetheless, the overall picture in the region has encouraging elements.

Latin America also presents a positive, if mixed, profile. Since the early 1980s constitutionally based, elected governments have been established almost everywhere in the region. Most Latin American governments have acknowledged the need for rule of law reform and are taking steps toward it, or at least proclaiming that they will. But judicial and police reform has run into walls of bureaucratic indifference and entrenched interests. A few countries, notably Chile and Costa Rica, have made progress, while others, such as El Salvador and Guatemala, may only now be getting serious about it. The will to reform has been lacking, however, in Argentina and Mexico, which have the necessary human and technical resources but whose political and economic development are being hampered by their weak rule of law.

Many Asian governments have begun to modify laws and legal institutions, primarily related to commercial affairs. This is the project of countries seeking to consolidate and advance economic progress, such as Malaysia, Taiwan, South Korea, and even China, as well as those hoping to get on the train, such as Vietnam. These reforms generally stop short of subordinating government's power to the law and are better understood as efforts to achieve rule by law than the rule of law. South Korea is almost alone in taking these efforts beyond the commercial domain and seriously attacking government impunity and corruption, as evidenced by the recent conviction of former South Korean Presidents Chun Doo-hwan and Roh Tae-woo on corruption charges. The Asian financial crisis highlighted the failure of the region's various rule of law reforms to bring transparency and accountability to the dealings of the ingrown circles of privileged bankers, businessmen, and politicians. Pressure for more reform, both from within Asia and from the international financial community, is growing.

The situation in the former Soviet Union is discouraging. Although the Baltic states have made major strides in depoliticizing and revitalizing their judicial systems, few other post-Soviet states have achieved much beyond limited reforms in narrow areas of commercial law. Their legal institutions have shed few of their Soviet habits and remain ineffective, politically subordinated, and corrupt. Russia's difficulties in achieving the rule of law are the weakest link in the postcommunist transformation of Russian society. The government has attempted a number of reform initiatives, including the drafting of new civil and criminal codes. These have been neutralized, however, by the ruling elite's tendency to act extralegally and by the new private sector's troubling lawlessness.

Although more than 30 sub-Saharan African countries have attempted political and economic transitions since 1990, rule of law reform is still scarce on the continent. The issue is coming to the fore in both those countries attempting to move halting transitions along and those hoping that "transitional justice" mechanisms such as truth commissions and war crimes tribunals can help overcome the bitter legacy of the past. By far the most positive case is South Africa, where a far-reaching program to transform the administration of justice is under way. In at least a few other countries, including Botswana, Tanzania, and Uganda, less dramatic but still important progress has been made toward the reform of laws and law-related institutions, including the modernization of some commercial laws and stronger support for the judiciary. But in many countries of the region, the legal systems remain captive of the powers that be.

The Middle East shows the least legal reform activity of any region. Some Arab countries, among them Jordan, Lebanon, and Kuwait, are at least attempting reform in the commercial domain, such as in the mechanisms necessary to establish stock markets or otherwise attract foreign investment. Institutional change is more sporadic, ranging from the surprisingly bold reform plans announced by the government of Oman to Egypt's judicial reforms, whose seriousness is still unclear.

Rule of law reform is at least a stated goal of many countries. Globally there has been a great deal of legal reform related to economic modernization and a moderate amount of law-related institutional reform, but little deep reform of the higher levels of government. Around the world, the movement toward rule of law is broad but shallow.

## Legal Aid

Most governments attempting rule of law reform are not doing so on their own. Assistance in this field has mushroomed in recent years, becoming a major category of international aid. With a mix of altruism and self-interest, many Western countries have rushed to help governments in Eastern Europe and the former Soviet Union carry out legal and institutional reforms. Russia's legal and judicial reforms, for example, have been supported by a variety of U.S. assistance projects, extensive German aid, a $58 million World Bank loan, and numerous smaller World Bank and European Bank for Reconstruction and Development initiatives, as well as many efforts sponsored by Great Britain, the Netherlands, Denmark, and the European Union. Asia and Latin America are also major recipients of rule of law aid, with a focus on commercial law in Asia and on criminal and commercial law in Latin America. Africa and the Middle East have received less attention, reflecting the smaller degree of reform that countries there have undertaken.

A host of U.S. agencies underwrite such aid, including the U.S. Agency for International Development, the Justice and Commerce Departments, and the Securities and Exchange Commission. Coordination is poor and turf battles are common. The rapid expansion of U.S. rule of law aid exemplifies the only partially successful U.S. response to the challenges of the post–Cold War era. Many programs have sprung up to address these emerging issues, but officials have done far too little to ensure that they are well designed, consistent, and coherent.

Almost every major bilateral donor, a wide range of multilateral organizations—especially development banks—and countless foundations, universities, and human rights groups are getting into the act. In most countries, U.S. rule of law assistance is a small part of the aid pool, although Americans frequently assume it is of paramount importance. They mistakenly believe that rule of law promotion is their special province, although they are not alone in that. German and French jurists also tend to view their country as the keeper of the flame of civil code reform. British lawyers and judges point to the distinguished history of the British approach. Transitional countries are bombarded with fervent but contradictory advice on judicial and legal reform.

Donors sometimes determine rule of law reform priorities. Enormous amounts of aid are granted for writing or rewriting laws, especially commercial laws. Hordes of Western consultants descend on transitional societies with Western legal models in their briefcases. Judicial training courses run by Western groups have become a cottage industry, as have seminars on conflict resolution. Aid providers are expanding their rule of law efforts to reach parliaments, executive branch agencies, and local governments. Assistance also extends to civic groups that use law to advance particular interests and nongovernmental organizations that push for reform.

**The Net Effect**

The effects of this burgeoning rule of law aid are generally positive, though usually modest. After more than ten years and hundreds of millions of dollars in aid, many judicial systems in Latin America still function poorly. Russia is probably the single largest recipient of such aid, but is not even clearly moving in the right direction. The numerous rule of law programs carried out in

Cambodia after the 1993 elections failed to create values or structures strong enough to prevent last year's coup. Aid providers have helped rewrite laws around the globe, but they have discovered that the mere enactment of laws accomplishes little without considerable investment in changing the conditions for implementation and enforcement. Many Western advisers involved in rule of law assistance are new to the foreign aid world and have not learned that aid must support domestically rooted processes of change, not attempt to artificially reproduce pre-selected results.

Efforts to strengthen basic legal institutions have proven slow and difficult. Training for judges, technical consultancies, and other transfers of expert knowledge make sense on paper but often have only minor impact. The desirability of embracing such values as efficiency, transparency, accountability, and honesty seems self-evident to Western aid providers, but for those targeted by training programs, such changes may signal the loss of perquisites and security. Major U.S. judicial reform efforts in Russia, El Salvador, Guatemala, and elsewhere have foundered on the assumption that external aid can substitute for the internal will to reform.

Rule of law aid has been concentrated on more easily attained type one and type two reforms. Thus it has affected the most important elements of the problem least. Helping transitional countries achieve type three reform that brings real change in government obedience to law is the hardest, slowest kind of assistance. It demands powerful tools that aid providers are only beginning to develop, especially activities that help bring pressure on the legal system from the citizenry and support whatever pockets of reform may exist within an otherwise self-interested ruling system. It requires a level of interventionism, political attention, and visibility that many donor governments and organizations cannot or do not wish to apply. Above all, it calls for patient, sustained attention, as breaking down entrenched political interests, transforming values, and generating enlightened, consistent leadership will take generations.

The experience to date with rule of law aid suggests that it is best to proceed with caution. The widespread embrace of the rule of law imperative is heartening, but it represents only the first step for most transitional countries on what will be a long and rocky road. Although the United States and other Western countries can and should foster the rule of law, even large amounts of aid will not bring rapid or decisive results. Thus, it is good that President Ernesto Zedillo of Mexico has made rule of law development one of the central goals of his presidency, but the pursuit of that goal is certain to be slow and difficult, as highlighted by the recent massacre in the south of the country. Judging from the experience of other Latin American countries, U.S. efforts to lighten Mexico's burden will at best be of secondary importance. Similarly, Wild West capitalism in Russia should not be thought of as a brief transitional phase. The deep shortcomings of the rule of law in Russia will take decades to fix. The Asian financial crisis has shown observers that without the rule of law the Asian miracle economies are unstable. Although that realization was abrupt, remedying the situation will be a long-term enterprise.

These lessons are of particular importance concerning China, where some U.S. policy makers and commentators have begun pinning hope on the idea that promoting the rule of law will allow the United States to support positive economic and political change without taking a confrontational approach on human rights issues. But China's own efforts to reform its law are almost 20 years old and have moved slowly, especially outside the economic domain. Statements by U.S. officials and increased flows of rule of law assistance are unlikely to speed up the process, judging from the rule of law programs that have been operating in China for years. Rule of law promotion should be part of U.S. policy toward China, but it will not increase U.S. influence over that country. Nor will it miraculously eliminate the hard choices between ideals and interests that have plagued America's foreign policy for more than two centuries.

## Note

The Carnegie Endowment gratefully acknowledges the permission of the Council on Foreign Relations to reprint this article, which originally appeared in *Foreign Affairs*, vol. 77, no. 2 (March/April 1998).

# CHAPTER ELEVEN

# Promoting the Rule of Law Abroad: The Problem of Knowledge (2003)

WHEN RULE OF LAW aid practitioners gather among themselves to reflect on their work, they often express contradictory thoughts. On the one hand, they talk with enthusiasm and interest about what they do, believing that the field of rule of law assistance is extremely important. Many feel it is at the cutting edge of international efforts to promote both development and democracy abroad. On the other hand, when pressed, they admit that the base of knowledge from which they are operating is startlingly thin. As a colleague who has been closely involved in rule of law work in Latin America for many years said to me recently, "we know how to do a lot of things, but deep down we don't really know what we are doing." Although some practitioners harbor no doubts and promote the rule of law abroad with a great sense of confidence, most persons working in the field openly recognize and lament the fact that little really has been learned about rule of law assistance relative to the extensive amount of on-the-ground activity.

This fact raises an interesting puzzle the current rule of law promotion field—which started in the mid-1980s in Latin America and now extends to many regions, including Eastern Europe, the former Soviet Union, Asia, and sub-Saharan Africa—is already older than its precursor was, the law and development movement of the 1960s and early 1970s, when that earlier movement ran out of steam and closed down. The law and development movement died out above all because of a too obvious gap between its ambitions and its achievements. Yet the current rule of law field—which has some important similarities to but also differences from the law and development movement—is still expanding as it approaches the end of its second decade, despite an apparent lack of knowledge at many levels of conception, operation, and evaluation.

The answer to the puzzle may lie not so much in differences between the substance of the two movements—though those differences are real—than in differing contexts. The law and development movement was launched in the optimistic days of the early 1960s, when hopes for democracy and development were high for the newly decolonized states of Africa and Asia, and for the developing world as a whole. Yet as the law and development movement unfolded, that broader context of optimism deteriorated quickly. Democratic experiments failed in many parts of the developing world in the 1960s and the broader hope for rapid developmental gains ran into contrary realities in many countries. By the end of that decade, the modernization paradigm on which U.S. foreign aid of the 1960s, including the law and development movement, had been based was already in serious doubt and a pessimistic assessment of foreign aid caused much retooling and retraction.

In contrast, the optimistic context of the crucial early years of the current rule of law aid movement—the heady period of the end of the Cold War—has held up somewhat longer. Although simplistic thinking about the ease and naturalness of the many dual transitions around the world to democracy and market economics has met with many disappointments, the international aid community has not (yet) experienced a major disillusionment with the underlying assumptions about aid for democracy and market economics from which the rule of law aid movement operates.

It may be then that a still-favorable, though increasingly shaky, context holds together the rule of law assistance movement. This should not prevent us, however, from pushing at this question about knowledge: What is the problem of knowledge that aid practitioners allude to in private? What is it that practitioners do not know that they feel they should know as they engage in rule of law promotion projects around the world? What about the many "lessons learned" that are dutifully reported in institutional documents? And to the extent there really is a problem of knowledge, what causes it and what might ameliorate it?

### Self-Evident but Uncertain Rationales

The problem of knowledge in rule of law promotion can be considered as a series of deficits at various analytic levels, descending in generality. To start, there is a surprising amount of uncertainty about the basic rationale for rule of law promotion. Aid agencies prescribe rule of law programs to cure a remarkably wide array of ailments in developing and postcommunist countries, from corruption and surging crime to lagging foreign investment and growth. At the core of this burgeoning belief in the value of rule of law work are two controlling axioms: The rule of law is necessary for economic development and necessary for democracy. When held up to a close light, however, neither of these propositions is as axiomatic as it may at first appear.

It has become a new credo in the development field that if developing and postcommunist countries wish to succeed economically they must develop the rule of law. One form of this economic rationale for rule of law work focuses on foreign investment: If a country does not have the rule of law, the argument goes, it will not be able to attract substantial amounts of foreign investment and therefore will not be able to finance development. Leaving aside the first question of whether foreign investment is really always a requirement for development (since it is not clear, for example, that the economic success of a number of the major Western economies, such as the American and Japanese economies, was based on substantial amounts of inward foreign investment), there is a notable lack of proof that a country must have a settled, well-functioning rule of law to attract investment. The argument has an undeniable common sense appeal—investors will want predictability, security, and the like. Yet the case of China flies squarely in the face of the argument—the largest recipient of foreign direct investment in the developing world happens to be a country notorious for its lack of Western-style rule of law. It is clear that what draws investors into China is the possibility of making money either in the near or long term. Weak rule of law is perhaps one negative factor they weigh in their decision of whether to invest, but it is by no means determinative. A recent study of the rule of law and foreign investment in postcommunist countries points to a similar conclusion. Weak rule of law is not a major factor in determining investment flows, and the more important causal relationship may be in the reverse direction: The presence of at least certain types of foreign investors may contribute to the development of the rule of law through their demands for legal reforms.[1]

A broader form of the argument about the relationship between the rule of law and economic development emphasizes an array of rule of law components—such as the need for legal predictability, the enforcement of contracts, and property rights—as necessary for the functioning of a modern market economy. Again the appeal of this argument is obvious and probably contains elements of truth. But as Frank Upham has argued in a study of the supposed relationship between an idealized apolitical, rule-based system of law and the economic development of the United States and Japan, the relationship is by no means as clear-cut as many might hope.[2] Similarly, a review by Rick Messick of studies that attempt to find causal relationships between judicial reform and development notes that "the relationship is probably better modeled as a series of on-and-off connections, or of couplings and decouplings," in other words the causal arrows go both directions and sometimes do not appear at all.[3] It is not possible here to survey all the literature on what is in fact an extremely complex, multifaceted question about the relationship of the rule of law and economic development. The central point is that simplistic assertions such as have become common among aid agencies to the effect that the "rule of law" grosso modo is necessary for development are at best badly oversimplified and probably misleading in many ways. The case of China again points to some of the shortcomings of the assertion. Many countries being told that they must have Western style of rule of law before they can achieve significant economic growth look with envy at China's sustained economic growth of the past twenty years and wonder why the prescription did not apply there.

Things are similarly murky on the political side of the core rationale. Unquestionably the rule of law is intimately connected with liberal democracy. A foundation of civil and political rights rooted in a functioning legal system is crucial to democracy. But again, the idea that specific improvements in the rule of law are necessary to achieve democracy is dangerously simplistic. Democracy often, in fact usually, co-exists with substantial shortcomings in the rule of law. In quite a few countries that are considered well-established Western democracies—and that hold themselves out to developing and postcommunist countries as examples of the sorts of political systems that those countries should emulate—one finds various shortcomings: (1) court systems that are substantially overrun with cases to the point where justice is delayed on a regular basis; (2) substantial groups of people, usually minorities, are discriminated against and unable to find adequate remedies within the civil legal system; (3) the criminal law system chronically mistreats selected groups of people, again, usually minorities; and (4) top politicians often manage to abuse the law with impunity, and political corruption is common.

Of course one can interpret this to mean that because of the deficiencies in the rule of law these countries are imperfect democracies. This is true enough, but the point is that they are widely accepted in the international community as established democracies. Yet their aid agencies are telling officials in the developing and postcommunist world that well-functioning rule of law is a kind of tripwire for democracy. It would be much more accurate to say that the rule of law and democracy are closely intertwined but that major shortcomings in the rule of law often exist within reasonably democratic political systems. Countries struggling to become democratic do not face a dramatic choice of "no rule of law, no democracy" but rather a series of smaller, more complicated choices about what elements of their legal systems they wish to try to improve with the expectation of achieving what political benefits.

In short, the axiomatic quality of the two core rationales of the current wave of rule of law assistance efforts—that the rule of law is necessary for economic development and democracy—is misleading when used as a mechanistic, causal imperative by the aid community. Rule of law aid practitioners can probably prescribe rule of law programs with a safe belief that these initiatives may well be helpful to both economic development and democratization, but they really do not know to what extent there are direct causal connections at work and whether similar resources directed elsewhere might produce greater effect on economic and political conditions.

**The Elusive Essence**

Rule of law aid providers seem confident that they know what the rule of law looks like in practice. Stated in shorthand form, they want to see law applied fairly, uniformly, and efficiently throughout the society in question, to both public officials as well as ordinary citizens, and to have law protect various rights that ensure the autonomy of the individual in the face of state power in both the political and economic spheres. Their outlook on the rule of law can certainly be criticized for its narrowness. They do not have much interest in non-Western forms of law, in traditional systems of justice, or, in the case of some American rule of law experts, even in civil law. But it is important to go beyond that fairly obvious weakness to a different aspect of the problem of knowledge: Rule of law aid practitioners know what the rule of law is supposed to look like in practice, but they are less certain what the essence of the rule of law is.

By their nature as practitioners intent on producing tangible, even measurable changes in other societies, rule of law aid specialists need to concretize the appealing but inevitably somewhat diffuse concept of the rule of law. In the broader field of democracy assistance, the pattern has been for democracy promoters to translate the overarching idea of democracy into an institutional checklist or template that they can pursue through a series of specific aid intiatives.[4] Similarly, rule of law promoters tend to translate the rule of law into an institutional checklist, with primary emphasis on the judiciary.

The emphasis on judiciaries is widespread in the rule of law field, with the terms *judicial reform* and *rule of law reform* often used interchangeably. The emphasis derives from the fact that most rule of law promotion specialists are lawyers and when lawyers think about what seems to be the nerve center of the rule of law they think about the core institutions of law enforcement.

Yet it is by no means clear that courts are the essence of a rule of law system in a country. Only a small percentage of citizens in most Western rule of law systems ever have direct contact with courts. In a certain sense courts play a role late in the legal process—it might well be argued that the making of laws is the most generative part of a rule of law system. Yet rule of law programs have not much focused on legislatures or the role of executive branch agencies in law-making processes. The question of which institutions are most germane to the establishment of the rule of law in a country is actually quite complex and difficult. Yet for the last ten to fifteen years, rule of law programs have given dominant attention to judiciaries, without much examination of whether such a focus is really the right one.

The uncertainty goes beyond the question of "which institutions?" Indeed, doubt exists about whether it is useful to conceive of and attempt to act upon rule of law development in primarily institutional terms. Clearly law is not just the sum of courts, legislatures, police, prosecutors, and other formal institutions with some direct connection to law. Law is also a normative system that resides in the minds of the citizens of a society. As rule of law providers seek to affect the rule of law in a country, it is not clear if they should focus on institution building or instead try to intervene in ways that would affect how citizens understand, use, and value law. To take a simple example, many rule of law programs focus on improving a country's courts and police on the assumption that this is the most direct route to improve compliance with law in the country. Yet some research shows that compliance with law depends most heavily on the perceived fairness and legitimacy of the laws, characteristics that are not established primarily by the courts but by other means, such as the political process. An effort to improve compliance thus might more fruitfully take a completely different approach.

In sum, the question of where the essence of the rule of law actually resides and therefore what should be the focal point of efforts to improve the rule of law remains notably unsettled. Rule of law should be the focal point of efforts to improve the rule of law remains notably unsettled. Rule of law practitioners have been following an institutional approach, concentrating on judiciaries, more out of instinct than well-researched knowledge.

### How Does Change Occur?

Even if we leave aside the problem of where the essence of the rule of law resides and accept the institutionalist approach that has become the norm, we see that rule of law aid providers face a problem of knowledge with regard to the very basic question of how change in systems actually occurs. Aid providers know what endpoint they would like to help countries achieve—the Western-style, rule-oriented systems they know from their own countries. Yet, they do not really know how countries that do not have such systems attain them. That is to say they do not know what the process of change consists of and how it might be brought about.

In launching and implementing the many rule of law programs of recent years, rule of law aid specialists have blurred this lack of knowledge by following what has been the approach to achieving change in the broader field of democracy assistance: attempting to reproduce institutional endpoints. This consists of diagnosing the shortcomings in selected institutions—that is, determining in what ways selected institutions do not resemble their counterparts in countries that donors believe embody successful rule of law—and then attempting to modify or reshape those institutions to fit the desired model. If a court lacks access to legal materials, then those legal materials should be provided. If case management in the courts is dysfunctional, it should be brought up to Western standards. If a criminal procedure law lacks adequate protections for detainees, it should be rewritten. The basic idea is that if the institutions can be changed to fit the models, the rule of law will emerge.

This breathtakingly mechanistic approach to rule of law development— a country achieves the rule of law by reshaping its key institutions to match those of countries that are considered to have the rule of law—quickly ran into deeply embedded resistance to change in many countries. The wave of judicial and police reform efforts in many Latin American countries sponsored by the United States in the second half of the 1980s, for example, initially bounced off institutions that had deep-seated reasons, whether good or bad, for being the way they were and little inclination to accept the reformist ideas brought from the outside.

The sobering experience with the early wave of efforts to promote institutional change produced two responses in the rule of law aid community. The first was a great deal of attention to what quickly came to be called "will to reform."[5] The new wisdom held that absent sufficient will to reform on the part of key host country officials, efforts to reform judiciaries, police, and other key institutions would be futile. It was up to rule of law aid providers to find and support "change agents" in the institutions, with the predominant assumption being that such agents would reside in the leadership of the institutions in question.

The sudden focus on will to reform was a way of restating the problem of how change occurs—aid providers should not presume change will naturally occur once institutions are introduced to the right way of doing things. Instead, change will occur when some of the key people inside the system want it to occur and those persons are given enabling assistance that allows them to carry out their will.

Though taken within the rule of law aid community as a crucial new insight, the focus on will to reform was a smaller step forward than it initially appeared. Major questions abound, still unanswered. For example, how does will to reform develop? Can it be generated and if so how? Should we assume that institutions change through gradualist reform processes willed by persons inside the system? Does public pressure play a major role? What about abrupt, drastic change provoked by persons outside the institutions who are dissatisfied with their function or who have their own goals about what institutions to have?

The other response to the initial wave of disappointments was the introduction within the rule of law aid community of the concepts of incentives and interests. After bouncing off a number of reform-resistant institutions, rule of law aid providers began saying that it was necessary to understand the underlying interests of institutional actors and to try to reshape the incentives to which these actors responded. This represented progress and allowed some analytic insights, which while rather basic were at least better than completely technocratic approaches. Aid providers began confronting the unpleasant fact, for example, that poorly performing judicial systems in many countries served the interests of powerful actors in various ways (for example, not serving as a means of justice for poor persons seeking to uphold land claims) and that the persons in those systems had no incentives to change their ways and had some significant incentives not to. But it was hard to go beyond new insights to new methods to produce change. Realizing that incentive structures are distorted is one thing; doing something about it is another. To some extent, casting the problem of change in terms of interests and incentives has ended up being more a restatement of lack of knowledge about how change occurs than an answer to it.

### What Effects Will Change Have?

Although rule of law aid providers lack knowledge about what might produce broad-scale change in the role and function of law in a society that seems to lack the rule of law, they nevertheless do succeed in helping produce change in some specific areas. When they do, however, they often do not really know what effects those changes will have on the overall development of the rule of law in the country.

Consider several examples. A focus of many judicial reform programs has been to speed up the processing of cases by slow, inefficient courts. Such programs highlight administrative reforms, usually featuring the much-favored tool of case-tracking software. The aid providers' assumption is that efficient processing of cases is one small but vital element of the rule of law and improving that processing will improve the rule of law. Yet even in this well-defined, circumscribed area there is a surprising amount of uncertainty. For example, it is possible that if the processing of cases speeds up in a country where justice has long been quite poorly served, the number of cases filed with the courts might skyrocket, clogging the courts anew and effectively negating the reform achieved. Or, if the system has significant unfairness built into it, such as political bias or control, does increasing the speed of cases through the system actually represent a gain for the rule of law? This question arose vividly in Egypt in the second half of the 1990s where the United States devoted significant resources to helping the Egyptian judiciary improve its case management and speed up its processing of cases.

Another example concerns the spillover effects of improvement in one part of the system to other parts. A key belief animating some programs of commercial law reform in authoritarian or semi-authoritarian contexts is that if international aid efforts can help improve the quality of justice on commercial matters, this will augment justice in other domains and thus represent a kind of stealth method of promoting the rule of law in a broader political sense. The Western aid organizations supporting rule of law reforms in China and Vietnam regularly invoke this argument. It is of great appeal to donors who on the one hand seek to pave the way for business reforms that will facilitate commerce but on the other hand want to defend themselves against charges that they are assisting authoritarian regimes. Though attractive, the argument is not grounded in any systematic research and represents a typical example in the rule of law world of an appealing hypothesis that is repeated enough times until it takes on the quality of a received truth.

One more example concerns means of increasing judicial independence. Rule of law aid providers have given considerable attention to trying to find ways to increase judicial independence in Latin America and now are tackling the issue in other regions. Believing that one of the stumbling blocks is the hold on the process of judicial selection and promotion by politicized, corrupted ministries of justice, they have pushed for and supported efforts to establish semi-autonomous judicial councils to take over these functions. The idea has common sense appeal, but despite an accumulating record of experience there has been little effort to date to examine in any systematic fashion whether the various new judicial councils have improved the situation. The first such study indicates that the results are not impressive.[6] Anecdotal evidence from Argentina and other countries suggests that as often happens with institutional solutions to deeper problems, the underlying maladies of the original institutions end up crossing over and infecting the new institutions.

These are just several of many possible examples that indicate that even when aid programs are able to facilitate fairly specific changes in relevant institutions, it is rarely clear what the longer-term effects of those changes are on the overall development of the rule of law in the country in question.

## Limitations of Lessons Learned

In analyzing the levels and extent of the problem of knowledge in the field of rule of law assistance, I do not mean to imply that no learning is taking place. Aid practitioners, especially those who are close to the field efforts and have extensive experience in projects in at least several countries, often accumulate considerable knowledge about how to go about promoting the rule of law. Yet the knowledge tends to stay within the minds of individual practitioners and not get systematized or incorporated by the sponsoring institutions.

Aid institutions do seek to come up with "lessons learned" and to present them in official reports as evidence that they are taking seriously the need to reflect critically on their own work. Yet most of the lessons learned presented in such reports are not especially useful. Often they are too general or obvious, or both. Among the most common lessons learned, for example, are "programs must be shaped to fit the local environment" and "law reformers should not simply import laws from other countries." The fact that staggeringly obvious lessons of this type are put forward by institutions as lessons learned is an unfortunate commentary on the weakness of many of the aid efforts.

There is also the persistent problem of lessons learned not actually being learned. Experienced practitioners have consistently pointed, for example, to the fact that judicial training, while understandably appealing to aid agencies, is usually rife with shortcomings and rarely does much good.[7] Yet addicted to the relative ease of creating such programs and their common sense appeal, aid organizations persist in making judicial training one of the most common forms of rule of law assistance. Similarly, it has become painfully clear on countless occasions that trying to promote the rule of law by simply rewriting another country's laws on the basis of Western models achieves very little, given problems with laws not adapted to the local environment, the lack of capacity to implement or enforce the laws, and the lack of public understanding of them. Yet externally supported law reform efforts in many countries, especially those efforts relating to the commercial domain, often continue to be simplistic exercises of law copying. The problem of reforms being blocked by underlying interests and incentives turns out not only to apply to institutions in the aid-recipient countries but to the aid agencies themselves.

## Obstacles to Knowledge

Confronted with the lack of systematic, well-grounded knowledge about how external aid can be used to promote the rule of law in other countries, aid officials have usually responded by arguing that the field is relatively young and still in the early stage of learning. As the years pass, however, this explanation is losing force. If one takes together the law and development movement and the current rule of law promotion field, over thirty years of activity are now under the bridge, surely enough time for real learning to take place. It is apparent therefore that some embedded obstacles to the accumulation of knowledge exist below the surface. At least five can be identified at a quick glance.

First, there is the unavoidable fact that the rule of law is an area of great conceptual and practical complexity. Understanding how law functions in a society, the roles it plays, and how it can change is extremely difficult, especially in societies that are not well understood by aid providers from many points of view. Foreign aid providers have found it hard enough to develop effective ways of analyzing and acting upon much more delimited challenges, such as increasing the supply of potable drinking water or vaccinations in poor societies. Grasping the problem of the shortcomings of law throughout the developing and postcommunist worlds is an enormous intellectual and practical challenge.

Related to this is a second problem—the tremendous particularity of the legal systems, or perhaps better stated, the functioning of law, in the countries of Latin America, Asia, Africa, Eastern Europe, and the former Soviet Union where rule of law promoters are at work. A rule of law aid provider traveling to Guyana, Yemen, Madagascar, or some other country to set up an assistance project is faced with the daunting challenge of understanding the realities of law in that particular society. He or she is unlikely to be able to draw much up-to-date, detailed, comprehensive, and insightful information about the problem because the availability of such knowledge tends to be highly sporadic. Even to the extent that some such information exists, drawing the connection between it and the question of "what to do?" is akin to stringing a very long, thin line between two distant points.

The third obstacle is that aid organizations have proven themselves to be ill-adept at the task of generating and accumulating the sort of knowledge that would help fill the gap. They profess great interest in lessons learned but tend not to devote many resources to serious reflection and research on their own efforts.[8] They are by nature forward-looking organizations, aimed at the next project or problem. Personnel tend to change positions regularly, undermining the building up of institutional knowledge. They are criticized by others if they are seen as devoting too much time to study and not enough to knowledge.

They are criticized by others if they are seen as devoting too much time to study and not enough to action. And they work in a context of broader doubt about the value of aid, which has led to a tremendous set of conscious and unconscious defensive walls being built up around their activities, including rule of law work.

Fourth, if aid organizations are themselves not sponsoring the kind of applied policy research that would build knowledge in the rule of law promotion domain, neither are political science departments or law schools. This kind of research is eminently applied in nature and thus tends not to attract scholars, who have few professional incentives to tackle questions that arise from and relate to aid activities. Remarkably little writing has come out of the academy about the burgeoning field of rule of law promotion in the last twenty years. And only a small part of that existing literature is written by scholars who have had significant contact with actual aid programs.

A fifth obstacle is the fact that many lawyers—who tend to dominate the operational side of rule of law aid—are not oriented toward the empirical research necessary for organized knowledge accumulation. They often have relatively formalistic views of legal change and are slow to take up the developmental, process-oriented issues that have come to inform work in other areas of socioeconomic or sociopolitical change. Also, lawyers working on rule of law aid programs sometimes feel in tension with the aid organizations of which they are part. They are a minority legal subculture in organizations unfamiliar with and often not wholly comfortable with legal development work. This leads the rule of law aid practitioners to feel they lack the space necessary for searching studies of rule of law aid and to be wary of other development specialists attempting to raise hard questions about this work.

## When Is a Field a Field?

The rapidly growing field of rule of law assistance is operating from a disturbingly thin base of knowledge at every level—with respect to the core rationale of the work, the question of where the essence of the rule of law actually resides in different societies, how change in the rule of law occurs, and what the real effects are of changes that are produced. The lessons learned to date have for the most part not been impressive and often do not actually seem to be learned. The obstacles to the accumulation of knowledge are serious and range from institutional shortcomings of the main aid actors to deeper intellectual challenges about how to fathom the complexity of law itself.

Thus far the field of rule of law assistance has expanded less because of the tangible successes of such work than because of the irresistible apparent connection of the rule of law with the underlying goals of market economics and democracy that now constitute the dual foundation of contemporary international aid. With a recognizable set of activities that make up the rule of law assistance domain (primarily judicial reform, criminal law reform, commercial law reform, legal education work, and alternative dispute resolution), a growing body of professional specialists, and a consistent place on the international aid agenda, rule of law assistance has taken on the character of a coherent field of aid. Yet it is not yet a field if one considers a requirement for such a designation to include a well-grounded rationale, a clear understanding of the essential problem, a proven analytic method, and an understanding of results achieved. Doubtless many types of work with law in developing and postcommunist countries are valuable and should be part of the international community's engagement with these countries. However, whether rule of law promotion is in fact an established field of international aid or is even on the road to becoming one remains uncertain.

## Notes

Originally published as Carnegie Working Paper 34 (January 2003).

1. See John Hewko, "Foreign Direct Investment: Does the Rule of Law Matter?" Carnegie Endowment Working Paper no. 26 (Washington, D.C.: Carnegie Endowment for International Peace, April 2002).
2. See Frank Upham, "Mythmaking in the Rule of Law Orthodoxy," Carnegie Endowment Working Paper no. 30 (Washington, D.C.: Carnegie Endowment for International Peace, September 2002).
3. Rick Messick, "Judicial Reform and Economic Development: A Survey of the Issues," *The World Bank Research Observer* 14(1) (February 1999): 117–36.
4. On the democracy template, see Thomas Carothers, *Aiding Democracy Abroad: The Learning Curve* (Washington, D.C.: Carnegie Endowment for International Peace, 1999), ch. 5.
5. The first major shift to a focus on will to reform came after a review in the early 1990s by the U.S. Agency for International Development (USAID) of its own rule of law programs. See Harry Blair and Gary Hansen, *Weighing in on the Scales of Justice: Strategic Approaches for Donor-Supported Rule of Law Programs*, USAID Program and Operations Assessment Report no. 7 (Washington, D.C.: USAID, 1994).
6. See Linn Hammergren, "Do Judicial Councils Further Judicial Reform? Lessons from Latin America," Carnegie Endowment Working Paper no. 28 (Washington, D.C.: Carnegie Endowment for International Peace, June 2002).
7. See, for example, the critical analysis of judicial training programs in Linn Hammergen, *Judicial Training and Justice Reform* (Washington, D.C.: USAID Center for Democracy and Governance, August 1998).
8. One noteworthy exception is the study of legal and judicial reform by Linn Hammergren, sponsored by USAID and released as four papers in 1998.

SECTION FOUR

# *The State*
# *of Democracy*

FOR MOST OF THE FIRST DECADE after the end of the Cold War, the dominant outlook in the democracy promotion community was expansive and optimistic. Democracy was "on the march" in the world, and democracy-building work was helping move democracy along its successful path. Many practitioners acknowledged that democracy was not going to be easy to achieve, but a contagious optimism, often verging on triumphalism, was the spirit of the day.

By the late 1990s, however, it was increasingly evident that many of the efforts to achieve positive political change around the developing and postcommunist worlds were proving much harder and more problematic than expected. No positive ideological alternative to democracy was gaining ground, and citizens in most parts of the world were still professing belief in democracy as an ideal. But in numerous countries, old authoritarian structures were proving persistent or were reconstructing themselves in new semi-authoritarian forms. In other places, the old concentrations of political power were genuinely gone, but the new systems taking their place were weak and performing poorly. All over, citizens were wondering whether what democracy they had recently achieved was actually improving their day-to-day life.

This cooling off of the democratic trend has continued to the point where today democracy's "third wave" has broken into sharply discordant parts. The postcommunist world, for example, is split into two contrasting halves. In Central and Eastern Europe, and parts of Southeastern Europe, democracy, though riddled with problems, is taking hold. In contrast, the former Soviet Union is largely a democratic wasteland, dominated by an insalubrious assortment of authoritarian and semi-authoritarian regimes. In Africa, a small but important set of countries is making real political progress. However, a larger number is failing to realize the hopes of the transitions away from one-party rule launched in the early 1990s. The picture is similarly uneven in Latin America, Asia, and the Middle East. Although it seemed for a brief time that the arrival of the twenty-first century might be defined by democracy's global triumph, it is clear now that this century will instead be the proving period for making democracy work on a worldwide scale.

The first essay in this section, "Promoting Democracy in a Postmodern World," which I wrote in 1995, is a personal reflection on the uncomfortable disjunction between the often idealized image of democracy that Western activists promote abroad and the less shiny reality of real-life politics at home. I wrote the second piece, "Democracy without Illusions," in 1997 as an initial effort to call attention to the fact that all was not well with the third wave and to urge a lowering of expectations about it. As the cooling trend continued in the next several years, I developed those thoughts into a broader critique of the underlying analytic framework democracy promoters were using in what I believed were often wrongly labeled "transitional countries." That essay, "The End of the Transition Paradigm," provoked many responses and the *Journal of Democracy* published four of them in a subsequent issue. They are included here, as well as my reply to them. Closing out this section is a review of Fareed Zakaria's recent book, *The Future of Freedom* (published by W.W. Norton in 2003). In that work, Zakaria grapples with the same issue of democracy's troubled progress in the developing and postcommunist worlds. He arrives at a different diagnosis and suggested response, which I take issue with in my review.

# CHAPTER TWELVE

# Promoting Democracy in a Postmodern World (1996)

I WAS IN KAZAKHSTAN not long ago, on a project funded by the U.S. Agency for International Development to assist the Kazakh Parliament with its drafting of an electoral law. The trip was going smoothly until a critical moment occurred. I was working closely with a senior member of the Parliament, a wise and patient man who approached his work with great seriousness. I had just reviewed a number of provisions of the draft law and highlighted some choices open to his drafting committee. He looked at me gravely, pushing slowly aside with one hand the raft of possibilities I had been outlining, and stated with quiet firmness, "We want our Parliament to be just like your Congress." Our eyes met for a meaningful moment as I tried to think of something to say other than the three words that had immediately come screaming into my mind: "No, you don't!" I mumbled something to the effect that our Congress was in fact not perfect, that there was much value in exploring a range of ways to organize legislatures and draft laws. My host's eyes narrowed as he listened to my words, words that I knew sounded like evasion. The American expert has come all this way to say he has no model?

Among those Americans involved in the business of promoting democracy abroad—a minor growth industry populated by people from nongovernmental organizations, consulting firms, think tanks, universities, and the U.S. government itself, who career around the world helping to draft constitutions, observe elections, reform judiciaries, strengthen parliaments, build civil societies, empower local governments, and train journalists—the relation between the proffered ideal and the actual state of democracy at home is rarely much discussed. As a result, little attention has been given to the surprising and in some ways paradoxical fact that the United States, and to a lesser extent Western Europe, have moved into a particularly active phase of promoting democracy in other countries precisely at a time when the health of their own democratic systems is clouded with doubt.

It would be too much to say that democracy is in a state of crisis in the United States or Western Europe. But it is unquestionably troubled. Leaving aside the many serious social problems in the United States and the continuing inability of Western European economies to create jobs, one can point to a set of interrelated political problems in many well-established democracies. Political parties command increasingly feeble loyalty from citizens. The ruling politicians seem in most Western democracies either to be a stagnant gang of old faces or a series of one-term leaders who go rapidly from incoming boom to outgoing bust. Political participation has weakened and taken on superficial, commercialized forms. In general, the political sphere is often no longer much respected or valued. Antipolitical personalities and ideas have growing appeal, with the underside of antipolitics often not far from antidemocracy.

Very little of this vague but troubling situation appears in the world of U.S. democracy promotion programs abroad. What gets presented in such programs is generally a high school civics version of democracy. Democracy is portrayed as a gleaming edifice made up of larger-than-life institutions and structures. It is also characterized as a self-evident truth, with the resulting assumption that democratic values, once properly introduced, will take hold naturally and cement into perpetuity the proper institutional system. This view admits that a few problems may be found in the practice of democracy in the United States, but such problems are only wrinkles around the edges that do not raise questions about the core.

In U.S. assistance programs on political party development, for example, I have gotten used to watching the visiting American experts diagnose the shortcomings of the party systems of the host countries. They shake their heads smilingly but sadly at the proliferation of parties that has followed the initial ascent into democracy. They devise strategies to reduce those unworkable proliferations into two- or three-party systems, in which parties are to be defined by mild ideological shadings rather than along potentially explosive religious, ethnic, or regional lines. Yet I never hear the American experts seriously explore the waning legitimacy and significance of political parties in the well-established two- or three-party systems in the West. The juxtaposition of the absolute confidence with which the U.S. party model is presented and the parlous state of our own parties is remarkable. Similarly, I have observed many parliamentary assistance programs in which U.S. experts help foreign parliamentarians revise their committee systems, train their staff, improve their information services, or even hold mock congressional hearings, all to help mold their legislatures in the form of the U.S. Congress. Yet I have never witnessed a detailed presentation on why the U.S. Congress has performed so poorly over the past ten years, why it is held in such low regard by many Americans, and how parliaments in transitional societies might avoid its shortcomings.

I do not mean to say that we have nothing to offer the world, that the deficiencies of our own democracy disqualify us from venturing out into the world to help others make their societies more democratic. But it does seem that we are promoting democracy in ways that are habitually two-dimensional and even disingenuous. This may in part be due to our understandable desire to be positive. One hates to disembark in a newly democratizing country and immediately disgorge a heavy load of bad news about all the difficulties that lie ahead. It also probably reflects the fact that those directly involved in promoting democracy tend to be a relatively homogeneous group of people who have done fairly well by democracy in the United States and are less immediately aware of or affected by its shortcomings than many others might be.

But the main cause of the persistent disjunction between realities at home and ideals abroad is something else. To the extent that democracy promoters concern themselves with the fact that all is not well with democracy in America and Western Europe, they assume that such problems are the symptoms of "mature democracies" and that prior to the current malaise in Western politics there was a long, golden period in which democracy enjoyed its fruition. Their related assumption is that the many newly democratizing countries around the world will experience a similar pattern of development. First these countries will build the basic institutions of democracy, then they will live out their own golden periods, and only after they are far down the democratic road will the various elements of the democratic malaise affecting the West be relevant to them. Stated in more conceptual terms, the view is that Western political life is in a transition to some ill-defined postmodern state and that its strains are characteristic features of this emergent postmodernism. The newly democratizing countries, in contrast, are at a prior stage—they are striving to become modern. They must grapple with modernism before they need worry about postmodernism. They must learn to walk, in other words, before they need worry about stumbling.

One obvious criticism of this outlook is that there never was a golden period of democracy in the United States or in other Western countries; all periods of Western democracy have been fraught with problems. Yet although it is true that democracy has always been highly imperfect, the problems outlined above do appear to reflect a distinct syndrome of postmodern fatigue with democracy—and perhaps with politics itself.

The deeper flaw of this outlook lies with the notion that the postmodern fatigue is a narrow political phenomenon based on the experience of life in developed Western democracies. In fact the symptoms of postmodern fatigue are just one part of a much broader social, intellectual, and political trend that has penetrated societies in different stages of political development in many parts of the world, particularly Latin America and the formerly communist world. The core psychological components of the shift from modernism to postmodernism—the movement from alienation to detachment, from irony to cynicism, and from the loss of meaning to the loss of interest in meaning—are hardly limited to Western democracies. Nor are the basic sociopolitical elements: the technologically fueled evolution of individualism, the growing fascination with putatively apolitical solutions to political problems, and the tendency to view political choices as a derivative of economic frameworks rather than the reverse.

Thus the many democratic transitions of recent years in Latin America, Eastern Europe, and the former Soviet Union, and possibly even Africa and Asia, may seem at first glance like efforts by other societies to achieve the plateau of Western political modernism. In fact, however, they are much more complex transitions in which societies already suffused with many of the attitudes and ideas of postmodernism are attempting to develop the structures and processes of liberal democracy. They are, in short, learning to walk while they already know intellectually all about stumbling. The idea that in promoting democracy abroad we should put aside for some much later date consideration of the characteristic problems of "mature democracies" is wrong.

### Ideological Certainties

In parallel to their tendency to hold out an idealized version of U.S. democracy to foreigners, Americans abroad tend to read into the many democratic transitions of recent years far too much ideological certainty. They often view such transitions as societywide epiphanies, large-scale conversions to liberal democratic values. This view is tied to the deeper, seductive idea that late-twentieth-century history is defined by the triumph of liberal democracy. Yet the democratic trend in the world, significant as it is, should be understood as much in terms of failure as of triumph.

In Latin America, for example, the regionwide shift from dictatorial regimes to elected, civilian governments in the 1980s was born from the dual failure of right-wing authoritarians to govern effectively and of left-wing movements to win broad credibility. The shift to democracy can scarcely be described in triumphal terms; rather, a region beset with economic woes, corruption, mismanagement, and profound social inequities turned to democracy as the political lender of last resort. In Eastern Europe and the former Soviet Union, the engine of political change in the late 1980s was the abject political and economic failure of communism. Similarly, the unexpected democratic trend in Africa of the early 1990s grew out of the prolonged, resounding failure of one-party rule in that continent. Only in East Asia has the democratic trend arisen in societies that have been developing successfully and self-confidently.

With this important but limited exception, therefore, "failure of the alternatives" appears to be a more useful controlling concept than "triumph of an idea" in explaining the widespread democratic trend of recent years. Democracy was certainly a positive choice for many troubled societies, something that some people fought for out of deep conviction. But the democratic trend did not result from a rising ideology outshining an array of vigorous rivals. Instead it was more a process of elimination—as the other ideological choices collapsed, democracy was the only one left standing.

Viewing the democratic trend in this way highlights the fact that the recent political transitions are highly pragmatic, or perhaps more accurately, highly functionalist experiments. People around the world are trying out democracy to see what it can deliver to them. What they want it to deliver depends somewhat on the particular country involved, but material interests usually dominate. They want a life that matches the expectations raised by images of Western prosperity that now circulate so pervasively around the world. They want a government that can accomplish basic tasks with a semblance of competence and honesty. They want to be left alone at the political level but taken care of at the social and economic levels. In supporting democratization they are not so much hoping for the establishment of a new, participatory, civic-oriented relationship between citizens and the state as for what might be called the professionalization of the state. They do not dream of humanizing politics so much as of obviating the need for politics itself.

The American tendency to read into recent political transitions around the world too much ideological certainty is reflected in, and causes problems for, U.S. assistance programs aimed at democracy promotion. The problems often begin at the early stage of political transitions, when opposition individuals or groups are challenging existing nondemocratic regimes. In such situations, Americans are quick to assume that anyone challenging a dictatorship is a democrat. They project the simple framework of democracy versus dictatorship upon local power struggles, which, though often concerned with political liberalization, are also closely linked with historical conflicts between different regional, ethnic, or religious factions. They are then surprised when the people they support turn out to be primarily interested in gaining and consolidating power rather than building democracy. And they fail to realize how much the United States is perceived in the countries in which it is engaged as taking sides in historical power struggles rather than advancing the abstract principles of democracy.

These problems continue as democratic transitions proceed. Once the old regime is out and a new government comes to power through elections or general affirmation, U.S. assistance organizations undertake civic education throughout the country. Such programs rest on the idea that the common person in a transitional society yearns for democracy but just does not know much about what democracy is. Civic educators funded by the United States fan out through the countryside armed with brochures, pamphlets, charts, and books translated into the local language, which explain what political rights are, what voting is, what parliaments do in democracies, what the separation of powers means, and so on.

But much of this heartfelt educational work assumes away the essential task. It assumes that the people in a transitional society want to become democratic and just need to know more about how to do so. In fact, however, in societies currently in the midst of democratic transitions, many citizens feel a strong skepticism about the utility of politics itself and a disinclination to be stirred by any ideological education, particularly one in which political values are presented as self-evident truths rather than correlated with clear individual interests. Civic educators are dismayed when political apathy follows hard on the heels of initially energizing democratic transitions. Rather than question the tenets of their educational approach, they simply prescribe larger doses of the same medicine.

It is not surprising that Americans tend to see the recent wave of political transitions in primarily ideological terms. We are a nation that defines itself through ideology, and we are prone to view the world through our own ideological lens. Nonetheless, in failing to see that many of these transitions reflect as much a spirit of antipolitical functionalism as ideological conviction, we are missing an important connection. An essential feature of the troubled condition of democracy in the United States and Western Europe is precisely that of the rise of apolitical or even antipolitical attitudes. Citizens of these countries increasingly view their political systems not as repositories of value but as service mechanisms to be evaluated only in terms of the material goods they deliver. In the established democracies, antipolitical attitudes are eating away at existing systems of liberal democratic governance. In the transitional countries, such attitudes are complicating the efforts to establish democratic systems. In either case, however, the underlying phenomenon is strikingly similar. The fact that Americans tend not to draw this connection highlights the earlier point that they often fail to relate the condition of democracy at home to their understanding of democracy abroad. And the fact that this connection exists means that the political challenges facing democratizing societies are not fundamentally different from those confronted by mature democracies.

## A Place in the World

In a broad, metaphorical sense, the manifold efforts by Americans to promote democracy abroad express a basic perception about America's place in the world. And the disjunctions that mark these assistance efforts reflect a deep division built into the common perception. On the one hand, many Americans believe that the world is becoming or should become more like America, and that it is their job to go out in the world to push that process along. Yet at the same time many Americans believe that there is a tremendous gulf between themselves and the world. They believe that America is fundamentally different from other countries; the mere fact of foreignness seems utterly strange, almost unnatural to them.

This division in our idea of our place in the world is rooted in our own national self-conception. We believe that America is a unique country but, at the same time, a universal model. It is unique as the oldest democracy. The idea of America as the "city on the hill" remains surprisingly strong despite the uncertainties that many Americans have about the country's future and the widespread critical view of the actual functioning of its political system. Americans view their country as the self-made miracle that any person or society can emulate with hard work and the right intentions. That there may well be an inherent contradiction between being simultaneously unique and universal seems to escape our notice. Our self-appointed place in the world rests uneasily on the conscious or unconscious denial of that contradiction. But although it is denied, the contradiction has haunted our entire experience of international engagement. It lies behind the disconcerting condition that we know so well of having been highly engaged politically, economically, militarily, and culturally in the world for generations, yet having remained so much an island nation despite it all.

The current historical juncture affords us an opportunity to change our basic psychological relationship to the world. By "juncture" I am referring not only to the end of the Cold War but to the full set of transitional features of the international sphere, including the trend toward democracy in many countries, the increasing internationalization of economic systems, and the overly hyped but nonetheless significant "information revolution." We have engaged in much talk about the implications of the end of the Cold War and of the other distinctive features of this new period. But the changes we have made in our international outlook have been surprisingly few and generally limited to the level of formal policy modifications. It is the psychological underpinnings of our relationship to the world that must change. Democracy promotion, as a defining metaphor for that relationship, is one place to start.

Within American political culture, pride in the unique stability of America's democratic system has hardened over the generations into a tendency to equate the particular forms of our political institutions with democracy itself. Missing from our political life is much real debate about how our crucial political values, such as representation and pluralism, might be better served by different institutional forms or configurations. In fact, we maintain a remarkable attachment to the particular institutional forms of our democracy, such as our highly flawed Congress, even as the underlying principles upon which they were built atrophy from ill service.

We have been carrying this overattachment to forms and underattachment to principles with us when we go abroad promoting democracy. We need to concentrate less on helping to reproduce certain institutional forms in other countries and more on fostering the underlying values and principles of democracy. For example, when faced with a dysfunctional parliament in a transitional society we should not immediately think in terms of a checklist of institutional modifications needed to make that parliament resemble our Congress—such as increasing the number of staff, expanding the library, changing the rules of procedure, or strengthening the committee system. Instead, we need to help empower those people and organizations who wish to fight to change the patterns of representation, and let them work out their precise institutional objectives. Or, if we are trying to assist the development of political parties in another country, we should refrain from our habitual tendency to send American political consultants to teach those parties to be U.S.-style political machines replete with media expertise, a penchant for polls, and a winning-is-all approach. Instead, we should try to help stimulate debate and inquiry into the full range of possible types of political association, on the assumption that we do not have the final answer with respect to the forms and functions of political parties.

In short, the challenge of promoting democracy abroad turns out to bear important similarities to the challenge of reinvigorating democracy at home. If we have been falling short in our approaches abroad, it is perhaps because we have not been seriously engaged in the task at home. Reconfiguring our relationship to the world in this new international era can only follow from a reconfiguring of our own relationship to the democratic principles and values we espouse.

### Note

The Carnegie Endowment gratefully acknowledges the permission of *Dissent* to reprint this article, which originally appeared in *Dissent* (Spring 1996).

# CHAPTER THIRTEEN

# Democracy
# without Illusions
# (1997)

## From Revolution to Retrenchment

THOUGH OFTEN OVERSOLD, the trend toward democratic government that began in southern Europe in the mid-1970s, swept through Latin America in the 1980s, and spread to many parts of Asia, the former Soviet Union, Eastern Europe, and Africa in the late 1980s and early 1990s has been an important phenomenon. Together with the demise of Soviet-sponsored communism and the globalization of the international economic system, it propelled the world from the postwar period into a new era. The spread of democracy has by no means eradicated political repression or conflict, but it has tremendously increased the number of people who enjoy at least some freedom and fostered hope that the next century might be less fraught with political rivalry and destruction than the present one.

In the last several years, however, what enthusiasts at the start of the decade were calling "the worldwide democratic revolution" has cooled considerably. The headlines announcing that country after country was shrugging off dictatorial rule and embarking on a democratic path have given way to an intermittent but rising stream of troubling reports: a coup in Gambia, civil strife in the Central African Republic, flawed elections in Albania, a deposed government in Pakistan, returning authoritarianism in Zambia, the shedding of democratic forms in Kazakhstan, sabotaged elections in Armenia, eroding human rights in Cambodia. There is still sometimes good news on the democracy front, such as

155

Boris Yeltsin's defeat of the Russian communists last summer, but a counter-movement of stagnation and retrenchment is evident.

Given the relevance of democracy's fortunes to the state of international relations, the new countermovement raises significant questions, starting with the basic one of whether it is only a scattering of predictable cases of backsliding or instead presages a major reverse trend. Furthermore, the rise of retrenchment prompts inquiry into where it is taking countries in which it is occurring, whether it signals the emergence of a new contender to the liberal democratic model, and what it says about when and why democracy succeeds.

Retrenchment also poses serious questions for U.S. policy. As democratization advanced around the globe in the 1980s and early 1990s, successive U.S. administrations increasingly emphasized support for democracy as a foreign policy goal. The tendency reached its zenith—rhetorically, at least—when the Clinton administration proclaimed the promotion of democracy "the successor to a doctrine of containment." It is thus imperative to ask whether retrenchment signals a failure of U.S. policies on democracy promotion and what it may mean for U.S. foreign policy in the years ahead.

## Retrenchment's Reach

Democratic stagnation and retrenchment have been most pronounced in the former Soviet Union, Africa, and the Middle East. Several former Soviet republics have made genuine democratic progress since the USSR's dissolution in 1991, but in the rest of the fifteen, pluralism was stillborn or is losing ground. The 1996 Russian presidential elections were a milestone, yet political life in Russia is still only very partially democratic and not especially stable. The dominant ideology is a form of state nationalism in which elements of pluralism mix uneasily with authoritarian structures and impulses carried over from the communist era. The Baltic states have established working democratic systems, and Ukraine and Moldova are at least holding on to a certain degree of pluralism and openness in politics.

Elsewhere in the former Soviet Union, Belarus has quietly sunk into dictatorship. The Central Asian states are a dispiriting collection of politically retrograde entities. Uzbekistan, Turkmenistan, and Tajikistan are under absolutist rule, with Tajikistan still wracked by civil strife. President Nursultan Nazarbayev of Kazakhstan has punctured his promises of democracy with a march toward strongman rule over the last two years, capped by his replacement of presidential elections with a referendum on his continued rule. Even President Askar Akayev of Kyrgyzstan, the darling of Western donors for his initial reforming path, is showing incipient authoritarian tendencies, evident in the problematic parliamentary and presidential elections of 1995. Hopes for democracy in the Transcaucasus have faded, with both Armenia and Azerbaijan holding seriously flawed elections in the last two years. Pluralism is surviving in Georgia, but political stability seems to depend almost exclusively on one man, Eduard Shevardnadze.

In sub-Saharan Africa, the surge away from one-party regimes toward democracy has fragmented. Democratization is still advancing, or at least has not been reversed, in some nations, including not only South Africa but Mali, Malawi, Namibia, and Benin. At the same time, many of the more than 30 countries that experienced political openings early in the decade have gone seriously off course. Some have descended into civil conflict, and in Rwanda and Burundi, the violence has been horrifying. Coups have halted liberalization in Nigeria, Gambia, and Niger. Elsewhere, in Cameroon, Gabon, Chad, Burkina Faso, and Togo, entrenched strongmen have manipulated or co-opted supposedly transitional elections so as to reconsolidate their power. Fraud, severe administrative disorder, or a lack of permitted opposition parties have marred many elections, as in Côte d'Ivoire, Tanzania, and Kenya. Even where legitimate balloting has taken place, some of the newly elected leaders have disappointed, like President Frederick Chiluba of Zambia, who has returned to the authoritarian habits of his predecessors. On the whole, sub-Saharan Africa is more pluralistic today than it was ten years ago, and democracy may well take root in a number of African countries. The hopes for a continentwide shift to democracy, however, have not been fulfilled.

The Middle East, the world's least democratic region, felt a liberalizing breeze in the late 1980s and early 1990s. Various governments undertook cautious, gradual political openings in response both to popular discontent generated by worsening economic woes and to democratic change worldwide. In Morocco and Jordan, the openings have slowly advanced and a certain space for pluralism has been created, although in both countries constitutional monarchs retain the bulk of power. Other states have suffered serious setbacks or stagnation. The transition to democracy in Algeria, once held out as a model for Arab countries, was abruptly derailed in 1992 by a military takeover after Islamist victories in national elections and has since degenerated into a vicious civil war. Yemen's surprising experiment with democratization in the early 1990s, undertaken as part of the unification of the previously separate states of North and South Yemen, collapsed in 1994 when the south tried to secede and civil war flared. In Egypt, President Hosni Mubarak has resisted rising internal pressure for political reform and left many wondering if he can navigate the country through increasingly polarized waters. Around the region, deeply entrenched conservative elites fearful of Islamic fundamentalists have largely choked off nascent liberalization.

In Eastern Europe, Latin America, and Asia, the democratic trend has fared better but the picture is still very mixed. Democracy has advanced considerably in Central and Eastern Europe. Poland, the Czech Republic, and Hungary, in particular, have taken huge strides. Romania has also made progress, including the surprising opposition sweep in the November national elections, although its slower and more uneven change reflects its relatively more oppressive rule before 1989. Bulgaria, Albania, and Slovakia enjoy some openness and pluralism, but their political paths are tortuous. Bulgaria has suffered from political and economic ineptitude in all its major factions. Albanian President Sali Berisha and Slovakian Prime Minister Vladimir Meciar have only limited tolerance for opposition and flirt with autocracy. "Retrenchment" is an inadequate word for the political and human horrors that have ravaged the former Yugoslavia since 1991. Dictatorial regimes in Serbia and Croatia dominate the area, and the prospects for peaceful pluralism in Bosnia remain extremely shaky in spite of internationally supervised national elections in September.

To the surprise of many observers, Latin America has experienced few outright reversals among the more than a dozen transitions to elected, civilian government that occurred in the 1980s. Haiti suffered a coup in 1991, but U.S. military intervention overturned the regime and reinstalled the elected president, Jean-Bertrand Aristide. Peru experienced a setback in 1992 with President Alberto Fujimori's temporary suspension of democratic rule in an *autogolpe*, and the country remains in a gray area between dictatorship and democracy. Guatemala, Venezuela, and Paraguay have all had close brushes in recent years with military coups, but elected governments are still in place.

The question for Latin America is not whether democracy can be maintained in form but whether it can be achieved in substance. In a few countries, primarily ones with some democratic tradition, such as Costa Rica, Chile, and Uruguay, it is possible to speak of the consolidation of democracy. In most of the region, however, severe deficiencies mark political life—weak capacity and performance of government institutions, widespread corruption, irregular and often arbitrary rule of law, poorly developed patterns of representation and participation, and large numbers of marginalized citizens.

The recent progress of Asia's far from all-encompassing but nonetheless notable democratic trend has been as various as the trend's original causes and manifestations. Taiwan and South Korea remain examples of relatively successful democratic transitions following from successful economic transformations. Democratization in the Philippines, Thailand, and Mongolia is holding steady or even advancing on some counts, in spite of serious corruption in the former two countries and the burdensome legacy of Soviet rule in the latter.

Asia's other recent experiments with political liberalization or democratization are question marks. Political life in Cambodia has deteriorated sharply since the United Nations–sponsored 1993 elections, with widespread human rights abuses and large-scale government corruption. Political tensions are high in Pakistan following the ouster of Prime Minister Benazir Bhutto in November amid charges of corruption and abuse of power. Bangladesh seemed headed for a return to military rule early last year but held legitimate elections in June and for the time being continues with an elected government. Casting its shadow over democracy's prospects throughout Asia is China, the first Asian case of backtracking from the liberalization of the late 1980s.

## Strongmen in New Clothing

Democratization's stall is serious but not fatal. It is significant enough that pessimists can claim it proves the fragility of democracy, the rise of political chaos, and the imperfectibility of humanity. However, it is sufficiently limited that optimists can say it is merely an expected "market correction" that does not undermine the longer-term global movement toward democracy. Democratic stagnation and retrenchment are likely to continue in many countries but without broadening to such a degree as to settle the debate between pessimists and optimists—a debate, in any case, rooted as much in clashing political faiths as empirical realities.

Although the new countermovement away from democracy is still emerging, its impact clearly varies by region. Stagnation and retrenchment have been only moderate in regions with relatively strong historical sociopolitical ties to the Western industrialized democracies—Latin America, Central Europe, and the Baltic states—and in East Asia, the one region of the developing world that has enjoyed sustained economic growth. But the toll has been heavy elsewhere— the former Soviet Union, sub-Saharan Africa, the Middle East, and southeastern Europe. What appeared to many enthusiasts a few years back to be a grand unifying movement may, at least over the next several decades, heighten the political divide between the Western world (including Latin America, Eastern Europe, and parts of the former Soviet Union) and the non-Western one. This is not a prophecy of a clash of civilizations but a warning against facile universalism.

Despite the diversity of the countries in which democracy has stagnated or been rolled back, most have ended up in a similar state—not with full-fledged dictatorships but with a particular style of semi-authoritarian regime. Their leaders act on authoritarian instincts and habits, usually developed during a lifetime under dictatorship. Yet in recent years they have been exposed to the heady international side of democratic transitions—the visits of senior officials from powerful countries and prestigious multilateral organizations, the expanded flows of aid and investment, and the favorable stories in the Western press. They come to crave the attention, approval, and money that they know democracy attracts from the Western international community. As a result, their rule becomes a balancing act in which they impose enough repression to keep their opponents weak and maintain their own power while adhering to enough democratic formalities that they might just pass themselves off as democrats.

In this ambiguous climate, opposition groups have some latitude but little real strength, newspapers and radio offer independent voices but television is state-dominated, trade unions are permitted but the government co-opts them, elections are plausible but preceded by campaigns in which incumbents enjoy huge advantages of resources and media time, the legislature contains heterogeneous forces but possesses minimal authority, and the judiciary operates with some independence at the local level but is politically controlled at the top. The many new semi-authoritarian regimes are often highly personalistic, although the leaders draw their power from entrenched economic and political structures. The regimes usually depend on their militaries or internal security forces to ensure political stability but are not military regimes per se. The leaders rarely articulate much in the way of conservative or liberal ideology, relying on opportunistic nationalism and populism to sway the people.

In some countries, particularly in Central Asia and sub-Saharan Africa, strongmen have given up the pretense of presenting themselves to the world as democrats and claim to be practicing Asian-style "soft authoritarianism" a la Singapore or Malaysia. A strong hand is necessary for national development, they insist, and democracy can come only after development. This line is often popular, at least at first, in countries where flailing pluralistic governments and the increased crime, corruption, and poverty that frequently follow political openings have left citizens disillusioned. The Singapore model also has appeal among Western advisers and observers, many of whom wonder whether developing countries are "ready for democracy" and believe, without admitting to it, that a strong hand is just what is needed.

Few if any of the many newly established or reestablished semi-authoritarian regimes, however, bear much resemblance to the soft authoritarian governments of Asia. Rather than building up meritocratic civil services, the new semi-authoritarians usually indulge in rampant patronage. Rather than investing heavily in education and trying to minimize inequality, they fritter away scarce revenues on pet projects of dubious value and allow elites to increase their already disproportionate share of the national wealth. In place of discipline and seriousness of national purpose they offer disguised improvisation and pompous rhetoric. In the end, arguments for development before democracy are little more than attempted cover for the dictatorial ambitions of autocrats like Islam Karimov of Uzbekistan and Henri Konan-Bédié of Côte d'Ivoire.

The emptiness of their pretensions underlines the fact that no positive alternative to democracy has yet emerged in the post–Cold War world. Soft authoritarianism is still practiced in only a handful of states. Democratic retrenchment is not the consequence of the spreading allure of Asian-style authoritarianism or of any newer competitor to democracy; it offers only variations on old, unproductive patterns of authoritarianism.

## Boom and Bust

With its startling pace and unexpected breadth, the democratic trend of the 1980s and early 1990s seemed to sweep away decades of research on how democracy develops. Democratic transitions popped up in the most unexpected places, apparently depending on remarkably little—not the political history or culture of a country, literacy levels, the existence of a middle class, or the level or distribution of wealth. So long as the elites in a country embraced the democratic ideal—something elites everywhere seemed to be doing—democracy would spring into being. In the space of a few years, democracy appeared to go from the political equivalent of an arcane religious faith, attainable only after laborious study, to a pop religion spread through televangelism and mass baptisms.

At the enthusiasm's height, Western observers proclaimed every country attempting a political opening, no matter how partial, "in transition to democracy." Stagnation and retrenchment have brought them back to earth. Above all, the backsliding makes clear how difficult democracy is to achieve. The leading cause in many instances is as straightforward as it is inescapable: Elites are able to reconsolidate their rule after a political opening because of the political and economic resources they command and the weakness of fledgling opposition forces.

In some societies, especially in Central Europe and South America, openings involved real shifts in the basic configuration of power following delegitimation of old structures or mass popular mobilization. Yet in many cases the openings were highly controlled and top-down, reflecting ruling elites' desire to relieve rising pressure for change or to impress Western governments rather than a commitment to cede significant authority. Breaking down the entrenched antidemocratic power structures common around the world and preventing new leaders from falling into bad old habits have proved perplexing tasks.

Recent events highlight the folly of ignoring the broad set of social, political, and economic factors bearing on democratization. There is certainly no list of absolute preconditions for democracy. Yet neither are all countries equally likely to manage to establish a pluralistic, open political life in the next several decades. Per capita income at least in the middle range helps. So does past experience with multiparty politics and other democratic practices. Finally, being part of a region that looks to the Western industrialized countries for social and political models or that seeks integration with the West aids countries embarked on a democratic experiment. No country's culture, history, or economic circumstances bar it from democracy. Poor nations far from Western influence and with no history of political pluralism or openness may well succeed in making themselves democratic. But relatively affluent countries that have had some experience with political liberalization and that identify closely with the West will have a much better chance.

The political strains that market reform has created are a factor that one might expect to provoke democratic stagnation and retrenchment. When in the late 1980s and early 1990s many countries began to implement economic and political liberalization programs simultaneously, a large group of observers, particularly critics of the "Washington consensus" on market reform, questioned the feasibility of the undertaking. They pointed to the numerous short-term pressures that economic liberalization programs typically generate—heightened unemployment, rising prices for basic foodstuffs and other previously subsidized goods, and increases in poverty and inequality—and asked whether fragile newly elected governments would be able to cope.

Such strains are apparent in almost every society that has implemented market reforms, and they will unquestionably make the consolidation of democracy that much more complicated. They do not, however, appear to have been a major cause of the political backtracking of the last several years. Backsliding has not been concentrated in countries undergoing economic liberalization. If anything, serious market reform programs are more common in regions where democratization is generally not retreating—Central Europe, the Baltic states, South America, and East Asia—than in ones where it is. Moreover, in countries in which retrenchment has coincided with attempted market transitions, like Zambia, Albania, and Slovakia, it has been mainly a matter of rulers indulging their authoritarian tendencies, not of rising popular pressures overwhelming weak democratic institutions.

## Modest Contributions

During the first Clinton administration, the president and his top foreign policy aides held out democratic "enlargement" as a guiding principle of their foreign policy. The experience of those years with respect to democracy around the world, however, was as much contraction as enlargement. This uncomfortable fact was absent from administration talk about foreign policy. Officials repeatedly hailed a few prominent examples of democratic progress—Haiti, Russia, and South Africa—and all but ignored the many cases of stagnation and retrenchment.

Some, seeing the political backsliding as a yardstick of failure, may be tempted to blame the Clinton administration for democracy's problems abroad. Such a view, however, relies on the same flawed assumption that has underlain Clinton dogma—that U.S. policy is significantly responsible for democracy's advance or retreat in the world. In fact, only in a very limited number of cases is the United States able to mobilize sufficient economic and political resources to have a major impact on the political course of other countries. The Clinton administration, like the Bush administration before it, has played a reasonably active supporting role for the cause of democracy beyond U.S. borders. In many countries, Washington's diplomatic encouragement and material aid to democratic reformers have made a modest contribution to democratic progress. In a few countries, the United States' role has even been quite significant. American support for Boris Yeltsin since 1991 has helped him survive politically and thus helped Russia keep to the path of reform, although the Clinton administration let Yeltsin off too easy on Moscow's war in Chechnya. U.S. diplomatic and economic support for reformers in Ukraine has bolstered that country's shaky efforts to achieve democracy and capitalism. Although triggered more by politics at home than a desire to promote democracy abroad, the U.S. intervention in Haiti made pluralism possible there. Clinton administration opposition to attempted military coups in Latin America, such as those in Guatemala and Paraguay, has helped discourage democratic reversals in that region.

At the same time, the U.S. government could have done more for democracy in some countries without sacrificing countervailing interests. In Bosnia last year, the administration failed to enforce the provisions of the 1995 Dayton agreement strongly enough to ensure free and fair elections. U.S. policy toward Croatia and Serbia has not sufficiently emphasized the importance of pluralism for long-term peace in the Balkans. It appears the administration will allow President Levon Ter-Petrosian of Armenia to get away with his sabotage of the recent presidential elections and continue reaping the political benefits of being a leading recipient of U.S. aid. In Kazakhstan, the U.S. government talked a great deal in the early 1990s about promoting democracy but raised few protests when President Nazarbayev began dispensing with democratic niceties. And in Albania, the administration failed to anticipate and was slow to react to President Sali Berisha's undermining of parliamentary elections last May.

Clinton's critics, with some cause, long for greater muscularity and decisiveness in foreign policy. But even if renewed along those lines, U.S. policy will not change the basic course of events in Algeria, Azerbaijan, Bangladesh, Bulgaria, Chad, Uzbekistan, or most of the other countries in which political openings or transitions have been troubled or truncated. Moreover, the pattern of much of the recent democratic slippage makes a productive response more difficult. In most cases there has been no sharp, highly visible break, such as a military coup, to attract outsiders' attention and spur interested countries to action. Instead, there have been intermittent negative signals of varying severity and clarity: a problematic but not openly fraudulent election, sporadic harassment of outspoken journalists, increasing reports of government corruption and arbitrary behavior, the dismissal of moderate reformers from the cabinet.

Countries where such patterns are unfolding make poor targets for campaigns of foreign pressure based on economic sanctions or the withholding of foreign aid. Western donors have difficulty agreeing on such campaigns even in drastic circumstances; they are highly unlikely to do so in response to partial political backsliding. Nor does the specter of greater economic hardship for the masses move most budding authoritarians faced with relinquishing any of their power; they and their biggest supporters are usually the last to suffer. Aid conditionality has worked best when focused on a single major goal, as when donors in 1992 pressured then-President H. Kamuzu Banda to hold a national referendum on Malawi's future political structure. Such goals are hard to pinpoint in the gradual slide that has characterized recent retrenchments.

Assistance programs specifically designed to strengthen democratic processes and institutions have also proved to be a problematic response to retrenchment. Democracy-related assistance, which has become a valuable component of the foreign aid of the United States and many other Western democracies over the last ten years, can help countries that are moving toward democracy make more rapid, effective transitions. But when the host government is not genuinely committed to reform, such aid is undermined. It may keep besieged opposition groups and civic organizations alive but cannot be expected to change the overall direction of politics. In many retrenching countries, the United States and other Western donors have closed down most of their democracy-related programs because of legitimate concerns about wasting funds, legitimating the illegitimate, or being associated with a failure.

## Revisiting Interests

Rising democratic stagnation and retrenchment forces the U.S. government to reexamine questions not only of how much the United States can actually foster democracy abroad but of how strong its interests in the matter actually are. The Clinton administration implies that America has a blanket interest in the promotion of democracy abroad, but such a policy line runs up against increasingly harsh realities these days.

During the Cold War, Washington frequently subordinated its interest in democracy and human rights abroad to the dominant goal of opposing communism. As the Cold War ended, the attractive idea gained ground in the policy community that U.S. moral and pragmatic interests abroad were fusing; thus the promotion of democracy would now complement rather than conflict with national economic and security interests. Washington still had relationships with so-called friendly tyrants, as in the Persian Gulf states, but these seemed to be a holdover and generally on the decline. In some regions, a convergence of U.S. policy interests is indeed occurring. With regard to Latin America, for example, nearly all arms of the U.S. government, with the possible exception of unreconstructed elements in the intelligence agencies, now accept that democratic governments are more favorable than repressive military leaders for U.S. economic, security, and political interests alike.

Yet the rise in retrenchment makes clear that tradeoffs between U.S. ideals and interests abroad are not fading away and may even be multiplying. Since the 1993 coup in Nigeria, the Clinton administration has shied away from pushing democracy there, mindful that Nigeria is a major supplier of oil to the United States and that a unilateral U.S. embargo on Nigerian oil would end up benefiting European oil companies and causing little economic harm to Nigeria. The muted response to Kazakhstan's move toward authoritarianism reflects recognition of President Nazarbayev's cooperation in making his country nuclear-weapons-free and his support for enormous private American investments in the Kazakh oilfields. In Croatia, the administration raises little fuss about President Franjo Tudjman's repressive ways, at least in part because he has backed U.S. policy on Bosnia. In some countries, moreover, U.S. policy makers fear that pushing for democracy entails unacceptable risks for the inhabitants. The violence in Rwanda and Burundi shows how catastrophically wrong political openings can go in ethnically driven societies.

In some cases, and especially with the last group, subordinating the desire for democracy is a reasonable decision given the nature of the other interests at stake. In other cases, however, such as in the Balkans and parts of the former Soviet Union, the U.S. government shows signs of slipping back into favoring friendly tyrants for the wrong reasons—because they appear to be men of action, because they are willing to do its bidding, and because they are good at flattering high-level visitors.

## Down to Earth

Recent events do not negate the fact that in this century the world has experienced a broad trend toward democracy, of which the upswing of the last twenty years is a crucial part. The current retrenchment is not a widespread reversal of the overall democratic trend, nor does it announce some rising contender to the liberal democratic model. Nonetheless, the reality of retrenchment is stripping away the illusions that have surrounded the pro-democratic enterprise of recent years. It has exposed the chimera of instantaneous democracy, revealing the difficulties and the significant chance of failure in democratic transitions. Similarly, although there is no fixed set of preconditions and democracy is certainly not an exclusively Western province, the pattern of retrenchment shows that factors such as the level of affluence, experience with pluralism, and the degree of Western sociopolitical influence are relevant to democracy's prospects in a particular society. Finally, retrenchment has undermined the seductive idea that the spread of democracy will rapidly efface basic political differences between established Western democracies and governments in non-Western regions. Democratization will not be an end-of-the-century global deliverance from the strife, repression, and venality that afflict political life in so many parts of the world.

The new political tide does not mean that democracy promotion will cease to be an important part of a post–Cold War U.S. foreign policy. U.S. ideals and interests abroad often converge around democracy, and the United States is a much more credible advocate for democracy now that it is not engaged in the superpower rivalry. Yet retrenchment is a sobering tonic for U.S. policy makers and pundits who made overreaching claims for America's influence on the political direction of other countries. The shedding of illusions is painful but potentially beneficial. It may help the second Clinton administration bring its rhetoric into line with reality on this front and drop the unproductive quest to unify U.S. foreign policy around a single sweeping idea. The debates of recent years over a new organizing concept that can fill the void left by containment's demise must give way to the recognition that only a course marked by steady presidential engagement, serious strategic focus, and substantial resource commitments can produce a foreign policy that commands Americans' support and the world's respect.

## Note

The Carnegie Endowment gratefully acknowledges the permission of the Council on Foreign Relations to reprint this article, which originally appeared in *Foreign Affairs*, vol. 76, no. 1 (January/February 1997).

# CHAPTER FOURTEEN

# The End of the
# Transition Paradigm
# (2002)

IN THE LAST QUARTER of the twentieth century, trends in seven different regions converged to change the political landscape of the world: (1) the fall of right-wing authoritarian regimes in Southern Europe in the mid-1970s; (2) the replacement of military dictatorships by elected civilian governments across Latin America from the late 1970s through the late 1980s; (3) the decline of authoritarian rule in parts of East and South Asia starting in the mid-1980s; (4) the collapse of communist regimes in Eastern Europe at the end of the 1980s; (5) the breakup of the Soviet Union and the establishment of fifteen post-Soviet republics in 1991; (6) the decline of one-party regimes in many parts of sub-Saharan Africa in the first half of the 1990s; and (7) a weak but recognizable liberalizing trend in some Middle Eastern countries in the 1990s.

The causes, shape, and pace of these different trends varied considerably. But they shared a dominant characteristic—simultaneous movement in at least several countries in each region away from dictatorial rule toward more liberal and often more democratic governance. And though differing in many ways, these trends influenced and to some extent built on one another. As a result, they were considered by many observers, especially in the West, as component parts of a larger whole, a global democratic trend that thanks to Samuel Huntington has widely come to be known as the "third wave" of democracy.[1]

This striking tide of political change was seized upon with enthusiasm by the U.S. government and the broader U.S. foreign policy community. As early as the mid-1980s, President Ronald Reagan, Secretary of State George Shultz, and other high-level U.S. officials were referring regularly to "the worldwide democratic revolution." During the 1980s, an active array of governmental, quasigovernmental, and nongovernmental organizations devoted to promoting democracy abroad sprang into being. This new democracy-promotion community had a pressing need for an analytic framework to conceptualize and respond to the ongoing political events. Confronted with the initial parts of the third wave—democratization in Southern Europe, Latin America, and a few countries in Asia (especially the Philippines)—the U.S. democracy community rapidly embraced an analytic model of democratic transition. It was derived principally from their own interpretation of the patterns of democratic change taking place, but also to a lesser extent from the early works of the emergent academic field of "transitology," above all the seminal work of Guillermo O'Donnell and Philippe Schmitter.[2]

As the third wave spread to Eastern Europe, the Soviet Union, sub-Saharan Africa, and elsewhere in the 1990s, democracy promoters extended this model as a universal paradigm for understanding democratization. It became ubiquitous in U.S. policy circles as a way of talking about, thinking about, and designing interventions in processes of political change around the world. And it stayed remarkably constant despite many variations in those patterns of political change and a stream of increasingly diverse scholarly views about the course and nature of democratic transitions.[3]

The transition paradigm has been somewhat useful during a time of momentous and often surprising political upheaval in the world. But it is increasingly clear that reality is no longer conforming to the model. Many countries that policy makers and aid practitioners persist in calling "transitional" are not in transition to democracy, and of the democratic transitions that are under way, more than a few are not following the model. Sticking with the paradigm beyond its useful life is retarding evolution in the field of democratic assistance and is leading policy makers astray in other ways. It is time to recognize that the transition paradigm has outlived its usefulness and to look for a better lens.

## Core Assumptions

Five core assumptions define the transition paradigm. The first, which is an umbrella for all the others, is that any country moving *away* from dictatorial rule can be considered a country in transition *toward* democracy. Especially in the first half of the 1990s, when political change accelerated in many regions, numerous policy makers and aid practitioners reflexively labeled any formerly authoritarian country that was attempting some political liberalization as a "transitional country." The set of transitional countries swelled dramatically, and nearly 100 countries (approximately 20 in Latin America, 25 in Eastern Europe and the former Soviet Union, 30 in sub-Saharan Africa, 10 in Asia, and 5 in the Middle East) were thrown into the conceptual pot of the transition paradigm. Once so labeled, their political life was automatically analyzed in terms of their movement toward or away from democracy, and they were held up to the implicit expectations of the paradigm, as detailed below. To cite just one especially astonishing example, the U.S. Agency for International Development (USAID) continues to describe the Democratic Republic of Congo (Kinshasa), a strife-wracked country undergoing a turgid, often opaque, and rarely very democratic process of political change, as a country in "transition to a democratic, free market society."[4]

The second assumption is that democratization tends to unfold in a set sequence of stages. First there occurs the *opening,* a period of democratic ferment and political liberalization in which cracks appear in the ruling dictatorial regime, with the most prominent fault line being that between hard-liners and soft-liners. There follows the *breakthrough*—the collapse of the regime and the rapid emergence of a new, democratic system, with the coming to power of a new government through national elections and the establishment of a democratic institutional structure, often through the promulgation of a new constitution. After the transition comes *consolidation,* a slow but purposeful process in which democratic forms are transformed into democratic substance through the reform of state institutions, the regularization of elections, the strengthening of civil society, and the overall habituation of the society to the new democratic "rules of the game."[5]

Democracy activists admit that it is not inevitable that transitional countries will move steadily on this assumed path from opening and breakthrough to consolidation. Transitional countries, they say, can and do go backward or stagnate as well as move forward along the path. Yet even the deviations from the assumed sequence that they are willing to acknowledge are defined in terms of the path itself. The options are all cast in terms of the speed and direction with which countries move on the path, not in terms of movement that does not conform with the path at all. And at least in the peak years of the third wave, many democracy enthusiasts clearly believed that, while the success of the dozens of new transitions was not assured, democratization was in some important sense a natural process, one that was likely to flourish once the initial breakthrough occurred. No small amount of democratic teleology is implicit in the transition paradigm, no matter how much its adherents have denied it.[6]

Related to the idea of a core sequence of democratization is the third assumption—the belief in the determinative importance of elections. Democracy promoters have not been guilty—as critics often charge—of believing that elections equal democracy. For years they have advocated and pursued a much broader range of assistance programs than just elections-focused efforts. Nevertheless, they have tended to hold very high expectations for what the establishment of regular, genuine elections will do for democratization. Not only will elections give new postdictatorial governments democratic legitimacy, they believe, but the elections will serve to broaden and deepen political participation and the democratic accountability of the state to its citizens. In other words, it has been assumed that in attempted transitions to democracy, elections will be not just a foundation stone but a key generator over time of further democratic reforms.

A fourth assumption is that the underlying conditions in transitional countries—their economic level, political history, institutional legacies, ethnic make-up, sociocultural traditions, or other "structural" features—will not be major factors in either the onset or the outcome of the transition process. A remarkable characteristic of the early period of the third wave was that democracy seemed to be breaking out in the most unlikely and unexpected places, whether Mongolia, Albania, or Mauritania. All that seemed to be necessary for democratization was a decision by a country's political elites to move toward democracy and an ability on the part of those elites to fend off the contrary actions of remaining antidemocratic forces.

The dynamism and remarkable scope of the third wave buried old, deterministic, and often culturally noxious assumptions about democracy, such as that only countries with an American-style middle class or a heritage of Protestant individualism could become democratic. For policy makers and aid practitioners this new outlook was a break from the long-standing Cold War mindset that most countries in the developing world were "not ready for democracy," a mindset that dovetailed with U.S. policies of propping up anticommunist dictators around the world. Some of the early works in transitology also reflected the "no preconditions" view of democratization, a shift within the academic literature that had begun in 1970 with Dankwart Rustow's seminal article, "Transitions to Democracy: Toward a Dynamic Model."[7] For both the scholarly and policy communities, the new "no preconditions" outlook was a gratifyingly optimistic, even liberating view that translated easily across borders as the encouraging message that, when it comes to democracy, "anyone can do it."

Fifth, the transition paradigm rests on the assumption that the democratic transitions making up the third wave are being built on coherent, functioning states. The process of democratization is assumed to include some redesign of state institutions—such as the creation of new electoral institutions, parliamentary reform, and judicial reform—but as a modification of already functioning states.[8] As they arrived at their frameworks for understanding democratization, democracy aid practitioners did not give significant attention to the challenge of a society trying to democratize while it is grappling with the reality of building a state from scratch or coping with an existent but largely nonfunctional state. This did not appear to be an issue in Southern Europe or Latin America, the two regions that served as the experiential basis for the formation of the transition paradigm. To the extent that democracy promoters did consider the possibility of state building as part of the transition process, they assumed that democracy building and state building would be mutually reinforcing endeavors or even two sides of the same coin.

## Into the Gray Zone

We turn then from the underlying assumptions of the paradigm to the record of experience. Efforts to assess the progress of the third wave are sometimes rejected as premature. Democracy is not built in a day, democracy activists assert, and it is too early to reach judgments about the results of the dozens of democratic transitions launched in the last two decades. Although it is certainly true that the current political situations of the transitional countries are not set in stone, enough time has elapsed to shed significant light on how the transition paradigm is holding up.

Of the nearly 100 countries considered as transitional in recent years, only a relatively small number—probably fewer than twenty—are clearly en route to becoming successful, well-functioning democracies or at least have made some democratic progress and still enjoy a positive dynamic of democratization.[9] The leaders of the group are found primarily in Central Europe and the Baltic region—Poland, Hungary, the Czech Republic, Estonia, and Slovenia—although there are a few in South America and East Asia, notably Chile, Taiwan, and Uruguay. Those that have made somewhat less progress but appear to be still advancing include Brazil, Bulgaria, Mexico, Ghana, the Philippines, Romania, Slovakia, and South Korea.

By far the majority of third-wave countries have not achieved relatively well-functioning democracy or do not seem to be deepening or advancing whatever democratic progress they have made. In a small number of countries, initial political openings have clearly failed and authoritarian regimes have resolidified, as in Uzbekistan, Turkmenistan, Belarus, and Togo. Most of the transitional countries, however, are neither dictatorial nor clearly headed toward democracy. They have entered a political gray zone.[10] They have some attributes of democratic political life, including at least limited political space for opposition parties and independent civil society, as well as regular elections and democratic constitutions. Yet they suffer from serious democratic deficits, often including poor representation of citizens' interests, low levels of political participation beyond voting, frequent abuse of the law by government officials, elections of uncertain legitimacy, very low levels of public confidence in state institutions, and persistently poor institutional performance by the state.

As the number of countries falling in between outright dictatorship and well-established liberal democracy has swollen, political analysts have proffered an array of "qualified democracy" terms to characterize them, including semidemocracy, formal democracy, electoral democracy, façade democracy, pseudodemocracy, weak democracy, partial democracy, illiberal democracy, and virtual democracy.[11] Some of these terms, such as "façade democracy" and "pseudodemocracy," apply only to a fairly specific subset of gray-zone cases. Other terms, such as "weak democracy" and "partial democracy," are intended to have much broader applicability. Useful though these terms can be, especially when rooted in probing analysis such as O'Donnell's work on "delegative democracy," they share a significant liability: By describing countries in the gray zone as types of democracies, analysts are in effect trying to apply the transition paradigm to the very countries whose political evolution is calling that paradigm into question.[12] Most of the qualified democracy terms are used to characterize countries as being stuck somewhere on the assumed democratization sequence, usually at the start of the consolidation phase.

The diversity of political patterns within the gray zone is vast. Many possible subtypes or subcategories could potentially be posited, and much work remains to be done to assess the nature of gray-zone politics. As a first analytic step, two broad political syndromes can be seen to be common in the gray zone. They are not rigidly delineated political-system types but rather political patterns that have become regular and somewhat entrenched. Although they have some characteristics in common, they differ in crucial ways and basically are mutually exclusive.

The first syndrome is feckless pluralism. Countries whose political life is marked by feckless pluralism tend to have significant amounts of political freedom, regular elections, and alternation of power between genuinely different political groupings. Despite these positive features, however, democracy remains shallow and troubled. Political participation, though broad at election time, extends little beyond voting. Political elites from all the major parties or groupings are widely perceived as corrupt, self-interested, and ineffective. The alternation of power seems only to trade the country's problems back and forth from one hapless side to the other. Political elites from all the major parties are widely perceived as corrupt, self-interested, dishonest, and not serious about working for their country. The public is seriously disaffected from politics, and while it may still cling to a belief in the ideal of democracy, it is extremely unhappy about the political life of the country. Overall, politics is widely seen as a stale, corrupt, elite-dominated domain that delivers little good to the country and commands equally little respect. And the state remains persistently weak. Economic policy is often poorly conceived and executed, and economic performance is frequently bad or even calamitous. Social and political reforms are similarly tenuous, and successive governments are unable to make headway on most of the major problems facing the country, from crime and corruption to health, education, and public welfare generally.

Feckless pluralism is most common in Latin America, a region where most countries entered their attempted democratic transitions with diverse political parties already in place yet also with a deep legacy of persistently poor performance of state institutions. Bolivia, Ecuador, Guatemala, Honduras, Nicaragua, and Panama all fall into this category, as did Venezuela in the decade prior to the election of Hugo Chávez. Argentina and Brazil hover uneasily at its edge. In the postcommunist world, Albania, Bosnia, Moldova, and Ukraine have at least some significant signs of the syndrome, with Bulgaria and Romania teetering on its edge. Nepal is a clear example in Asia; Bangladesh, Mongolia, and Thailand may also qualify. In sub-Saharan Africa, a few states, such as Guinea-Bissau, Madagascar, and Sierra Leone, may be cases of feckless pluralism, though alternation of power remains rare generally in that region.

There are many variations of feckless pluralism. In some cases, the parties that alternate power between them are divided by paralyzing acrimony and devote their time out of power to preventing the other party from accomplishing anything at all, as in Bangladesh. In other cases, the main competing groups end up colluding, formally or informally, rendering the alternation of power unhelpful in a different manner, as happened in Nicaragua in the late 1990s. In some countries afflicted with feckless pluralism, the political competition is between deeply entrenched parties that essentially operate as patronage networks and seem never to renovate themselves, as in Argentina or Nepal. In others, the alternation of power occurs between constantly shifting political groupings, short-lived parties led by charismatic individuals or temporary alliances in search of a political identity, as in Guatemala or Ukraine. These varied cases nonetheless share a common condition that seems at the root of feckless pluralism—the whole class of political elites, though plural and competitive, are profoundly cut off from the citizenry, rendering political life an ultimately hollow, unproductive exercise.

### Dominant-Power Politics

The most common other political syndrome in the gray zone is dominant-power politics. Countries with this syndrome have limited but still real political space, some political contestation by opposition groups, and at least most of the basic institutional forms of democracy. Yet one political grouping—whether it is a movement, a party, an extended family, or a single leader—dominates the system in such a way that there appears to be little prospect of alternation of power in the foreseeable future.

Unlike in countries beset with feckless pluralism, a key political problem in dominant-power countries is the blurring of the line between the state and the ruling party (or ruling political forces). The state's main assets—that is to say, the state as a source of money, jobs, public information (via state media), and police power—are gradually put in the direct service of the ruling party. Whereas in feckless pluralism judiciaries are often somewhat independent, the judiciary in dominant-power countries is typically cowed, as part of the one-sided grip on power. And while elections in feckless-pluralist countries are often quite free and fair, the typical pattern in dominant-power countries is one of dubious but not outright fraudulent elections in which the ruling group tries to put on a good-enough electoral show to gain the approval of the international community while quietly tilting the electoral playing field far enough in its own favor to ensure victory.

As in feckless-pluralist systems, the citizens of dominant-power systems tend to be disaffected from politics and cut off from significant political participation beyond voting. Since there is no alternation of power, however, they are less apt to evince the "a pox on all your houses" political outlook pervasive in feckless-pluralist systems. Yet those opposition political parties that do exist generally are hard put to gain much public credibility due to their perennial status as outsiders to the main halls of power. Whatever energies and hopes for effective opposition to the regime remain often reside in civil society groups, usually a loose collection of advocacy nongovernmental organizations and independent media (often funded by Western donors) that skirmish with the government on human rights, the environment, corruption, and other issues of public interest.

The state tends to be as weak and poorly performing in dominant-power countries as in feckless-pluralist countries, although the problem is often a bureaucracy decaying under the stagnancy of de facto one party rule rather than the disorganized, unstable nature of state management (such as the constant turnover of ministers) typical of feckless pluralism. The long hold on power by one political group usually produces large-scale corruption and crony capitalism. Due to the existence of some political openness in these systems, the leaders do often feel some pressure from the public about corruption and other abuses of state power. They even may periodically declare their intention to root out corruption and strengthen the rule of law. But their deep-seated intolerance for anything more than limited opposition and the basic political configuration over which they preside breed the very problems they publicly commit themselves to tackling.

Dominant-power systems are prevalent in three regions. In sub-Saharan Africa, the widely hailed wave of democratization that washed over the region in the early 1990s has ended up producing many dominant-power systems. In some cases, one-party states liberalized yet ended up permitting only very limited processes of political opening, as in Burkina Faso, Cameroon, Equatorial Guinea, Gabon, Kenya, Mauritania, and Tanzania. In a few cases, old regimes were defeated or collapsed, yet the new regimes have ended up in dominant-party structures, as in Zambia in the 1990s, or the forces previously shunted aside have reclaimed power, as in Congo (Brazzaville).

Dominant-power systems are found in the former Soviet Union as well. Armenia, Azerbaijan, Georgia, Kazakhstan, and Kyrgyzstan fall in this category. The other Central Asian republics and Belarus are better understood as out-and-out authoritarian systems. The liberalization trend that arose in the Middle East in the mid-1980s and has unfolded in fits and starts ever since has moved some countries out of the authoritarian camp into the dominant-power category. These include Algeria, Egypt, Iran, Jordan, Morocco, and Yemen. Dominant-power systems are scarce outside of these three regions. In Asia, Cambodia and Malaysia count as examples. In Latin America, Paraguay may be one case, and Venezuela is likely headed toward becoming a second.

Dominant-power systems vary in their degree of freedom and their political direction. Some have very limited political space and are close to being dictatorships. Others allow much more freedom, albeit still with limits. A few "transitional countries," including the important cases of South Africa and Russia, fall just to the side of this syndrome. They have a fair amount of political freedom and have held competitive elections of some legitimacy (though sharp debate on that issue exists with regard to Russia). Yet they are ruled by political forces that appear to have a long-term hold on power (if one considers the shift from Yeltsin to Putin more as a political transfer than an alternation of power), and it is hard to imagine any of the existing opposition parties coming to power for many years to come. If they maintain real political freedom and open competition for power, they may join the ranks of cases, such as Italy and Japan (prior to the 1990s) and Botswana, of longtime democratic rule by one party. Yet due to the tenuousness of their new democratic institutions, they face the danger of slippage toward the dominant-power syndrome.

As political syndromes, both feckless pluralism and dominant-power politics have some stability. Once in them, countries do not move out of them easily. Feckless pluralism achieves its own dysfunctional equilibrium—the passing of power back and forth between competing elites who are largely isolated from the citizenry but willing to play by widely accepted rules. Dominant-power politics also often achieves a kind of stasis, with the ruling group able to keep political opposition on the ropes while permitting enough political openness to alleviate pressure from the public. They are by no means permanent political configurations; no political configuration lasts forever. Countries can and do move out of them—either from one to the other or out of either toward liberal democracy or dictatorship. For a time in the 1990s, Ukraine seemed stuck in dominant-power politics but may be shifting to something more like feckless pluralism. Senegal was previously a clear case of dominant-power politics but, with the opposition victory in the 2000 elections, may be moving toward either liberal democracy or feckless pluralism.

Although many countries in the gray zone have ended up as examples of either feckless pluralism or dominant-power politics, not all have. A small number of "transitional countries" have moved away from authoritarian rule only in the last several years, and their political trajectory is as yet unclear. Croatia, Indonesia, Nigeria, and Serbia are four prominent examples of this type. Some countries that experienced political openings in the 1980s or 1990s have been so wracked by civil conflict that their political systems are too unstable or incoherent to pin down easily, although they are definitely not on a path of democratization. The Democratic Republic of Congo, Liberia, Sierra Leone, and Somalia all represent this situation.

### The Crash of Assumptions

Taken together, the political trajectories of most third-wave countries call into serious doubt the transition paradigm. This is apparent if we revisit the major assumptions underlying the paradigm in light of the above analysis.

First, the almost automatic assumption of democracy promoters during the peak years of the third wave that any country moving away from dictatorship was "in transition to democracy" has often been inaccurate and misleading. Some of those countries have hardly democratized at all. Many have taken on a smattering of democratic features but show few signs of democratizing much further and are certainly not following any predictable democratization script. The most common political patterns to date among the transitional countries—feckless pluralism and dominant-power politics—include elements of democracy but should be understood as alternative directions, not way stations to liberal democracy. The persistence in official U.S. democracy-promotion circles of using transitional language to characterize countries that in no way conform to any democratization paradigm borders in some cases on the surreal—including not just the case of Congo cited above but many others, such as Moldova

("Moldova's democratic transition continues to progress steadily"), Zambia ("Zambia is . . . moving steadily toward . . . the creation of a viable multiparty democracy"), Cambodia ("policy successes in Cambodia towards democracy and improved governance within the past 18 months are numerous"), and Guinea ("Guinea has made significant strides toward building a democratic society").[13] The continued use of the transition paradigm constitutes a dangerous habit of trying to impose a simplistic and often incorrect conceptual order on an empirical tableau of considerable complexity.

Second, not only is the general label and concept of "transitional country" unhelpful, but the assumed sequence of stages of democratization is defied by the record of experience. Some of the most encouraging cases of democratization in recent years—such as Mexico, South Korea, and Taiwan—did not go through the paradigmatic process of democratic breakthrough followed rapidly by national elections and a new democratic institutional framework. Their political evolutions were defined by an almost opposite phenomenon—extremely gradual, incremental processes of liberalization with an organized political opposition (not soft-liners in the regime) pushing for change across successive elections and finally winning. And in many of the countries that did go through some version of what appeared to be a democratic breakthrough, the assumed sequence of changes—first settling constitutive issues then working through second-order reforms—has not held. Constitutive issues have reemerged at unpredictable times, upending what are supposed to be later stages of transition, as in the recent political crises in the Central African Republic, Chad, and Ecuador.

Moreover, the various assumed component processes of consolidation—political party development, civil society strengthening, judicial reform, and media development—almost never conform to the technocratic ideal of rational sequences on which the indicator frameworks and strategic objectives of democracy promoters are built. Instead they are chaotic processes of change that go backwards and sideways as much as forward, and do not do so in any regular manner.

The third assumption of the transition paradigm—the notion that achieving regular, genuine elections will not only confer democratic legitimacy on new governments but continuously deepen political participation and democratic accountability—has often come up short. In many transitional countries, reasonably regular, genuine elections are held, but political participation beyond voting remains shallow and governmental accountability is weak. The wide gulf between political elites and citizens in many of these countries turns out to be rooted in structural conditions, such as the concentration of wealth or certain sociocultural traditions, that elections themselves do not overcome. It is also striking how often electoral competition does little to stimulate the renovation or development of political parties in many gray-zone countries. Such profound pathologies as highly personalistic parties, transient and shifting parties, or stagnant patronage-based politics appear to be able to coexist for sustained periods with at least somewhat legitimate processes of political pluralism and competition.

These disappointments certainly do not mean that elections are pointless in such countries or that the international community should not continue to push for free and fair elections. But greatly reduced expectations are in order as to what elections will accomplish as generators of deep-reaching democratic change. Nepal is a telling example in this regard. Since 1990, Nepal has held many multiparty elections and experienced frequent alternation of power. Yet the Nepalese public remains highly disaffected from the political system, and there is little real sense of democratic accountability.

Fourth, ever since "preconditions for democracy" were enthusiastically banished in the heady early days of the third wave, a contrary reality—the fact that various structural conditions clearly weigh heavily in shaping political outcomes—has been working its way back in. Looking at the more successful recent cases of democratization, for example, which tend to be found in Central Europe, the Southern Cone, or East Asia, it is clear that relative economic wealth, as well as past experience with political pluralism, contributes to the chances for democratic success. And looking comparatively within regions, whether in the former communist world or sub-Saharan Africa, it is evident that the specific institutional legacies from predecessor regimes strongly affect the outcomes of attempted transitions.

During the 1990s, a number of scholars began challenging the "no preconditions" line, with analyses of the roles that economic wealth, institutional legacies, social class, and other structural factors play in attempted democratic transitions.[14] Yet it has been hard for the democracy-promotion community to take this work on board. Democracy promoters are strongly wedded to their focus on political processes and institutions. They have been concerned that trying to blend that focus with economic or sociocultural perspectives might lead to the dilution or reduction of democracy assistance. And having set up as organizations with an exclusively political perspective, it is hard for democracy-promotion groups to include other kinds of expertise or approaches.

Fifth, state building has been a much larger and more problematic issue than originally envisaged in the transition paradigm. Contrary to the early assumptions of democracy aid practitioners, many third-wave countries have faced fundamental state-building challenges. Approximately twenty countries in the former Soviet Union and former Yugoslavia have had to build national state institutions where none existed before. Throughout much of sub-Saharan Africa, the liberalizing political wave of the 1990s ran squarely into the sobering reality of devastatingly weak states. In many parts of Latin America, the Middle East, and Asia, political change was carried out in the context of stable state structures, but the erratic performance of those states complicated every step.

Where state building from scratch had to be carried out, the core impulses and interests of powerholders—such as locking in access to power and resources as quickly as possible—ran directly contrary to what democracy building would have required. In countries with existing but extremely weak states, the democracy-building efforts funded by donors usually neglected the issue of state building. With their frequent emphasis on diffusing power and weakening the relative power of the executive branch—by strengthening the legislative and judicial branches of government, encouraging decentralization, and building civil society—they were more about the redistribution of state power than about state building. The programs that democracy promoters have directed at governance have tended to be minor technocratic efforts, such as training ministerial staff or aiding cabinet offices, rather than major efforts at bolstering state capacity.

## Letting Go

It is time for the democracy-promotion community to discard the transition paradigm. Analyzing the record of experience in the many countries that democracy activists have been labeling transitional countries, it is evident that it is no longer appropriate to assume:

- that most of these countries are actually in a transition to democracy;
- that countries moving away from authoritarianism tend to follow a three-part process of democratization consisting of opening, breakthrough, and consolidation;
- that the establishment of regular, genuine elections will not only give new governments democratic legitimacy but foster a longer term deepening of democratic participation and accountability;
- that a country's chances for successfully democratizing depend primarily on the political intentions and actions of its political elites without significant influence from underlying economic, social, and institutional conditions and legacies;
- that state building is a secondary challenge to democracy building and largely compatible with it.

It is hard to let go of the transitional paradigm, both for the conceptual order and for the hopeful vision it provides. Giving it up constitutes a major break, but not a total one. It does not mean denying that important democratic reforms have occurred in many countries in the past two decades. It does not mean that countries in the gray zone are doomed never to achieve well-functioning liberal democracy. It does not mean that free and fair elections in transitional countries are futile or not worth supporting. It does not mean that the United States and other international actors should abandon efforts to promote democracy in the world (if anything, it implies that, given how difficult democratization is, efforts to promote it should be redoubled).

It does mean, however, that democracy promoters should approach their work with some very different assumptions. They should start by assuming that what is often thought of as an uneasy, precarious middle ground between full-fledged democracy and outright dictatorship is actually the most common political condition today of countries in the developing world and the postcommunist world. It is not an exceptional category to be defined only in terms of its not being one thing or the other; it is a state of normality for many societies, for better or worse. The seemingly continual surprise and disappointment that Western political analysts express over the very frequent falling short of democracy in transitional countries should be replaced with realistic expectations about the likely patterns of political life in these countries.

Aid practitioners and policy makers looking at politics in a country that has recently moved away from authoritarianism should not start by asking: "How is its democratic transition going?" They should instead formulate a more open-ended query, "What is happening politically?" Insisting on the former approach leads to optimistic assumptions that often shunt the analysis down a blind alley. To take one example, during the 1990s, Western policy makers habitually analyzed Georgia's post-1991 political evolution as a democratic transition, highlighting the many formal achievements and holding up a basically positive image of the country. Then suddenly, at the end of the decade, the essential hollowness of Georgia's democratic transition became too apparent to ignore, and Georgia is now suddenly talked about as a country in serious risk of state failure or deep sociopolitical crisis.[15]

A whole generation of democracy aid is based on the transition paradigm, above all the typical emphasis on an institutional "checklist" as a basis for creating programs, and the creation of nearly standard portfolios of aid projects consisting of the same diffuse set of efforts all over—some judicial reform, parliamentary strengthening, civil society assistance, media work, political party development, civic education, and electoral programs. Much of the democracy aid based on this paradigm is exhausted. Where the paradigm fits well—in the small number of clearly successful transitions—the aid is not much needed.

Where democracy aid is needed most, in many of the gray-zone countries, the paradigm fits poorly.

Democracy promoters need to focus on the key political patterns of each country in which they intervene, rather than trying to do a little of everything according to a template of ideal institutional forms. Where feckless pluralism reigns, this means giving concentrated attention to two interrelated issues: how to improve the variety and quality of the main political actors in the society and how to begin to bridge the gulf between the citizenry and the formal political system. Much greater attention to political party development should be a major part of the response, with special attention to encouraging new entrants into the political party scene, changing the rules and incentive systems that shape the current party structures, and fostering strong connections between parties and civil society groups (rather than encouraging civil society groups to stay away from partisan politics).

In dominant-power systems, democracy promoters should devote significant attention to the challenge of helping encourage the growth of alternative centers of power. Merely helping finance the proliferation of nongovernmental organizations is an inadequate approach to this challenge. Again, political party development must be a top agenda item, especially through measures aimed at changing the way political parties are financed. It should include efforts to examine how the overconcentration of economic power (a standard feature of dominant-power systems) can be reduced as well as measures that call attention to and work against the blurring of the line between the ruling party and the state.

In other types of gray-zone countries, democracy promoters will need to settle on other approaches. The message for all gray-zone countries, however, is the same—falling back on a smorgasbord of democracy programs based on the vague assumption that they all contribute to some assumed process of consolidation is not good enough. Democracy aid must proceed from a penetrating analysis of the particular core syndrome that defines the political life of the country in question, and how aid interventions can change that syndrome.

Moving beyond the transition paradigm also means getting serious about bridging the long-standing divide between aid programs directed at democracy building and those focused on social and economic development. USAID has initiated some work on this topic but has only scratched the surface of what could become a major synthesis of disparate domains in the aid world. One example of a topic that merits the combined attention of economic aid providers and democracy promoters is privatization programs. These programs have major implications for how power is distributed in a society, how ruling political forces can entrench themselves, and how the public participates in major policy decisions. Democracy promoters need to take a serious interest in these reform efforts and learn to make a credible case to economists that they should have a place at the table when such programs are being planned. The same is true for any number of areas of socioeconomic reform that tend to be a major focus of economic aid providers and that have potentially significant effects on the underlying sociopolitical domain, including pension reform, labor law reform, antitrust policy, banking reform, and tax reform. The onus is on democracy aid providers to develop a broader conception of democracy work and to show that they have something to contribute on the main stage of the development assistance world.

These are only provisional ideas. Many other "next generation" challenges remain to be identified. The core point, however, is plain: The transition paradigm was a product of a certain time—the heady early days of the third wave—and that time has now passed. It is necessary for democracy activists to move on to new frameworks, new debates, and perhaps eventually a new paradigm of political change—one suited to the landscape of today, not the lingering hopes of an earlier era.

## Notes

The author would like to thank Jeffrey Krutz for his research assistance relating to this article and Daniel Brumberg, Charles King, Michael McFaul, Marina Ottaway, Chris Sabatini, and Michael Shifter for their comments on the first draft.

The Carnegie Endowment gratefully acknowledges the permission of the Johns Hopkins University Press to reprint this article, which originally appeared in the *Journal of Democracy*, vol. 13, no. 1 (January 2002).

1. Samuel P. Huntington, *The Third Wave: Democratization in the Late Twentieth Century* (Norman: University of Oklahoma Press, 1991).
2. Guillermo O'Donnell and Philippe C. Schmitter, *Transitions from Authoritarian Rule: Tentative Conclusions About Uncertain Democracies* (Baltimore: Johns Hopkins University Press, 1986).
3. Ruth Collier argues that a similar transition paradigm has prevailed in the scholarly writing on democratization. "The 'transitions literature,' as this current work has come to be known, has as its best representative the founding essay by O'Donnell and Schmitter (1986), which established a framework that is implicitly or explicitly followed in most other contributions." Ruth Berins Collier, *Paths Toward Democracy: The Working Class and Elites in Western Europe and South America* (Cambridge: Cambridge University Press, 1999), p. 5.
4. "Building Democracy in the Democratic Republic of Congo," www.usaid.gov/democracy/afr/congo.html. Here and elsewhere in this article, I cite USAID documents because they are the most readily available practitioners' statements of guidelines and political assessments, but I believe that my analysis applies equally well to most other democracy-promotion organizations in the United States and abroad.

5. The conception of democratization as a predictable, sequential process of incremental steps is vividly exemplified in USAID's "managing for results" assessment system. See *Handbook of Democracy and Governance Program Indicators* (Washington, D.C.: USAID, August 1998).

6. Guillermo O'Donnell argues that the concept of democratic consolidation has teleological qualities, in "Illusions about Consolidation," *Journal of Democracy* 7 (April 1996): 34–51. A response to O'Donnell's charge is found in Richard Gunther, P. Nikiforos Diamandouros, and Hans-Jürgen Puhle, "O'Donnell's 'Illusions': A Rejoinder," *Journal of Democracy* 7 (October 1996): 151–59.

7. See, for example, Giuseppe Di Palma, *To Craft Democracies: An Essay on Democratic Transitions* (Berkeley: University of California Press, 1991). Dankwart Rustow's article "Transitions to Democracy: Toward a Comparative Model," originally appeared in *Comparative Politics* 2 (April 1970): 337–63.

8. USAID's current listing of the types of governance programs in its democracy-assistance portfolio, for example, contains no examples of work on fundamental state building. See "Agency Objectives: Governance," www.usaid.gov/democracy/gov.html.

9. An insightful account of the state of the third wave is found in Larry Diamond, "Is the Third Wave Over?" *Journal of Democracy* 7 (July 1996): 20–37.

10. Larry Diamond uses the term *twilight zone* to refer to a sizeable but smaller set of countries—electoral democracies that are in a zone of "persistence without legitimation or institutionalization," in *Developing Democracy: Toward Consolidation* (Baltimore: Johns Hopkins University Press, 1999), p. 22.

11. David Collier and Steven Levitsky, "Democracy with Adjectives: Conceptual Innovation in Comparative Research," *World Politics* 49 (April 1997): 430–51.

12. Guillermo O'Donnell, "Delegative Democracy," *Journal of Democracy* 5 (January 1994): 55–69.

13. These quotes are all taken from the country descriptions in the democracy-building section of the USAID web site, www.usaid.gov/democracy.html.

14. See, for example, Michael Bratton and Nicolas van de Walle, *Democratic Experiments in Africa: Regime Transitions in Comparative Perspective* (Cambridge: Cambridge University Press, 1997); Valerie Bunce, *Subversive Institutions: The Design and Destruction of Socialism and the State* (Cambridge: Cambridge University Press, 1999); Ruth Collier, *Paths Toward Democracy*; Dietrich Rueschmeyer, Evelyne Huber Stephens, and John D. Stephens, *Capitalist Development and Democracy* (Chicago: Chicago University Press, 1992); Adam Przeworski, *Democracy and the Market: Political and Economic Reforms in Latin America and Eastern Europe* (Cambridge: Cambridge University Press, 1991); and Adam Przeworski and Fernando Limongi, "Political Regimes and Economic Growth," *Journal of Economic Perspectives* 7 (Summer 1993): 51–69.

15. See Charles King, "Potemkin Democracy," *The National Interest* 64 (Summer 2001): 93–104.

# CHAPTER FIFTEEN

# Debating the Transition Paradigm (2002)

## In Partial Defense of an Evanescent "Paradigm"

### BY GUILLERMO O'DONNELL

*Guillermo O'Donnell is the Helen Kellogg Professor of Government and International Studies at the University of Notre Dame. His most recent book is* Counterpoints: Selected Essays on Authoritarianism and Democratization *(University of Notre Dame Press, 1999).*

THOMAS CAROTHERS HAS WRITTEN a timely and important essay that deserves wide attention. His goal is the healthy one of sparking discussion among both scholars and those who are "practitioners" of democracy—government officials, civil society activists, or professionals who work in the field of democracy promotion. Since I am a scholar, I will focus on what Carothers has to say concerning academic writings about transitions and democratization.

To begin with, I am in an odd situation. I am flattered that Carothers mentions me as coauthor of the "seminal work" on transitions.[1] Since he follows this reference with a series of criticisms aimed at what he calls the "transition paradigm," readers might assume that I will dispute most of what he says. In fact, I agree with many of his arguments. The reason for this apparent paradox is that Carothers lumps together, under the heading of the "transition paradigm," a large and uneven body of work, and then proceeds to concentrate his criticisms on some of the weakest parts of it. So I will try to set the record straight, both for the sake of fairness and because I believe that our discussions, to be fruitful, should be based on an accurate notion of what the scholarly literature actually says.

Carothers discusses three major and distinct issues: (1) The transition from authoritarian rule; (2) the aftermath of this transition; and (3) what some institutions (most of them belonging to or funded by Western governments) have been doing under the heading of "democracy promotion." Carothers argues that thinking on these three topics has been led astray by a faulty "analytic model of democratic transition" that derives in good measure from the "seminal" four-volume work already cited, especially the final volume, which I co-authored with Philippe Schmitter. Thus, given my putative co-parenthood of Carothers's transition paradigm, I feel compelled to recapitulate what Schmitter and I, and myself in further writings, said about transitions and democratization, while claiming innocence regarding some of the (presumed) descendants of our creature. Furthermore, as will be seen below, I agree with Carothers that, if the transition paradigm has taken the form that he describes, it is indeed mistaken and should be abandoned.

So let us examine the five "core assumptions" that according to Carothers constitute the "paradigm." The first, which he calls "an umbrella"[2] covering all the others, is that "any country moving away from dictatorial rule can be considered a country in transition toward democracy." I hasten to comment that our "seminal work" on transitions was not entitled *Transitions to Democracy*. Instead we called it *Transitions from Authoritarian Rule*, which is not the same thing at all. This was the result of a deliberate choice made by the three coeditors of the four volumes published under this title. It was also a corollary of the analysis that Schmitter and I offered in the fourth volume. Here we were explicit that these transitions do not necessarily lead to democracy; rather, they may as well lead to authoritarian regressions, to revolutions, or to hybrid regimes like those that occupy the "gray zone" which Carothers depicts. Indulging in a bit of wordplay, we said that two among the hybrid types that might appear were *democraduras* and *dictablandas*—essentially Carothers's "feckless-pluralist" and "dominant power" systems, respectively. If our work really was seminal, then one should take seriously our assertion that there was nothing predestined about these transitions, and our insistence that their course and outcome were open-ended and uncertain. We even stressed this view in the subtitle of this volume, which was *Tentative Conclusions about Uncertain Democracies*.

So we can hardly be found guilty of assuming that, as Carothers puts it, "democratization tends to unfold in a set sequence of stages."[3] This is Carothers's "second assumption," according to which the "paradigm" asserts that there is, or should be, first an "opening," then a "breakthrough," and then "consolidation"—a view that, as noted, we never shared. Carothers goes on to criticize the view that countries are moving, or should move, along a path in which "even the deviations from the assumed sequence . . . are defined in terms of the path itself. The options are all cast in terms of the speed and direction with which countries move on the path, not in terms of movement that does not conform with the path at all." I strongly agree with this criticism—and why not, for it closely echoes the warning against "illusions about consolidation" that I published in the *Journal of Democracy* in 1996![4]

Two years before that, moreover, I wrote in the *Journal of Democracy* that, even when an opening and breakthrough produce a democratic regime, its features, workings, and social impacts may be quite different from those of formally institutionalized democracies, and that such "delegative" regimes should not be seen as "en route" to "democratic consolidation."[5] So when Carothers complains about "democracy enthusiasts" who hold the naive view that democratization is inevitable, I cannot help but agree with him, even as I wonder just who these enthusiasts are. Instead of referring to "the" paradigm, it would have been useful if Carothers had specified which paradigm he means—if such a thing ever existed—and who has proposed or adopted it.

Still in relation to the "set sequence of stages," Carothers later mentions countries which, contrary to what the "paradigm" asserts, "did not go through the paradigmatic process of democratic breakthrough followed rapidly by national elections and a new democratic institutional framework." Even though the overuse of the (undefined) idea of paradigm raises doubts about how to interpret this sentence, in *Transitions from Authoritarian Rule* Schmitter and I dwelt at length on the differences between what we called transitions by collapse (which seem to be the ones to which Carothers refers) and pacted, usually protracted transitions. Furthermore, in the third volume of this work Alfred Stepan wrote a chapter in which he looked in detail at the various transitional paths that countries may take.[6] Since then, this very question has received attention in a large body of academic literature which takes as its starting point the recognition that, *contra* Carothers, there is no "paradigmatic" process of transition.

### The Role of Elections

I turn next to the third "assumption," which has to do with elections. Carothers invites us to reject the idea that "regular, genuine elections will not only give new governments democratic legitimacy but foster a longer term deepening of democratic participation and accountability." With apologies for the repetition, let me point once again to early concepts such as *democradura* and delegative democracy, for they show that at least part of the academic literature did not attribute such magical powers to elections. In addition, interested readers of the present exchange should consult the April 2002 issue of the *Journal of Democracy* for scholarly essays on hybrid regimes, competitive authoritarianism, electoral authoritarianism, delegative democracy, and other "gray-zone" cases. The authors of these essays do anything but wax naive about what they see in a host of countries where elections are held, but where democracy itself remains tenuous or simply nonexistent.

Here I want to emphasize a point on which I side with the putative "transition paradigm" and against Carothers's criticisms. I do think that fair elections are extremely important. This is not because such elections will necessarily lead to wonderful outcomes. It is because these elections, per se and due to the political freedoms that must surround them if they are to be considered fair (and, consequently, if the resulting regime is to be democratic),[7] mark a crucial departure from the arbitrariness of authoritarian rule. When some fundamental political freedoms are respected, this means great progress in relation to authoritarian rules and gives us ample reason to defend and promote fair elections.

The existence of fair elections also helps us to draw a relatively clear line between what Carothers calls cases of "feckless pluralism" and what he calls cases of "dominant-power" politics. The former, as Carothers rightly notes, are afflicted by bad governance and often by widespread popular alienation. Yet insofar as they hold fair elections we can classify these cases (by definition, including Carothers's) as democratic regimes. These may or may not be democratic states or countries that are under an appropriate rule of law; they are democratic regimes—no less and no more than that.

By contrast, Carothers's "dominant-power systems" are not democracies. These are authoritarian regimes that may have an electoral base, but where elections are not fair and there are severe restrictions on political freedoms. We see that the presence or absence of fair elections is important not only analytically to scholars but also practically to democracy promoters. Because of this I agree with Carothers that we should know more about the characteristics and likely patterns of change in the kinds of regimes he sketches. I also agree that this task will become easier if mistakes such as assuming that there is one single path or sequence of change are cleared away—particularly if, as Carothers believes is the case, such mistakes are widespread. However, this necessary task is not likely to be helped either by attributing magical properties to all kinds of elections or by denying the importance of fair ones.

## "Thoughtful Wishing" and Scholarship

The fourth assumption that Carothers attributes to the transition paradigm is one he puts this way: "underlying conditions in transitional countries. . .will not be major factors in either the onset or the outcome of the transition process."

There is a bit of history to recount here. When my colleagues and I began our work on transitions in the late 1970s and early 1980s, it was not in response to democratization in Latin America. It was in anticipation of these processes, before any had occurred in this region (with the partial exception of Peru), and while the mid-1970s transitions in Southern Europe still looked very uncertain. A characteristic of the authors of the four *Transitions* volumes is that all of us, whether directly in our own countries or through international networks of solidarity, were committed to help the demise of the authoritarian regimes that plagued these regions—ours was academic work with an intense political and moral intent.

In what Schmitter and I co-wrote, as well as in many other chapters of the four volumes, we made a considered decision to stress political factors without paying much attention to what might broadly be called socioeconomic ones. We believed that this way of thinking might be useful for stimulating transitions away from authoritarian regimes. In those times, most of the literature told us that we had to wait a long time until our countries reached the level of economic growth, or of development of the productive forces, or of modernization, or of maturation of the political culture, that would enable us to aspire to democracy. We found this rather discouraging. Thus, unabashedly engaging in "thoughtful wishing,"[8] we assumed that purposive political action could be effective, and that good analysis might be helpful to this end. So, yes, this initial literature is "politicist" in the sense criticized by Carothers, but the subsequent transitions did not entirely disprove it.

However, with regard to socioeconomic factors, let me recommend an excellent piece of academic research: the massive study recently completed by Adam Przeworski and his associates under the title *Democracy and Development.*[9] One robust conclusion of this work bears on two important—and distinct—issues that Carothers mistakenly conflates. The first issue refers to the likelihood of authoritarian breakdown and the emergence of a democratic regime; the second issue pertains to the probability that such a regime will persist. As regards the former question, Przeworski and his collaborators show that there is simply no statistical correlation between a country's level of socioeconomic development and the likelihood that it will experience an authoritarian breakdown followed by the onset of democracy. Yet when it comes to the question of democracy's durability, socioeconomic factors are significant—the mortality rate of poor democracies is higher than that of rich ones.[10] This, greatly summarized, is the present state of knowledge about Carothers's fourth assumption. At the very least it shows that it is misleading to speak of socioeconomic factors as if they have the same impact on the "onset" and the "outcome" of transitions.

The fifth and final alleged assumption is one which Carothers formulates as the belief that third-wave transitions "are being built on coherent, functioning states." It is true that in the original literature on transitions we did not explicitly discuss the problems that might arise from a weak or ineffective state. This was due in part to our belief that, in principle, this kind of state was more propitious than a strong one for easing the breakdown of an authoritarian regime and the eventual emergence of a democratic one. But in the early 1990s, well before economists took up the theme, many political scientists and sociologists began to argue that a reasonably effective and viable state is a crucial condition for, among other things, democratization. As is true of the other topics mentioned above, there is a large literature on this one, which Carothers unfortunately does not acknowledge.[11]

Limited space bars me from discussing many works which support my claim that the academic literature, despite its unevenness, rests on grounds far more solid than the evanescent "transition paradigm" that Carothers sketches. This is why I am more in agreement with Carothers's strictures than might have been surmised, considering the important weight that he gives to my work, individual and in collaboration, in the shaping of his "paradigm." No stringent test is required to disprove the attributed paternity of this rather pathetic creature; cursorily to survey the literature suffices.

And yet I commend Carothers's larger purpose. I agree with him that we need serious discussions, both in academia and in policy circles (and, I would add, in various nonprofit organizations), about the now-as-ever crucial issues of democracy and democratization throughout the world. For challenging us to undertake this discussion, Thomas Carothers deserves our thanks.

## Notes

The Carnegie Endowment gratefully acknowledges the permission of the Johns Hopkins University Press to reprint this article, which originally appeared in the *Journal of Democracy*, vol. 13, no. 3 (July 2002).

1. Guillermo O'Donnell, Philippe Schmitter, and Laurence Whitehead, eds., *Transitions from Authoritarian Rule*, 4 vols. (Baltimore: Johns Hopkins University Press, 1986).

2. Italics added. In note 3 to his essay "The End of the Transition Paradigm" in the January 2003 issue of the *Journal of Democracy*, Carothers further argues, quoting Ruth Collier, that the fourth volume of our *Transitions from Authoritarian Rule*

"established a framework that is implicitly or explicitly followed in most other contributions."

3. For what it is worth, other and arguably "seminal" early co-written or coedited volumes on the question of transition are also free of the kinds of mistakes and simplifications that exercise Carothers. See, for example, Larry Diamond, Juan J. Linz, and Seymour Martin Lipset, *Democracy in Developing Countries*, 4 vols. (Boulder, CO: Lynne Rienner, 1988–1989).

4. Guillermo O'Donnell, "Illusions About Consolidation," *Journal of Democracy* 7 (April 1996): 34–51. In this context. Carothers adds that "No small amount of democratic teleology is implicit in the transition paradigm, no matter how much its adherents have denied it" (p. 7) and proceeds to cite the essay just mentioned. This remark is odd, because there I argue about the teleological implications of the "consolidation" concept, which I criticize no less sharply than does Thomas Carothers. My view on this matter does not require me to "deny" anything; it is plainly consistent with the open-ended and nonsequential view of transitions *from* authoritarian rule presented in *Transitions*.

5. Guillermo O'Donnell, "Delegative Democracy," *Journal of Democracy* 5 (January 1994): 55–69. On his part, Philippe Schmitter has referred to "persistently unconsolidated democracies." See his "Dangers and Dilemmas of Democracy," *Journal of Democracy* 5 (April 1994): 57–74.

6. Alfred Stepan, "Paths Toward Redemocratization: Theoretical and Comparative Considerations," in Guillermo O'Donnell et al., eds., *Transitions from Authoritarian Rule: Comparative Perspectives*, pp. 64–84. Here and in the notes below, space constraints prevent me from offering the voluminous citations that would have been apposite.

7. I elaborate on this view in "Democracy, Law, and Comparative Politics," in *Studies in International Comparative Development* 36 (2001): 5–36.

8. This phrase comes from the preface written for our four volumes by Abraham Lowenthal, the director of the Latin American Program at the Woodrow Wilson International Center for Scholars in Washington, D.C., which generously housed and sponsored this project.

9. Adam Przeworski et al., *Democracy and Development: Political Institutions and Well-Being in the World, 1950–1990* (New York: Cambridge University Press, 2000).

10. Yet "poor democracies" are not condemned to breakdown. As Przeworski and his coauthors put it: "[Democracies] are brittle in poor countries. But they are not always sentenced to die: Education helps them survive independently of income, and a balance among the political forces makes them more stable." Adam Przeworski et al., *Democracy and Development*, 137.

11. Suffice to mention the detailed discussion of this matter in the influential book of Juan Linz and Alfred Stepan, *Problems of Democratic Transition and Consolidation: Southern Europe, Latin America, and Post-Communist Europe* (Baltimore: John Hopkins University Press, 1996); in addition, the literature on transitions in postcommunist countries discussed extensively this matter from its very beginning.

On my part, I first presented my views on the state and its crucial importance for democratization in a 1993 article whose title is itself indicative: "On the State, Democratization and Some Conceptual Problems: A Latin American View with Some Glances to Post-Communist Countries," *World Development* 21 (October 1993): 1355–69.

# The Democratic Path

## BY GHIA NODIA

*Ghia Nodia is chairman of the board of the Caucasian Institute of Peace, Democracy, and Development, and professor of political science at Ilya Chavchavadze State University of Language and Culture in Tbilisi, Georgia. His most recent contribution to the* Journal of Democracy *was "Ten Years After the Soviet Breakup: The Impact of Nationalism" (October 2001).*

WHEN I FIRST READ Thomas Carothers's essay, I agreed with all or nearly all that he had to say. But then a question began to nag me: What *really* was the target of his criticism? Or to put it another way: Did the sum total of the points that he made—and he was right to make them—add up to a demonstrated need for a "change of paradigm"?

Carothers offers an eloquent statement of the frustration that many feel as they look at countries that once were firmly authoritarian or even totalitarian and are such no more—yet that have not become fully democratic. This trend toward what Carothers calls the "gray zone" of ambiguity has replaced the optimism of the "third-wave" era, when democracy seemed to be going from strength to strength in region after region around the globe. Clearly there is a need to rethink the basic assumptions that we have been making about democratization for the last decade or so, and efforts toward this end have been attracting comment and arousing discussion. A few years ago, Fareed Zakaria made a splash by saying that democracy may not be such a great idea for some countries and recommended efforts to promote a supposedly more feasible "liberal constitutionalism" instead.[1] This general conclusion was too much for many to accept, even if they recognized the accuracy of the criticisms that Zakaria leveled against the simplistic ways in which too many Western analysts and democracy promoters understood the democratization process.

Carothers is aiming at many of the same targets as Zakaria but reaches far more modest conclusions. In assembling his bill of particulars, Carothers tends to quote reports from the U.S. Agency for International Development rather than works by theorists and scholars. His major practical recommendations boil down to: (1) stop making countries that have been successful in their democratic transitions the focus of democracy assistance; and (2) stop expecting most countries now labeled "transitional" to fit that description anymore, because their positions in the "gray zone" will perhaps not change anytime soon, if at all. They might make progress toward greater democracy, or they might not. Neither eventuality should surprise us.

If by proclaiming "the end of the transition paradigm" Thomas Carothers means that being "in democratic transition" has become a more or less permanent condition for many countries, then I agree with him. But this observation is only a start. A number of intellectual and practical challenges emerge *after* we say what Carothers says. If "transition" is no longer an apt metaphor for what these countries are experiencing, how *should* we conceptualize their condition? And what, if anything, should we do differently because we have stopped calling them by one name and are searching for another?

Carothers analyzes certain assumptions that he attributes to the "transition paradigm" but makes no mention of other and even broader assumptions that we should revisit. The most basic contention that lay at the basis of third-wave optimism was the notion that democracy is now the only "normal" political regime—the only game in the global village, if you will. At the end of the day, democracy is the only political regime that is fully compatible with modernity. One can reject democracy, but this implies some kind of rejection of modernity itself. The Muslim world, whose main problem seems to be finding an adequate response to modernity, and which has also had the least success in embracing democracy, is the most obvious example. For a time, certain East Asian regimes seemed to be challenging the democratic assumption with quasi-official teachings about uniquely "Asian values" as the ideological basis for successful modernization, but democratic progress in Taiwan and South Korea weakened that argument. Currently the doctrine of "Asian values" seems to be fading out of fashion.

This is the context in which gray-zone countries find themselves—and with reference to which their situation should be understood. The gray-zone regimes that Carothers has in mind are not openly challenging the democratic model as the one singularly best suited to modern conditions, nor are they trying to propose alternative grounds of political legitimacy. What they are doing, rather, is one of three things: (1) trying more or less sincerely to adopt this model but failing; (2) making a pretense of trying; or (3) engaging in a mixture of both good-faith failure and mere "going through the motions."

Such regimes typically feel pressure to at least appear democratic from two quarters. One is the "international community," which uses a variety of carrots and sticks to urge democratic compliance. The other is the more or less hardy local band of democrats, who use whatever influence they can muster to support democracy's cause at home. Where local democrats are weak, outside pressure can be crucial to sustaining hopes for democratic change and preventing full-scale relapses into authoritarianism. But beyond matters of will, there are often impediments of various kinds that hold countries back from becoming full-fledged liberal democracies. They then find themselves in some uncertain, incomplete, not fully defined state, that hazy zone of gray for which political theorists have not yet devised a proper name. Indeed, the very term *gray zone* suggests our problem in understanding the nature of such regimes.

### Two Meanings of "Normal"

But does the existence of this gray zone really cast a fundamental doubt on the assumption of democracy's exclusive claim to "normality" in the modern world? This depends on how we understand the word "normal." There are at least two interpretations, and we should be careful not to mix them up. One is purely normative: Democracy is the only acceptable political regime. There is a consensus among reasonable people that liberal democracy may have its problems but is clearly better than any of the alternatives.

But "normal" can also be used as a near-synonym for "natural." In this sense, democracy is thought to correspond better than any other regime to human nature itself, or to the nature of human society. If this is true, then it is not democracy but the lack of it that must be explained. Absent specific malign forces that bar people from having a democracy, they will have it. Or as John Mueller has written with specific reference to postcommunist transitions:

> The transitional experience in many of the postcommunist countries and elsewhere suggests that democracy as a form of government and capitalism as an economic form are really quite simple, even natural, and, unless obstructed by thugs with guns, they can emerge quite easily and quickly without any special development, prerequisites, or preparation. It seems to me that democracy is fundamentally about leaving people free to complain and that capitalism is fundamentally about leaving people free to be greedy.[2]

Nothing about the gray-zone experience challenges the normative supremacy of modern liberal democracy. On the contrary, the compelling power of democratic norms may explain why gray-zone countries have not simply slipped back into authoritarianism. But the existence of transitional countries where there is no transition does cast doubt on the idea that democracy is somehow "natural," and therefore presumably easy to achieve. In most of the countries that Carothers considers, people are free both to complain and to exercise their greed—arguably, they are even less restricted in this latter regard than people in established free-market democracies. Yet neither of these types of freedom has proven sufficient to produce liberal democracy on the Western model.

But does this mean that the concept of "democratic transition" makes no sense with regard to some countries, or merely that such transitions are more complicated than some of us had initially thought?

Others have criticized the teleological baggage with which the term *transition* has often been freighted. As Richard Rose and his colleagues argue: "To describe new democracies as being in transition is misleading; it implies that we know a society's starting-point, we know where it is today, and we know where it is heading."[3] If a country is not yet democratic, we cannot be fully sure that it will become such; therefore it is not right to say it is "in transition to" democracy. If it has already become democratic, then of course it is no longer in transition. Therefore transitions can only be known *ex post facto*. Until we know the end result, it is safer to speak simply of open-ended political change.

Yet Carothers goes farther, claiming that it is altogether wrong ever to speak of gray-zone countries under the rubric of democratic transition: "The most common political patterns to date among the 'transitional countries'—feckless pluralism and dominant-power politics—include elements of democracy but should be understood *as alternative directions, not way stations* to liberal democracy" (emphasis added). This is a formulation that I am quite unprepared to accept. Any given gray-zone country may or may not become a liberal democracy eventually, but the conditions in which these countries find themselves still can only be understood in terms of how near or far they are from democracy. Therefore the notion of the "path to democracy"—and with it the transition paradigm—remains valid.

We are dealing here, I think, with a problem that stems from the tendency of positivistic political science to treat political change in purely objective terms, as if it were a natural process. The logic runs something like this: We can talk about "democratic transition" as a kind of quasibiological process which—especially if U.S. funding or international pressure is applied—will lead to the conception and birth of a baby called "democracy." Transition is something like pregnancy. If a certain time has elapsed and the baby is not delivered, we should conclude that it was a false pregnancy or a stillbirth. In either case, the country at issue no longer deserves the special support and indulgence due a pregnant woman. I think it is this sort of approach that is Carothers's real target. He points out several times, after all, that the concept of transition makes sense only if it implies a process that goes through a consistently predictable set of stages.

My own view is that the positivistic approach is far from the only way to think about political transformations. The term *transition* makes sense not because its end result is teleologically predetermined, as if through a kind of social software or genetic coding, but because the idea of the right kind of end result—namely, democracy—is present in political discourse and exerts a powerful influence on events. Carothers does not deny that some gray-zone countries have abandoned outright dictatorship and introduced important elements of democracy, however incomplete. In other words, they have experienced political change that has been guided by the normative model of democracy. Is this not what is meant by a "democratic transition"?

The "muddling through" that we see today in many countries might be preparing them for further progress toward democracy, or it might not. We do not know, which is why we consigned them to the conceptual gray zone in the first place. But unless and until such countries come up with some kind of systemic alternative to democracy, it remains correct to try to understand their experience within the framework of democratic transition. Nor do I think that Carothers really proposes any other. He wants us to be modest in our expectations and skeptical about a positivist interpretation of the transition paradigm—both sensible attitudes, in my view—but he himself does not offer a new paradigm.

The truly important change toward which Carothers points us is the sober and fully conscious recognition of just how difficult a goal to achieve liberal democracy is. My impression is that political discourse within many a gray-zone country is replete with skepticism about whether the country is on the path to democracy, or even about whether it can actually become democratic. There often seems to be a tacit understanding that there are structural (or, if you like, "cultural") impediments that stand in the way of the arrival of "normal" democracy as it is known in the West.

Recognizing the existence of such impediments may lead to either of two attitudes. The first concludes that "democracy is not for us." This attitude will most likely express itself in the form of a nativist, and Western, or "antiglobalist" ideology. A regime informed by this attitude will probably not even try to appear democratic. If it does try to take on some formal features of democracy (including even elections, perhaps), it will do so in a palpably shallow and unconvincing way. The governments of Uzbekistan and Turkmenistan are like this. As Carothers points out, they are "out-and-out authoritarian systems" that use democratic rhetoric as window dressing.

There are many other countries, however, where most people acknowledge the presence of deep structural impediments to democracy but embrace it as a long-term goal nonetheless. It is these countries that are at issue here. Their major characteristics today are uncertainty and a sense of failure. Whether they are closer to "feckless pluralism" or "dominant-power politics," both elites and the public agree that their regimes are unsteady, unfinished, and unconsolidated. That explains why it is hard to find a name for them: It is much easier to label something that looks like a finished product than something in constant flux. Perhaps we should call these cases "failing transitions" or, in line with Carothers's terminology, "feckless transitions." The reference to "failure" is apt because such faltering transformations often exist against the backdrop of failing or structurally weak states. Indeed, in some cases it is extremely difficult to tell whether the failure of democracy or the failure of the state itself is the more basic difficulty (I am inclined to think it is more often the latter).

In stressing these points, I find myself in full agreement with Carothers. The focus of democratic theory—at least with regard to gray-zone countries—should not be on "how to defeat tyrants" or "how to introduce good legislation," but rather on how to deal with structural weaknesses such as a failing state or the malign legacy of an undemocratic political culture.

### Proving the Pudding

Yet the question remains: Do we have a new paradigm? Perhaps the real proof of the pudding is whether we have new policy recommendations. Should the countries at issue be advised to give up the democratic experiment altogether and work on creating something else, as Fareed Zakaria seemed to be suggesting? I do not think that is what Carothers intends. His policy advice is to focus on helping political parties and on bridging the gulf between citizens and the formal political system. These suggestions show that he remains fully within the transition paradigm: Some steps have already been taken (such as the creation of more or less democratic "formal political systems"), and now it is time to work on filling the form with appropriate substance.

Such ideas are hardly revolutionary. More importantly—and I say this as someone who has lived on the receiving end of "democracy assistance" for more than a decade—I do not find them very practical. The first Western political consultants who came among us after post-Soviet Georgia announced its plans to democratize took on the task of helping to develop proper political parties. These consultants failed spectacularly. Why? Most likely because, to borrow an image from Jonathan Swift's account of the Academy of Projectors in *Gulliver's Travels*, trying to build parties artificially with almost nothing but outside help is like trying to build a house from the roof downward. I am at an even greater loss to understand what "bridging the gap" between citizens and formal polities through outside assistance would mean in specific terms.

This opens up other big questions: What are the limits to "democracy assistance"? How much can outside help actually accomplish? What should be left to homegrown forces? I concur with Carothers about the importance of the two policy areas that he emphasizes, but I doubt that outside cash and consultants will be of much help. Here, perhaps, is where some paradigm-shifting is in order: Do not try to do what you cannot do; focus instead on areas where you have the best chance of getting results. But rejecting the concept of "transition" is of little relevance to such a reorientation.

**Notes**

The Carnegie Endowment gratefully acknowledges the permission of the Johns Hopkins University Press to reprint this article, which originally appeared in the *Journal of Democracy*, vol. 13, no. 3 (July 2002).

1. Fareed Zakaria, "The Rise of Illiberal Democracy," *Foreign Affairs* 76 (November–December 1997): 22–43.
2. John Mueller, "Democracy, Capitalism, and the End of Transition," in Michael Mandelbaum. ed.. *Post-Communism: Four Perspectives* (New York: Council on Foreign Relations, 1996), p. 104.
3. Richard Rose, William Mishler, and Christian Haerpfer, *Democracy and Its Alternatives: Understanding Post-Communist Societies* (Cambridge and Oxford: Polity, 1998), p. 7.

# Retaining the Human Dimension

### BY KENNETH WOLLACK

*Kenneth Wollack is president of the National Democratic Institute (NDI), a leading Washington, D.C.–based democracy-promotion organization that receives funding from the U.S. Agency for International Development (USAID) and the National Endowment for Democracy.*

IN "THE END OF THE TRANSITION PARADIGM," Thomas Carothers admonishes the democracy-promotion community for continuing to adhere to a naive and outdated notion of the democratization process in countries in political transition. This "transition paradigm," according to Carothers, has led policy makers to improperly assess political situations in many countries and has resulted in inappropriate or ineffective democracy-assistance programs.

Once again, Carothers has made a serious contribution to the policy discussion on an important topic. While those of us in the democracy-promotion community are not always in agreement with all of Carothers's views, we are fortunate to benefit from such constructive criticism. His assessments often spark much useful discussion within the National Democratic Institute (NDI) and similar organizations. Nevertheless, a number of Carothers's recent criticisms call for examination.

At first, I was tempted simply to concur with Carothers's critique but then argue that experienced democracy practitioners like NDI are innocent of the sins he enumerates. It is not my aim, however, to defend specific programs or organizations like NDI, but rather to offer a more general defense of democracy practitioners and funders. For the model of "democracy promoters" that Carothers presents is often as simplistic as the paradigm he suggests they blindly follow. It would be unhelpful to this debate (and exceedingly self-serving) to try to set organizations like NDI aside and join Carothers in pointing a finger at a group of anonymous democracy promoters.

The crux of Carothers's argument is that democracy promoters assume that many countries are in a transition to democracy despite clear evidence to the contrary. Given that most transitional countries actually fall, according to Carothers, into a vast "gray zone" between dictatorship and liberal democracy, internationally supported democracy assistance programs in these countries are naive at best and misguided at worst. In their adherence to this false "transition paradigm," democracy promoters, he asserts, impose a simplistic and overly optimistic conceptual order on a complex problem. To the extent that this happens, Carothers should be commended for pointing out a problem. Organizations like NDI have long opposed the very simplistic frameworks and templates that he describes.

Yet democracy promoters may not be as misguided as Carothers claims. Democracy promotion is a cause-oriented mission that requires a certain level of optimism and enthusiasm, but this should not disguise the often hard-headed realism that goes into program planning and work. The majority of democracy-assistance organizations see democracy promotion as but one part of a mix of foreign aid and development initiatives that includes economic and socioeconomic components. NDI and others are well aware of the complexity and volatility of political situations around the world. We work to identify specific country challenges and to design programs that take culture, tradition, and history into consideration. We also recognize the so-called "next generation" issues to which Carothers refers. These include anticorruption initiatives, economic reform, political finance reform, political party renewal and modernization, and information technology. Additionally, the encouragement of popular political participation among women, youth, and minorities and increased communication between citizens and elected officials are necessary to reduce apathy and disaffection among voters.

In reality, those of us who carry out democracy programs have never considered ourselves to be operating under a "transition paradigm," but even if we did, the situation would probably be more benign than Carothers makes it out to be. The real danger is not so much an inexact assessment of the state of democracy in a particular country, but the risk of poorly conceived and executed programs. While Carothers is right that democracy promotion, like any profession, is subject to mistakes and misjudgments, he fails to provide evidence for the larger claim that a faulty paradigm has undermined the whole endeavor. He argues that the transition paradigm is "retarding the evolution of democracy assistance," yet he does not address specific cases in which this may have occurred.

Carothers broadly criticizes several documents from the U.S. Agency for International Development (USAID) for presenting an inaccurate and misleading picture of democratic transitions in countries like Cambodia, the Democratic Republic of Congo, Guinea, and Zambia. In Georgia, he claims, the transition paradigm led to overly optimistic assumptions about democratic development. Yet Carothers's essay fails to examine how existing democracy programs are working to address challenges in these countries or to what degree these programs have been successful in accommodating changing political situations. With the support of USAID and the National Endowment for Democracy, NDI and others are asking the right questions in these countries and, I believe, are carrying out relevant programs:

- In Cambodia, programs are supporting civic groups and political parties that are challenging the "dominant-power politics" (Carothers's label) of the ruling Cambodian People's Party.
- In Guinea, interparty dialogue initiatives have enabled the opposition to gain visibility in public forums throughout the country.
- In the Democratic Republic of Congo, 23 opposition parties are receiving assistance as they participate in the Inter-Congolese Dialogue, a formal process designed to establish a timetable and conditions for a peaceful democratic transition.
- In Zambia, civic groups that strongly criticized recent electoral misconduct have benefited from outside assistance.
- In Georgia, civil society organizations and democratic reformers in the parliament are receiving support in their efforts to promote constitutional and electoral reforms, anticorruption initiatives, and decentralization.

While Carothers could undoubtedly question other democracy-related programs in these countries, the above-mentioned activities are surely consistent with the approach he advocates: an analysis of "key political patterns" and the development of "alternative centers of power." Moreover, not all programs are similarly run. Decentralization at USAID has resulted in dozens of USAID missions overseas, each of which approaches democracy promotion somewhat differently. A rigid conceptual framework, complete with indicators and strategic objectives, certainly exists, but it is not applied uniformly. Those who fund and implement democracy programs around the world are as varied as the political environments in which they operate.

Carothers's article also questions the terminology used to describe democratic transitions. It is true that many democracy activists use language similar to that comprising Carothers's "stages of democratization"—opening, breakthrough, and consolidation. But these are meant as shorthand descriptions of political situations—language used for organizing purposes—and not as immutable truths. For more than a decade, democracy practitioners have grown accustomed to working in what Carothers calls the "gray zone"—countries caught between authoritarianism and liberal democracy. This zone is hardly a new phenomenon that reflects a "crash of assumptions." More than ten years ago, democracy activists discovered that "breakthrough" elections in places like Pakistan. Zambia, and Albania did not lead to a consolidation stage of democracy. If there was a period in which we believed in a linear path to democratization, it was many years ago and very brief. In fact, if democracy promoters truly considered the transition toward, and the consolidation of, democracy as a "natural process," as Carothers asserts, we should have viewed our own program work—in fact, our very existence—as superfluous.

## New Approaches

In his essay, Carothers makes a number of recommendations for new approaches to democracy promotion. His call for greater political party development is particularly welcome. Political parties serve a function unlike any other institution in a democracy. By both aggregating and representing social interests, they provide a structure for political participation. They act as training grounds for political leaders who will eventually assume governing roles. They foster necessary competition and accountability in governance. In the legislative arena, they translate policy preferences into public policies. And it is political parties, acting through the legislative process, that the public must ultimately rely on to design anticorruption measures and oversee their enforcement. It should come as no surprise, then, that when political parties fail to fulfill their special roles, the entire democratic system is placed in jeopardy.

Despite the importance of parties to democratic development, in recent years civil society has become especially favored within the international democracy-assistance community. Indeed, civil society has been described as the well-spring of democracy. Thus, the international development community has buttressed civic groups and aided and abetted their rise, often from the ashes of discredited political parties. This has been a good and necessary endeavor; NDI has participated in such initiatives and continues to do so. At the same time, there is a distinct danger in focusing almost exclusively on civil society development. We have found, most starkly in places like Peru and Venezuela, that civil society activism without effective political institutions quickly creates a vacuum. It sows opportunities for populists and demagogues who seek to emasculate parties and legislatures, which are the cornerstones of representative democracy. The international community must respond to the need to build, sustain, and renew political parties. This "supply side" of the political equation deserves equal footing with civil society, the "demand side."

Over the past several years, there has gradually emerged a new recognition of the need to support political party development. In its new Inter-American Democratic Charter, the Organization of American States (OAS) affirms that the "strengthening of political parties is a priority for democracy." The World Bank has begun to explore ways to include legislatures as well as civic groups in the development of its Poverty Reduction Strategy Papers, which form the basis for concessional lending and debt relief in nearly 70 countries. And with the support of NDI, the three largest global groupings of political parties—the Liberal International, Socialist International, and Christian Democratic International—representing 340 parties in 140 countries, are joining forces to promote political party modernization, reform, and renewal. Despite these advances, there is still much left to be done before donors consider political parties as natural and indispensable partners in development.

Carothers reproves democracy-promotion organizations for possessing an exclusively political perspective and for failing to appreciate, let alone incorporate, economic issues that affect the democratization process. It is certainly true that democracy practitioners should have a better understanding of the linkages between economic and political reform. NDI has cosponsored a number of programs with the Center for International Private Enterprise on the "Politics of Economic Reform." In 1999, we brought together political and civic leaders from 17 emerging democracies in a conference called "Managing the Twin Transitions: Economic and Political Reform." More should be done to bridge political and economic issues.

Part of this responsibility, though, falls on the economic development community, which is comparatively flush with resources and has traditionally devalued, if not ignored, political development. In the past, economists hoped that development aid could achieve the kind of growth and opportunity that leads to social stability. In recent years, however, it has become apparent that a growing number of problems in the developing world are beyond the reach of traditional economic aid. While such problems frequently have economic consequences, they are often fundamentally political in nature. Rural dislocation, environmental degradation, and agricultural policies that lead to famine can be traced to political systems in which the victims have no political voice, government institutions feel no obligation to answer to the people, and special interests feel free to exploit resources without oversight or accountability. Truly sustainable development requires institutions and processes that provide the capacity to resolve problems without resort to violence or repression. International donor agencies and financial institutions have only begun to recognize this interconnectedness between political and economic reform. While Carothers is right to insist that democracy promoters should take greater account of the economic aspects of development, economic agencies also must gain a greater understanding of and appreciation for the political dimensions of development.

## The Human Dimension

In some ways, Carothers's article is a sophisticated statement of the obvious— that democracy, a highly desirable but elusive state of affairs, either has not taken hold or has been severely compromised in many places in the world, despite a general rhetorical commitment to it on the part of a hundred or more governments. But to assert that the "dominant paradigm" has outlived its usefulness may be an overreaction.

As Carothers correctly points out, there is too much oversimplification of complex issues. In the final analysis, however, it may be wrong to abandon the notion of a transition or movement toward democracy. Lost in the labyrinth of his new terminology and political categories is the human dimension of democratization. Carothers makes only a passing reference to the "hopeful vision" that the transition paradigm provides, citing this vision as an explanation for why democracy promoters are reluctant to abandon it. But for courageous democrats who are operating in authoritarian environments and gray zones, it is precisely this deep and abiding faith in the possibility of positive change that fuels their struggle. They are making real-life sacrifices in the belief that conditions can and will get better. It might very well be demoralizing and ultimately self-defeating for these democratic activists to abandon this faith for a world of "feckless pluralism" and "dominant powers."

As for the democracy promoters, we work in the Kosovos and Angolas and Algerias of the world not because we are the victims of faulty analysis, but because it seems right to have the same aspirations for Angolans and Algerians as we have for Serbians and Chileans—and for ourselves. People are driven to sacrifice time, money, and energy in the cause of democracy because, in the words of the late AFL-CIO president Lane Kirkland, "It is simply the right thing to do."

Carothers asserts that "given how difficult democratization is, efforts to promote it should be redoubled." Moreover, he offers concrete ways to improve democracy programming. Yet these messages seem to become lost in his article, leaving many readers with the impression that, for Carothers, positive democratic change in most countries is a quixotic goal. Let us hope that his next article will place greater emphasis on the reasons why democracy-promotion efforts should be sustained and expanded.

## Note

The Carnegie Endowment gratefully acknowledges the permission of the Johns Hopkins University Press to reprint this article, which originally appeared in the *Journal of Democracy*, vol. 13, no. 3 (July 2002).

# Tilting at Straw Men

## BY GERALD HYMAN

*Gerald Hyman is director of the Office of Democracy and Governance of the U.S. Agency for International Development's Bureau for Europe and Eurasia. The views expressed in this article are those of the author and do not necessarily reflect the views, opinions, or ideas of the U.S. government, USAID, its management, or its democracy practitioners.*

ALTHOUGH THOMAS CAROTHERS'S CRITIQUE of democracy promoters in the January 2002 *Journal of Democracy* was, in principle, directed at donors in general, all the examples and citations referred exclusively to the U.S. Agency for International Development (USAID). Carothers's critique would be trenchant, even devastating, if it accurately portrayed USAID's thinking on democracy. But it does not.[1] The article characterizes USAID's democracy practitioners as uncritically adhering to an increasingly outmoded "transition paradigm" based on five naive assumptions. That mischaracterization is a straw man, which is first created, then demolished. Undoubtedly, we at USAID are trying our best to promote transitions to democracy, but we do not adhere to any single transition paradigm and certainly not to the pastiche created by Carothers.

First, Carothers asserts that, notwithstanding the substantial and obvious evidence to the contrary, "democracy enthusiasts" continue to believe that "any country moving away from dictatorial rule is in transition toward democracy," and that the transition is inexorable. Furthermore, he argues that we have constructed a simplistic evolutionary scheme, and that our assistance programs are fashioned primarily to hasten the inevitable rather than to wrestle with a variety of possible outcomes, of which a successful democratic transition is only one, and indeed not a very likely one at that. No matter how optimistic we may be, no one who lives where we work could come to that conclusion. We are confronted day by day not only with successes but also with failures, setbacks, regressions, programmatic shortcomings, and "stagnant transitions."[2]

Indeed, as early as 1991, USAID's democracy policy stated, in its second sentence, what many considered obvious even then—that "progress toward democracy should not be expected to be 'linear, easily accomplished or effortlessly maintained.'"[3] Since 1991, even that caution has been replaced by the sobering reality that countries can move away from greater democracy and that democracy promotion is almost never easy, let alone inevitable. Still, notwithstanding the obstacles, we are firmly committed to democracy promotion. There is no excuse for some of the inflated claims that have appeared in USAID documents (which Carothers rightly criticizes), but the supposed predominance of a "transition paradigm" does not explain them.[4]

Second, since we are working to promote transitions to democracy and are charged by statute to "contribute to the development of democratic institutions and political pluralism,"[5] it is not surprising to find us thinking of ways to do so. Yet we certainly do not *assume* the "set sequence"—opening, breakthrough, and consolidation—that Carothers attributes to us as a second assumption.[6] In particular, we see "openings" not as events but as long, difficult, hard-won, incremental processes. Our assistance programs are often designed precisely for crafting small "openings" rather than finding them full-blown. And when there are "breakthroughs," they do not always (or even often) occur as they did in Europe or Eurasia, or possibly Indonesia and Nigeria—with the sudden collapse of the old order. Rather, breakthroughs are more often gradual, piecemeal, and linked to particular sectors rather than systemic. Finally, consolidation is more often a goal than a state. Unfortunately, it is a goal achieved all too infrequently, and many of USAID's most important policy documents emphasize the fallacy of assuming "set sequences" of reform.[7]

Nor do we subscribe to the third assumption, regarding "the determinative importance of elections." We make no apology for believing that there cannot be a true democracy without the general accountability of government to its citizens, and that elections are the only tested way to accomplish that. Simply put, there is no democracy without elections. Yet we do not believe that elections are determinative or that they are, by themselves, "a key generator of further democratic reforms." If anything, we have regularly urged in our documents and policy discussions against placing undue, unrealistic emphasis on (or faith in) elections. More than that, we have explicitly warned that, in certain contexts, elections can be premature and counterproductive from the point of view of both democracy and stability.[8] None of that is to gainsay the importance that we attach to elections and to political parties. In my opinion, however, we need to explore in greater depth why multiparty elections have not led more often to better representation or accountability, and to ask how we might craft strategies to achieve these ends.[9] We would very much welcome any help we could get in doing so.

Neither do we hold the fourth assumption attributed to us—that underlying economic, political, institutional, and social conditions "will not be major factors in either the onset or the outcome of the transition process," and that each country's trajectory will fit a set mold. To be sure, we are looking for general patterns, but we are fully cognizant of the various forms that democracy can take; the variety of social, cultural, and historical environments that shape or impede democracy; and the many paths political development can and will take. That is why USAID has in-country missions, each of which is responsible for designing country-specific programs. Moreover, that is why almost all our technical and policy documents emphasize that approaches need to be country-specific, consistent with social and economic conditions, and based on local realities, not idealized visions.[10] It is also why USAID Administrator Andrew Natsios emphasized in his March 2002 address at Monterrey, Mexico, that "you can't apply exactly the same matrix to every single country. . .local context always has to be taken into account." Yet it is probably fair to say that many of our programs in very different environments look quite similar. It is also fair to say, however, that similar-appearing programs may not really be so similar after all. The differences may be subtle, but that is Carothers's point—a point on which we all agree: Countries differ, sometimes subtly but nevertheless importantly, and democracy programs need to respond accordingly.

Finally, far from assuming that we are building inevitable transitions on "coherent, functioning states," we spend considerable energy trying to find ways to build precisely such states. The many meetings, external and internal, that we have held over the past few years on "failed states" and poor governance attest to our concern with this issue: For us, good governance is a problem, not an assumption. Indeed, we go Carothers one further. We do not limit our concern for good governance to the government or the state, but also include social institutions broadly defined, including those in civil society. To date, however, our concern has not been matched by adequate solutions, and we could use some assistance in addressing these problems.

As for the charge that our documents on governance list no examples of "work on fundamental state building," we do substantial work on state institutions, particularly local governments. It is true that we do not work as much any longer on national public administration as we once did, but that is because other better-endowed donors (particularly the World Bank) do so, and also because we are reluctant to work on "state building" where there is little political will for constructing a democratic state. Nevertheless, I believe we have substantially underestimated the general institutional decay in the countries in which we work, and I believe that work on national governance is an area we need to reconsider.

## Committed Realism

So, to parody the kind of slogans we used to hear from China, we do not assume the one goal (inevitable democracy), the three stages, or the five assumptions, even as we do our best to assist transitions to democratic governance. It is possible to be both deeply committed and seriously realistic, and we have tried our best to do so. Without a doubt, we need to address our failings, but they do not arise because we are besotted with the "transition paradigm" described by Carothers.

More importantly, although we find paradigms useful—while fully recognizing that they inevitably "oversimplify" their subjects—this has not, I believe, led to the shortcomings outlined by Carothers. Surely he agrees that analysis begins precisely by isolating—and thereby simplifying—admittedly complex problems. Analysis extracts, artificially, some elements or processes (preferably the fundamental ones), examines them in that artificial isolation, builds a conceptual model, then returns them to a more complex reality. This is hardly new. It captures the methodology of all science.[11] Clarifying our thinking by artificially constructing archetypes would hardly make us unique, even if those archetypes actually were "opening, breakthrough, and consolidation." The fact that reality is not fully captured by so simple a paradigm does not mean that even simple paradigms are not *useful* in thinking about a more complex reality. "To recognize, then, that the transition paradigm has outlived its usefulness," as Carothers argues, does not depend on some abstract notion of truth. It depends first on the purposes—the "usefulness" as he says—to which such a paradigm (however simple) is put, second on the limits of that utility, and third on our recognition of the more complex reality upon which such a paradigm might *usefully* shed some light.

The more useful paradigm, Carothers argues, would include a "gray zone" within which lie two "political syndromes"—feckless pluralism and dominant-power politics—that represent two of the "entrenched" alternatives to the inevitable transition paradigm. Neither is fully democratic or fully authoritarian, and neither is moving anywhere. They are not "rigidly delineated political-system types but rather political patterns that have become regular and somewhat entrenched." Feckless pluralism is a kind of flawed democracy in which relatively free and fair elections result only in the alternation of power between corrupt, self-interested, and ineffective political-party elites who "seem only to trade the country's problems back and forth from one hapless side to the other."

In principle, feckless pluralism would seem to carry its own electoral antidote: Throw out one or both of the feckless parties. In practice, the barriers to entry for new parties and the barriers to leadership positions for reformers within the existing (often highly centralized) parties are both extremely high. Still, there remains a question of whether, how, and when foreign donors should act to "perfect" other countries' "flawed democracies." But perhaps the most serious danger in feckless pluralism is that an exasperated electorate will choose not more internally democratic and potent parties, but rather a systemic alternative much closer to the dictatorial pole, the pattern that Carothers refers to as "dominant-power politics": limited political space and contestation in which . . . one political grouping . . . dominates . . . [with] little prospect of alternation of power in the foreseeable future." That pattern is, unfortunately, all too entrenched, and far from ignoring it, we are deeply engrossed in trying to do something about it.

More important, it is not clear from the article what kinds of programs would result from analyses based on these two "syndromes." Without more to go on, where do we go, strategically and programmatically, with "feckless pluralism" or "dominant-power politics"? It is a pity that Carothers did not spend more time addressing this question. In addition to these two, we have also been worried about alternative archetypes and processes over the past couple of years— for example, authoritarian regimes and military coups. None of these alternatives fits neatly into the "transition paradigm," nor do we think they do.

If anything, we have modulated substantially the emphasis on archetypes and typologies of states in favor precisely of looking at problems and processes. We have found that fitting countries into typologies often creates more disagreement and confusion than value. In the mid-1990s, we began developing and field-testing an analytical framework that embraced elements of four disciplines to analyze political dynamics and design appropriate democracy-promotion programs: political sociology and political anthropology to understand broad interactions of social structure, culture, and political systems; political economy to gain insights into the relations between actors and their interests, resources, choices, and strategies for maximizing gains; and institutional analysis to explore the design of institutional arenas, rules, and incentives in relation to which those actors operate.[12] Archetypes of all sorts, gray or otherwise, play a relatively small role in that analysis. Political institutions, processes, interests, and incentives are the dominant considerations. That framework is now the recommended approach to analysis and strategic programming at USAID. We train our staff in it. We have used it in more than two dozen countries. We believe it is a better approach than either the "transition paradigm" or the "gray zone."

### Dealing with Corruption and Conflict

We have also become increasingly concerned about corruption and conflict. Administrator Natsios has directed us to devise strategies that help deal with both. These are deep problems with profoundly deleterious (sometimes disastrous) consequences, heavily affected by the very social, historical, and cultural considerations that Carothers accuses us of ignoring. Moreover, President George W. Bush has just announced a New Compact for Development, a central component of which is a commitment to "good governance" that includes "rooting out corruption, upholding human rights and adhering to the rule of law." USAID is working with other U.S. government entities in designing how this element is to be measured.

Within USAID, Administrator Natsios has established a new office to deal with ways to better manage conflicts and, one would hope, to prevent or at least mitigate them. Everyone at USAID clearly understands the fundamental importance of social organization, culture, and history in shaping these pathologies. Our problem is to find ways of addressing them without being paralyzed by the complexity that these social (and other) considerations impose on us.

One way to address these issues is to isolate parts of their complex natures, propose some archetypal (albeit oversimplified) models to understand them, and then reassemble the parts and the archetypes. The models will almost certainly not fall neatly into the "transition paradigm," but they may well be informed by it, and they almost certainly will be similarly "simplistic." The alternative, once again, is to be paralyzed by complexity. The question is not whether we will simplify, but whether the simplification will be useful in helping us to disaggregate, and therefore to understand, the complexity. Of course, understanding the problem—getting the analysis right—is only the beginning. The bigger problem by far is finding ways to prevent conflict, reduce corruption, attenuate patrimonialism, and promote democracy. We have, in very early draft papers, been addressing these problems, and we could certainly use help on both the analytical and the programmatic sides.

In sum, the disappointing thing about Carothers's article is that it sets up a straw man in place of our thinking and does not address some of the problems with which he knows we have been struggling. We long ago moved beyond the "transition paradigm" as described by Carothers. We are now struggling to find strategies to deal with the limited authoritarian states and the motion without movement that he describes as feckless pluralism. We are also struggling with "deeply entrenched" patterns such as corruption, patrimonialism, incipient conflict, failed states, poor governance, and inadequate political parties. We have long benefited from Carothers's thinking, and we would benefit substantially if he, and others committed to democratization, could help us find strategies for dealing with these challenges.

## Notes

I am indebted to many people who have read, commented on, and criticized this article, particularly to Michele Schimpp, who gave me constant help and support notwithstanding her insightful reservations.

The Carnegie Endowment gratefully acknowledges the permission of the Johns Hopkins University Press to reprint this article, which originally appeared in the *Journal of Democracy*, vol. 13, no. 3 (July 2002).

1. Carothers's earlier critique of USAID democracy strategies similarly criticized an approach that USAID had already abandoned. See Thomas Carothers, *Aiding Democracy Abroad: The Learning Curve* (Washington, D.C.: Carnegie Endowment for International Peace, 1999), ch. 5.

2. Carothers, *Aiding Democracy Abroad*, p. 110.

3. USAID, *Democracy and Governance Policy* (Washington, D.C.: USAID, November 1991), p. 4.

4. An analysis of why such statements appear might have been more helpful than a simple recitation of them. This is not the place to explore those reasons in detail, but several are good starting points: the U.S. public disenchantment with foreign aid, the consequent search by every administration to find success stories, and the perverse interpretation of the Government Performance and Results Act. In addition, there are a variety of nonassistance foreign-policy considerations, as well as the tendency to emphasize the full half rather than the empty half of the glass and to give governments the benefit of the doubt in certain public documents, if only to nudge them into constructive action. None of these factors excuses exaggerations, and Carothers does us a service in pointing them out.

5. 22 USC §5401(b).

6. Carothers's position on both the first and second assumptions seems to be a bit ambivalent. As in the "The End of the Transition Paradigm," Carothers argues in *Aiding*

*Democracy Abroad* that USAID has "a democracy template," "a core strategy," "a model of democratization," and "a natural sequence of institutional modeling" (pp. 85–92). Yet in the same volume he concedes that democracy promoters are more sophisticated and nuanced: "At the same time, democracy promoters are facing the fact that democratic transitions often do not follow an orderly sequence. . . .Democracy promoters are identifying various political trajectories that follow political openings and transitional elections: institutional stagnation, backsliding to semiauthoritarianism, electoral breakdown, postconflict recovery, and others. They are beginning to design democracy aid portfolios to fit the specific dynamics and obstacles of these various contexts rather than working on the assumption of a natural sequence" (p. 334).

7. See, for example, USAID, *Constituencies for Reform: Strategic Approaches for Donor-Supported Civic Advocacy* (Washington, D.C.: USAID, February 1996), p. 51; USAID, *Weighing in on the Scales of Justice: Strategic Approaches for Donor-Supported Rule of Law Programs* (Washington, D.C.: USAID, February 1994), p. 12; USAID, *Conducting a DG [Democratic Governance] Assessment: A Framework for Strategy Development* (Washington, D.C.: USAID, November 2000); and *Democracy and Governance Policy*, p. 14.

8. See, for example, Krishna Kumar, "Bullets to Ballots: Electoral Assistance to Postconflict Societies," PN-ACA-900 (Washington, D.C.: USAID, Center for Development Information and Evaluation, 1997); and Krishna Kumar, ed., *Postconflict Elections, Democratization, and International Assistance* (Boulder, Colo.: Lynne Rienner, 1998).

9. Specifically, we need to understand why parties are becoming increasingly marginalized, even reviled, and how we might devise a strategy that will help produce more effective and accountable parties, both as vehicles of contestation and vehicles of governance.

10. See, for example, USAID, *Democracy and Governance: A Conceptual Framework* (Washington, D.C.: USAID, 1998), p. 3.

11. See, for example, the substantial literature employing Max Weber's concept of "ideal types" and the debate over Thomas Kuhn's *Structure of Scientific Revolutions* (Chicago: University of Chicago Press, 1962).

12. USAID, *Conducting a DG Assessment*.

# A Reply to My Critics

## BY THOMAS CAROTHERS

THE APRIL 2002 ISSUE of the *Journal of Democracy* contained four articles on "hybrid regimes," each of which explicitly or implicitly affirmed the main thesis of my article on "The End of the Transition Paradigm." In their estimable democratic fashion, the editors of the *Journal* have here assembled four contrary essays that take me to task in various ways. I wish to thank all four of these dissenters for engaging seriously with my ideas and the editors for giving me this space to reply.

Guillermo O'Donnell charges me with shortchanging the scholarly literature on democratization, and he highlights different ways in which literature does not conform to the transition paradigm that I criticize. In fact, however, there is little real difference between us. My article does not target the scholarly literature on democratization; it is about a set of ideas that many democracy-aid practitioners arrived at and began to apply in the late 1980s and early 1990s. That set of ideas was not derived, as O'Donnell writes, "in good measure" from his 1986 book (coauthored with Philippe Schmitter), *Transitions from Authoritarian Rule*.[1] Rather, as I said in my article, democracy promoters derived the paradigm "principally from their own interpretation of the patterns of democratic change taking place."

As I have written in more detail elsewhere, the scholarly and practitioner halves of the democracy world are noticeably, and probably unfortunately, separate.[2] Democracy promoters occasionally dip into academic writings on democratization but not in any systematic or concerted way. They borrowed a bit from the first wave of transitology literature in the second half of the 1980s, but it was largely a superficial transfer of ideas that got frozen into place around a few general concepts. For the most part, democracy promoters formed their paradigm around their own ideas about democracy and their observation of democratization as it was spreading in the world. On the other side of the fence, very few of the main theorists of democratization have delved in any depth into the world of democracy aid or integrated field-based insights from that domain into their work.

Thus O'Donnell may well be right about the important nuances and advances in the transitology literature from the mid-1980s to the present. But this does not say much about the practitioners' paradigm that I am analyzing. For example, he mentions the important work by Adam Przeworski on the relationship between economics and democracy. Przeworski published his first major book on the subject in 1991.[3] Yet it was not until the end of the 1990s that democracy promoters began exploring these connections in any serious way. The point is that the two worlds have not moved in tandem. In short, although O'Donnell's defense of the transitology literature is well argued, it is peripheral to the central thesis of my article.

Just as Ghia Nodia initially found himself agreeing with most of the points in my article, I had the same experience when I first read his thoughtful reply. But upon a second reading I identified what I believe is the core difference between us. In rejecting my argument that feckless pluralism and dominant-power politics should be understood as alternative (albeit undesirable) outcomes rather than as way stations to democracy, he insists that "the conditions in which these countries [what I call the 'gray-zone countries'] find themselves still *can only be understood in terms of how near or far they are from democracy*" (emphasis added). I am certainly not against holding countries up to established democratic standards and highlighting how they fall short. Such evaluations, however, are of limited utility for understanding many aspects of their political life, such as how they got into such a state and how they might get out.

Consider, for example, Kuwait, Nigeria, Ukraine, and Paraguay. Using the most widely accepted tool for assessing a country's proximity to democracy, the Freedom House survey, all four of these countries are in the same position—a rating of 4 in political rights. Thus, as Nodia would have it, they are the same distance from democracy, and this is the only way their political life should be understood. Yet this rating, while useful for some purposes, tells us very little about many relevant political characteristics, such as the shape and nature of their main political power structures, whether their regimes are decaying, stable, or strengthening, and the prospects for and likely path of future change.

A different way to interpret Nodia's argument is that since democracy is the only broadly legitimate political aspiration in the world today, we have to consider gray-zone countries as transitional countries because that is how they understand themselves. There are two problems, however, with this view. First, many leaders have learned to manipulate the transitional language to pursue political projects that have little to do with democracy, while defending themselves against critics by emphasizing how hard transition is and the need for patience. Second, if a country's leaders or people believe it to be on the path to democracy but concrete signs clearly indicate that it is heading elsewhere, the importance of that self-conception becomes open to doubt.

Nodia argues firmly for preserving the notion of the "path to democracy." But I have not suggested banishing it, only applying it with greater care. I was surprised and disappointed in this regard that Nodia did not address the question of whether he considers his own country, Georgia, to be on the "path to democracy" that he reaffirms. If he does, it would be interesting to hear his description of what defines such a path. If he does not, I would be curious as to how he would characterize Georgian politics without using some of the gray-zone concepts I suggest.

Nodia correctly notes that, unlike the view that Fareed Zakaria expressed in his 1997 article on illiberal democracy, I am not arguing that we should simply give up on democracy as an appropriate goal in many countries.[4] He incorrectly concludes from this fact, however, that I therefore remain "fully within the transition paradigm." He seems to be allowing remarkably little choice: If one believes in the possibility of democracy, one is ipso facto in the transition paradigm. I contend that it is possible to believe in the possibility of democracy while still recognizing that specific countries are not on the path toward it.

**The Practitioners**

Kenneth Wollack is eloquent in his defense of the democracy-aid community, and I certainly agree with him that many democracy promoters are dedicated, skillful people hard at work confronting complex political challenges all over the world. I think I am innocent, however, of his charge that I fail "to provide evidence for the larger claim that a faulty paradigm has undermined the whole endeavor"—largely because I did not make such a claim. I argued that an outdated paradigm is "retarding evolution in the field of democratic assistance," which is scarcely tantamount to saying that the whole endeavor has been vitiated. His overstatement of my position is unfortunately typical of a habit that I have encountered in the democracy-aid community—criticisms of the methods of democracy aid are interpreted as denunciations of the whole enterprise. I think the field of democracy aid is by now well-enough established that this sort of defensiveness is misplaced. I also believe that such defensiveness works against processes of learning and is thereby, I regret to say, retarding evolution in the field of democracy assistance.

I was stopped cold by Wollack's argument that "those who fund and implement democracy programs around the world are as varied as the political environments in which they operate." Democracy aid is dominated by a small number of basically like-minded North American and West European organizations. The programs that most of them have carried out over the years are marked by a tremendous similarity of basic approach and content, notwithstanding certain variations of method and style. The notion that, for example, the National

Democratic Institute for International Affairs, the International Republican Institute, and the International Foundation for Election Systems—three of the most important U.S. democracy-promotion groups—are as diverse and varied in their staffs, managements, boards of directors, ideas, and approaches as the many societies around the world where they work is simply untenable.

Like Nodia, Wollack mistakenly worries that I am in favor of abandoning the concept of democratic transition altogether. But he goes even further to express the concern that acknowledging the shortcomings of the transition paradigm will demoralize democratic activists and deny them their democratic aspirations. Again, this seems a weighty charge against a call for more accurate diagnoses of politically troubled countries. I strongly resist the idea that realistically assessing the political life of the many countries that are adrift after authoritarianism is inherently demoralizing or aspiration-denying. In my experience, citizens of such countries very much prefer that outsiders offer open, hard-edged discussion of the difficult realities they are facing rather than ritualistic incantations of the achievements and promise of democracy.

In his closing paragraph, Wollack provides some advice about what I should say in my future writings, urging me to set forth a more ringing call for increasing democracy aid. I feel obliged, therefore, to try to offer some advice for his future writings as well. I think it would be of wide interest if a representative of a major democracy-aid organization were to write an account that is not a chronicle of success stories but rather a more balanced examination that includes an analysis of the ways the organization has sometimes fallen short— with detailed case studies of the type Wollack recommends to me—and of what has been learned from those less-than-positive experiences. Such an article would be pathbreaking and, I believe, a useful, concrete example of the searching, self-reflective philosophy that Wollack says best describes the outlook of democracy promoters.

Gerald Hyman mounts a hearty defense of USAID's democracy work. Citing various USAID policy documents and official agency declarations, he portrays an organization that is programatically supple, adept at learning from experience, and well beyond any of the conceptual pitfalls I describe. It is a picture of an organization that I and many people around me wish we knew, but unfortunately do not. I note that my article was not intended specifically as a critique of USAID. The transition paradigm I analyze has been present in the work of many democracy-aid providers. USAID is by far the largest supplier of such funds in the world, however, and therefore inevitably tends to figure prominently in any broad discussion of the subject. I also note that my analysis of the transition paradigm is not something that I just made up after a casual perusal of the USAID web site. It is based on my experience over the past 15 years of working on, analyzing, and writing about democracy-aid programs in every region of the world where they are carried out, including many hundreds of formal and informal interviews and conversations with aid practitioners and recipients.

Hyman's central critique of my article is that the transition paradigm I outline is a straw man. In his opinion, to the extent USAID ever followed the paradigm, that time is long over. I received Hyman's reply while traveling in Eastern Europe. The day after I received it I was in a meeting with two people who work for USAID on democracy programs in one of the countries of the region. Early in the meeting they brought up my article. With Hyman's rebuttal fresh in my mind, I braced myself for still more criticism. Instead, they thanked me for writing the article, saying that it had been extremely useful for them in their recent efforts to convince some of their colleagues to move beyond what these two people saw as an outdated set of democracy programs in their country—programs firmly based on the transition paradigm. When I mentioned Hyman's reply and outlined for them the essence of his argument, they waved it away, saying that Washington is far from the field and that no one person in Washington can speak for the realities of USAID's work all over the world.

Therein lies my main reply to Hyman. He is one of a relatively small number of highly experienced democracy specialists at USAID in Washington who have been at the forefront of trying to improve and push ahead USAID's work in this domain. Their work has been valuable and has helped USAID take some important steps forward. But the sophisticated, nuanced understanding of democracy work that they have and that they put into some USAID policy documents and official declarations does not get easily translated into fact in the field. It is revealing in this regard that the evidence Hyman cites for USAID's sophistication in democracy programming is all from policy documents rather than from examples of actual programs.

There are hundreds, probably thousands (if one counts those working at USAID's partner organizations) of people involved in designing and implementing USAID's democracy-assistance programs. They vary tremendously in experience, knowledge, and expertise. For Hyman to talk in confident, blanket terms about a collective "we" in characterizing this world, as when he says, "we long ago moved beyond the 'transition paradigm,'" is not persuasive. The stubborn fact is that what Hyman sees as a straw man, I and other researchers keep meeting, quite alive and well, out in the world. There has certainly been an evolution in some places away from the most mechanical applications of the transition paradigm that were unfortunately all too common in the first half of the 1990s. But this evolution is hardly uniform or complete.

To cite just one recent example, in April, prior to my aforementioned trip to Eastern Europe, I was in a different part of the world and met with the USAID representatives in a country where USAID has been involved in democracy work for some time. They handed me an outline of the USAID democracy strategy in that country. It completely embodied the transition paradigm, starting with the generic strategic objective about democratic participation used by USAID in so many countries, through the four program clusters conforming exactly to USAID's four thematic priorities in democracy and governance work, all the way down to the dispersion of the small amount of available democracy funds among the many standard areas on the traditional democracy checklist. They ruefully acknowledged that the strategy was more a reflection of bureaucratic process than real strategic thinking, but they noted in its defense that one of USAID's top democracy experts had not long ago been out from Washington to help develop it.

Hyman himself makes clear the difficulty of the process of change within USAID even as he seeks to defend it. He mentions the analytic framework developed at USAID for assessing political contexts and developing democracy programs. This framework is a sophisticated tool and a valuable advance, but it has not yet been used in more than half the countries where USAID has been involved in democracy aid. And even where it has been used, it is only just starting to translate into significantly different programming. In sum, Hyman and I share many views about how democracy aid can and should evolve. What we disagree about is how far along USAID is on that path.

## Notes

The Carnegie Endowment gratefully acknowledges the permission of the Johns Hopkins University Press to reprint this article, which originally appeared in the *Journal of Democracy*, vol. 13, no. 3 (July 2002).

1. Guillermo O'Donnell and Philippe C. Schmitter, *Transitions from Authoritarian Rule: Tentative Conclusions about Uncertain Democracies* (Baltimore: Johns Hopkins University Press, 1986).

2. Thomas Carothers, *Aiding Democracy Abroad: The Learning Curve* (Washington, D.C.: Carnegie Endowment for International Peace, 1999), 90–4.

3. Adam Przeworski, *Democracy and the Market: Political and Economic Reforms in Eastern Europe and Latin America* (New York: Cambridge University Press, 1991).

4. Fareed Zakaria, "The Rise of Illiberal Democracy," *Foreign Affairs* 76 (November–December 1997): 22–43.

# CHAPTER SIXTEEN

# Zakaria's Complaint (2003)

FOLLOWING THE PATHS of Samuel Huntington, Francis Fukuyama, Robert Kaplan, and other authors of highly successful "state-of-the-world" articles, Fareed Zakaria has turned his much discussed 1997 *Foreign Affairs* essay, "The Rise of Illiberal Democracy," into a book.[1] With more than five years having elapsed in the passage, his slim volume is well-shielded against the possible charge that it is merely an "instant book." The intervening years also allowed a longer-term evaluation of how his original thesis is holding up.

Zakaria's original article hit a major nerve. Enthusiasm about "the world-wide democratic revolution" was rampant in the 1990s. Perceptively sensing that all was not well in the dozens of celebrated democratic transitions around the world, Zakaria punctured that enthusiasm with a sharp analytic arrow. He asserted that the global rush of democratization into previously undemocratic terrain was a dangerous thing. It was producing, he argued, a rash of illiberal democracies, defined roughly as countries where popularly elected leaders, unconstrained by any well-established institutions or habits of law-based liberalism, were trampling political and civil rights and generally making a hash out of democracy. A much better way to proceed, he said, was for a country first to pass through a sustained period of liberalizing autocracy, with gradual expansion of economic liberalization and the rule of law. Only once well down that road should the dangerous wilds of democracy be braved. Like Huntington's "Clash of Civilizations" and Kaplan's "The Coming Anarchy," Zakaria's article benefited from the inimitable tendency of America's chattering classes periodically to embrace thundering prognostications of gloom and doom as occasional respites from a congenitally optimistic national outlook.

In *The Future of Freedom*, Zakaria reasserts his core thesis and expands its reach. He applies it to Latin America, South Asia, and the Middle East, hitting each of these regional nails with the hammer of his much-admired East Asian model of economic and political development. And he turns his considerable critical faculties to bear on the deleterious consequences of what he believes is excessive democratization in established liberal democracies as well, at least in the United States (contemporary Europe is curiously absent from his *tour d'horizon*). Too much democracy, he charges, is the source of most of America's contemporary ills, from the decline of authority in American Christianity to the sad performance of American accountants at Enron and elsewhere. His analysis of America's problems verges into the realm of broad cultural criticism. It has that seductive but ultimately doubtful appeal of most such sweeping denunciations of the terrible erosion that modernization is inflicting on supposedly noble (and usually exclusionary) social traditions and standards. His arguments about the prospects for democracy in the rest of the world remain more analytically focused.

Zakaria's guiding formula, which can be summarized as "economic liberalization and the rule of law first, democracy later" may make sense in some contexts, but it is hardly the unerring guide he holds it out to be. Consider, for example, his favorite comparison in support of the formula: China versus Russia. He praises China's ruling communists, arguing that, thanks to their economic policies of the last twenty years, China is relatively well-positioned today to begin political liberalization and achieve "an extraordinary transformation toward genuine democracy." In contrast, he mercilessly criticizes Russia's post-1991 path, labeling it "Russia's democratic tragedy."

Perhaps in the late 1990s, when Russia was mired in a severe financial crisis and China's growth was humming along, this view seemed compelling. Today, however, it is less so. Russia is far from the economic basket case Zakaria makes it out to be, having implemented a number of significant reforms and enjoyed several consecutive years of solid growth (helped, but not solely caused, by high oil prices). And though Putin is a reluctant democrat with limited tolerance for opposition, Russia has increasingly rooted institutions of political pluralism and participation. Most of Russia's major transformative tasks—both economic and political—are behind it. In contrast, China's economic miracle is now bogged down in the swamp of vested interests that has accumulated around its static, overcentralized political structures. The Chinese government is still hesitating over the very idea of political liberalization, terrified that even small steps could unleash turmoil. According to Minxin Pei, whose work Zakaria

approvingly cites on Asia's other transitions, China faces an impending governance crisis of state incapacitation resulting from the Communist Party's failings and the absence of political competition.[2] The SARS crisis has only further
laid bare the dangers and brittleness of China's governance practices. In short,
if one asks which of these two countries is more likely to be a stable, functioning democracy twenty years from now, it is not at all obvious that the answer is
China.

Zakaria's application of his thesis to Latin America bounces off a region he
clearly knows only glancingly. He holds up Venezuela's regrettable president,
Hugo Chávez, as an example of the rise of illiberal democracy in the region.
Chávez indeed fits the mold, but his rise cannot be blamed on a rush to democracy without a preparatory period of liberal constitutionalism. Venezuela passed
through more than a hundred years of economic development, constitutionalism and various liberalizing (and nonliberalizing) autocrats before finally achieving democracy in the 1950s. The decay of that democratic system in the 1980s
and 1990s is a sad story, but one that is about irresponsible political elites and
misguided economic policies, not "premature democratization."

More generally, the histories of most Latin American countries are littered
with failed attempts to make a transition from liberal autocracies, even sometimes relatively economically successful ones, to democracy. Although it might
be nice if countries outside East Asia would mimic East Asia's path, many have
tried in one fashion or another and failed miserably. The one positive Latin
American example of movement from a liberalizing autocrat (at least liberal in
the economic sense) to sustained democracy is Chile, an example that Zakaria
invokes repeatedly. But Chile's post-Pinochet democratic success has as much
to do with Chile's long pre-Pinochet history of democracy as it does with the
economic groundwork Pinochet laid. Uruguay also made a successful transition to democracy in the same decade, without a Pinochet-style economic liberalization program as a precursor, drawing upon a similarly long earlier experience with democracy.

Zakaria is too quick to blame a rush to democracy for the rise of strongmen
presidents in many countries. The autocratic leaders in the Caucasus and Central Asia, for example, should be blamed on the legacy of Soviet political rule,
not precipitous elections. Zakaria has a point that in some abrupt transitions
away from dictatorship, it would surely be better to go slow on national elections and try first to build up a base of liberal restraints and the rule of law. But
what to do if the people of the society are pressing for democracy? Should the
U.S. government tell them not to? *Can* it?

Zakaria implies that it is the United States that has pushed the many politically transitional countries around the world in recent decades to launch hastily

into democratization, and that, if we had just held off that pressure, they might be enjoying a beneficial period of step-by-step liberalization. Yet Argentina's generals, Romania's Nicolae Ceausescu, Africa's many postcolonial strongman rulers, and numerous other dictators were not driven from power by the United States. They were pushed out by their own people, people desirous of democracy. And the idea that any of those countries might be better off today if such leaders had stayed around for another decade or two, dabbling in slow liberalization, is deeply misguided.

Deferred democratization, which occurs only after the long, slow achievement of constitutionalism, liberalism, and prosperity, has indeed worked well in some places and at some times, such as in parts of nineteenth-century Europe. The problem with this formula, however, is that the global political culture has changed. For better or worse (and I think much for the better), people all around the world have democratic aspirations. Unprepared though their societies may be for democracy, they yearn for a voice and a vote, not several preparatory generations of mild dictatorship. It might be easy to say, for example, that a country like Nigeria—ethnically divided, poor, lacking the rule of law—is badly positioned for democracy and would benefit from several decades of a firm-handed reformist autocrat. But it was Nigerians themselves who clamored for democracy when General Sani Abacha died in 1998, not a meddlesome United States pushing its own ideas on them. And even if Nigerians were somehow to agree they wanted to put off pluralism and opt for a wise, benign dictator, how likely is it that they would find such an admirable figure, given their repeated experience of authoritarians who promise to be reformists and turn into thugs?

Democracy may inspire people all around the world, but not Fareed Zakaria. He shudders almost visibly at the messiness of elections (which he likes to call "mass plebiscites"—the "mass" conveying his sense of the dangers lurking in the empowerment of the common man). The American Revolution was for him all about the rule of law, not democracy. In an observation that most Americans would find genuinely odd, he declares that the leading symbol of the American political system, and other successful Western political systems, is not democracy but the impartial judge. He returns repeatedly to the tensions that can arise between democracy and liberalism, arguing that, due to precipitous democratization, the two are coming apart. But he misses the central fact that the expansion of democracy around the world in the past twenty years, riddled though it is with shortcomings, has brought with it huge gains in liberty. Gross abuses of political and civil rights in many parts of Latin America, sub-Saharan Africa, central and eastern Europe, and the western parts of the former Soviet Union have dropped dramatically since the arrival of the democratic wave.

The sustained exposition of this book compared to Zakaria's original article also makes much clearer his soft spot for autocrats. The heroes of his narrative are Pakistan's President Pervez Musharraf, Indonesia's former President Suharto, China's communist leaders, Jordan's current and former kings and Tunisia's President Zine Al-Abidine Ben Ali. He gives them the benefit of every doubt. Many readers will be surprised to learn, for example, that Musharraf, whose authoritarian maneuverings made headlines last year, is in fact pursuing "a path of radical political, social, educational, and economic reform." Despite the torture chambers and pervasive, top-level corruption that marked Suharto's rule, he was "far more tolerant" and supportive of the rule of law than Indonesia's shaky but real democracy today. We should be grateful to China's leaders, he argues, for wisely and with great restraint keeping in check a dangerously "nationalistic, aggressive, and intolerant citizenry." And Tunisia's highly repressive police state, recently criticized by Freedom House for "an intensifying campaign of harassment against political opposition," is actually "reasonably open."

The two leaders who draw Zakaria's special ire are not dictators at all but Russia's two elected postcommunist presidents, Boris Yeltsin and Vladimir Putin. Zakaria just cannot say enough bad things about both of them. His bile toward Putin is especially surprising given that Putin's approach of combining economic reform with constrained democracy actually seems in many ways not far from Zakaria's ideal of liberal autocracy. Suharto can brutally suppress political liberties for decades, abuse the legal system for the massive enrichment of himself and his family, and stubbornly refuse to undertake any significant political reforms, yet earn Zakaria's praise as a liberal autocrat. Putin pursues serious economic reforms, steps on, but does not crush, political rights, and undertakes a genuine albeit limited program of rule-of-law reform yet is excoriated as an illiberal democrat. One comes away bewildered by Zakaria's use of the terms "liberal" and "illiberal." One has the nagging feeling that if Putin had just not committed the sin of actually being elected, he would be in Zakaria's pantheon of modernizing strongmen rulers.

*The Future of Freedom* falls short not just in diagnosis but also prescription. In a chapter on Islam in the modern world, Zakaria skillfully analyzes the grievous political plight of the Arab states and debunks some of the sloppy ideas about Islam that have bubbled up in the post–September 11 context. As he emphasizes, there is no generalized problem of democracy in Islamic societies, the problem is the failure of democracy in the Arab world. And although that failure has many roots, much of the blame can be laid at the feet of Arab leaders of the past forty or fifty years. But his prescription for solving the vexing dilemma that has seized much of Washington these days—how to democratize the Arab world?—is much less satisfying. Predictably, he calls for a strong dose of the East Asian elixir: a long period of economic liberalization to be followed only much later with political reform and democratization. Egypt, Zakaria thinks, is where we should start by pressing hard for economic reform.

That sounds good, but it overlooks the inconvenient fact that it is precisely the approach the United States has actually been taking for the last twenty years, to almost no effect. Over and over, the U.S. government has pushed and prodded President Hosni Mubarak to get serious about the economic reform program he initiated in the early 1980s. Halting progress has been made, but major structural reforms simply have not been carried out, and there is little sign they will come anytime soon. Why?

Content with his ringing formula of economics first, democracy later, Zakaria overlooks the fact that it is Egypt's stagnant, semi-authoritarian political system that has undermined efforts on economic reform. The static, patronage-ridden Egyptian state is choked with vested, antireformist economic interests that thrive in the protected political space around Mubarak. Lacking popular legitimacy that could come from genuine democratic processes, Mubarak badly needs the economic levers of reward and punishment that Egypt's statist economic structures give him to co-opt opponents and reward supporters. In an evasion that does deep damage to his central thesis, Zakaria ignores the fundamental conundrum that crops up in so many troubled countries—although economic failures do indeed often undermine efforts at democratization, the lack of democratic reforms often blocks efforts to make progress on economic reforms. The appealing formula of economics first, democracy later melts in the real-world cauldron that demands market reform and democratization now, together, difficult as that may be.

Zakaria's other brief forays into specific policy advice also suffer from a lack of serious examination of what policies the United States actually follows. For example, he bewails the fact that in U.S. dealings with developing countries, "elections trump everything," that Washington will forgive a foreign leader any number of sins as long as he or she is elected. That sounds like a telling critique, but it is a myth. It would certainly be news to Slobodan Milosevic, Aleksandr Lukashenko, Vladimir Meciar, Robert Mugabe, Hugo Chávez, Daniel arap Moi and many other noxious leaders of recent years that their having been elected gave them a free pass from the U.S. government. In the past ten years the United States has often been quite tough on these and other elected leaders it does not like and has sometimes intervened actively in election processes to try to hang them with their own ropes.

Zakaria urges the United States not to foster political change simply through elections but instead to support constitutionalism, the development of competing centers of power, such as strong legislatures and judiciaries, and civil society. But that is exactly what most U.S. democracy-promotion policies and programs already try to do. The percentage of election-related work in the overall pool of U.S. democracy aid has dropped significantly since 1990 to become only a small portion of the overall effort. As with his suggestions for the Middle East, Zakaria recommends mainly what the United States is already doing. His apparent lack of interest in really delving into the question of what U.S. policy actually is leads him to miss a more interesting issue: Given that U.S. and European democracy aid already largely conforms to what he recommends, does the parlous state of democracy in so many countries mean that this approach is incorrect, or that democracy-aid providers are simply being asked to tackle problems of a magnitude out of proportion to the resources given to them?

In the years since the publication of "The Rise of Illiberal Democracy," the course of global political events has made it much clearer that many of the attempted democratic transitions in what Huntington has called democracy's "third wave" are not faring well. Zakaria's article usefully attracted attention to the fact that much was not well in the world of new democracies at a time when few wanted to hear that news. He was also right to highlight the deep connections between economic development and democratic performance, providing a helpful corrective to some wishful thinking by democracy enthusiasts that socioeconomic realities could somehow be factored out of the democratization agenda.

But with the passage of time between article and book, not only has the seriousness of the Third Wave's travails become more apparent, but so has the heterogeneity of the problems that struggling democracies are encountering. Zakaria's diagnosis of illiberal democracy remains interesting and relevant. Some countries do indeed face this syndrome. But it is inadequate as a broadly applicable tool for understanding the dilemmas, dangers, and disappointments afflicting democracies all around the world. The recent near-collapse of Nepal's transition from monarchical rule, Moldova's slide back into protocommunist rule, Guatemala's turgid effort to break free from its military-dominated past, Côte d'Ivoire's tragic lapse into civil war, Albania's persistent political fecklessness, and dozens of other cases of badly troubled democracy have little to do with the phenomenon of illiberal democracy. They reflect a more complex cornucopia of problems and paradoxes, including the challenge of developing meaningful transfers of power in an age of a single dominant economic model, the question of whether the rapid expansion of civil society is overtaking traditional forms of political interest representation, and the devastating reality of the nearly universal collapse in the public credibility of political parties.

In the end, Zakaria's continued insistence in *The Future of Freedom* that the problem is simply too much democracy too soon has the feel of a meritorious, medium-sized idea being stretched much too thin. But this is the frequent flaw of trenchant articles whose success as provocations compel their return as books.

## Notes

The Carnegie Endowment gratefully acknowledges the permission of *The National Interest* to reprint this article, which originally appeared in *The National Interest*, vol. 72 (Summer 2003).

1.  Fareed Zakaria, *The Future of Freedom: Illiberal Democracy at Home and Abroad* (New York: W. W. Norton, 2003).
2.  Minxin Pei, "China's Governance Crisis," *Foreign Affairs* (September–October 2002).

# *Into the*
# *Middle East*

ONE REGION WAS conspicuously absent from the democratic wave of the
1980s and 1990s and from the priority target list of Western democracy promoters. That region, of course, was the Middle East. Yet quite suddenly in the
last two years, the U.S. government has shifted gears and now ranks a democratic transformation of the Middle East as one of its top foreign policy goals.
Europe has joined in, disagreeing with the United States on some important
elements of Middle East policy, but agreeing with the broader idea of making a
major pro-democratic push there.

The intervening factor of course was September 11, 2001. In its search for
explanations and solutions to the threat of terrorism, the U.S. policy community reached the conclusion that the political stagnation and repression prevalent in the Arab world was a primary underlying cause of violent, anti-Western
Islamic radicalism. From that conclusion a new policy credo emerged: Promoting democracy in the Middle East is necessary to eliminate the "roots of terrorism." The war in Iraq was, at least for some Bush aides, a first step in a new
policy of regional transformation. A significant motivation for some of the Bush
officials who pushed early on for the war and for some of the war's strongest
backers was the belief that by ousting Saddam Hussein, the United States could
bring democracy to Iraq and that a democratic Iraq would serve as a political
model for other Arab countries. But American's new pro-democratic policy
toward the Middle East is much broader than just the effort in Iraq; it now

consists of a host of diplomatic initiatives, aid programs, and other measures aimed at the entire region.

This sudden rush of U.S. and European attention to the lack of democracy in the Middle East is welcome and much overdue. Yet the policy challenge is unusually daunting: Well-entrenched authoritarian regimes dominate the region, and what political reform trends exist are mostly mild efforts at political liberalization designed more to safeguard against the possibility of deep-reaching political change rather than to encourage it. Moreover, the United States faces a serious problem of credibility in presenting itself to Arab audiences as a pro-democratic actor, given the U.S. government's long support for many of the authoritarian regimes in the region and what most Arabs believe is insufficient U.S. support for the political aspirations of the Palestinians.

The three essays in this section seek to bring some perspective and comparative insights to this new policy agenda. The first, "Democratic Mirage in the Middle East," I co-authored with my colleagues in the Democracy and Rule of Law Project at Carnegie during the run-up to the Iraq war. It is a response to what we viewed as excessive optimism on the part of some about the likelihood that an invasion of Iraq would produce a rapid democratization of Iraq and a subsequent democratic wave in the region. In 2002 and 2003, meetings in Washington, both inside and outside the government, on how to promote democracy in the Middle East began multiplying. Attending some of these sessions, I was struck how little specific thought most enthusiasts of the new democracy imperative had given to how democratization might actually occur in most Arab societies and what outside actors could actually do to promote such processes of change. "Is Gradualism Possible? Choosing a Strategy for Promoting Democracy in the Middle East" represents my attempt to outline some basic underpinnings of a pro-democracy strategy. The final essay, "Democracy: Terrorism's Uncertain Antidote" is an overall assessment of the Bush administration's overall new line on democracy in the Middle East.

# CHAPTER SEVENTEEN

# Democratic Mirage in the Middle East (2002)

BY MARINA OTTAWAY, THOMAS CAROTHERS,
AMY HAWTHORNE, AND DANIEL BRUMBERG

FROM WITHIN THE Bush administration and on the editorial pages of America's major newspapers, a growing chorus of voices is expounding an extraordinarily expansive, optimistic view of a new democratizing mission for America in the Middle East. The rhetoric has reached extraordinary heights. We are told that toppling Saddam Hussein would allow the United States to rapidly democratize Iraq and by so doing unleash a democratic tsunami across the Islamic World. Some believe that a pro-democracy campaign in the Middle East could produce a democratic boom comparable in magnitude and significance to the one produced by the end of the Cold War.

It is good that the question of democracy in the Middle East is finally receiving serious attention. Although the United States has, over the years, offered tepid encouragement for political reform in the Arab world and funded some democracy aid programs there, past efforts were timid, erratic, and not reinforced at senior diplomatic levels. For far too long, Washington coasted on the complacent and erroneous assumption that the stability of the autocratic regimes of the Middle East could at least protect U.S. national security. Now the pendulum has swung. U.S. officials no longer see these regimes as bulwarks against Islamic extremists but consider them responsible for the discontent that fuels terrorism and, in the case of Saudi Arabia, for the financing of extremist groups. But obstacles to democracy in the Middle East are many and go well beyond the autocratic nature of the present regimes to span a host of economic, sociopolitical, and historical factors. These realities do not mean the Middle

East will never democratize or that the United States has no role to play. But they do mean that the path will be long, hard, and slow and that American expectations and plans should be calibrated accordingly.

## Democratizing Iraq

It is hard not to feel the attraction of the tsunami idea—the tantalizing notion that with one hard blow in Iraq the United States can unleash a tidal wave of democracy in a region long known for resistance to such change. But can it? The United States can certainly oust Saddam Hussein and install a regime that is less repressive domestically and less hostile to U.S. interests. But democracy will not soon be forthcoming.

Experience in other countries where the United States has forcibly removed dictators or helped launch major postconflict democratic reconstruction indicates a strong need for caution. In Haiti, for example, the 1994 U.S. invasion and the subsequent large-scale reconstruction effort have not led to democracy but instead to political chaos, renewed repression, and dismal U.S.–Haiti relations. In post-Dayton Bosnia, the truly massive international reconstruction effort has produced peace and some socioeconomic gains, but only a tenuous political equilibrium that even six years later would collapse if international forces pulled out. Panama post–U.S. invasion might be construed as a more positive case, with post-Noriega politics having achieved some degree of pluralism. But Panama already had some genuine experience with pluralism before Noriega rose to power, and even so Panamanian politics today, though not dictatorial, are still mired in corruption, public disillusionment, and fecklessness. It should be noted that all these countries are small, making even forceful intervention manageable. Iraq, with its 23 million inhabitants, would require an intervention on a totally different scale.

The example of Afghanistan is especially sobering. Despite widespread optimism of the initial post-Taliban period and the Bush administration's ringing promises to lead the democratic reconstruction, the political situation in Afghanistan today is troubled and uncertain. The administration's failure to back up its promises with a genuine commitment to Afghanistan's reconstruction will badly undercut similar promises made about Iraq.

Like Afghanistan, Iraq is a country torn by profound ideological, religious, and ethnic conflicts. Before democratization can even begin, the United States would have to assemble a power-sharing agreement among ethnic Kurds, Shiites, and Sunni Muslims. Because no obvious leader is waiting in the wings and the exiled Iraqi opposition is chronically divided, Washington would have to provide the political and, most importantly, military and security infrastructure necessary for holding a new government together. In short, the United States would have to become engaged in nation building on a scale that would dwarf any other such effort since the reconstruction of Germany and Japan after World War II. And it would have to stay engaged not just years, but decades, given the depth of change required to make Iraq into a democracy. Thus far the Bush administration has given no indication that it is ready to commit to such a long-term, costly endeavor. All this does not mean that Iraq can never become democratic. But the idea of a quick and easy democratic transformation is a fantasy.

## Tsunami?

Equally doubtful is the idea that a regime change in Iraq would trigger a democratic tsunami in the Middle East. The notion that the fabled "Arab street" would respond to the establishment of a U.S.-installed, nominally democratic Iraqi regime by rising up in a surge of pro-democratic protests, toppling autocracy after autocracy, and installing pro-Western, pluralist regimes is far-fetched. No one can predict with any certainty what the precise regional consequences of a U.S. action would be, but they would likely have as many or more negative than positive effects on the near-term potential for democracy.

For example, an invasion would very likely intensify the anti-Americanism already surging around the region, strengthening the hands of hard-line political forces. Autocratic Arab regimes that refused to support the American war effort could benefit from a wave of Arab nationalism and find their position strengthened, at least for a period. Domestic advocates of reform would come under suspicion as unpatriotic. Conversely, by supporting the invasion, several autocratic regimes, including Saudi Arabia and Egypt, might win a reprieve from any new U.S. pressure to democratize.

The formation of a new, more moderate regime in Iraq would unlikely have the inspirational effect some predict. Many Arabs, rather than looking to Iraq as a model, would focus on the fact that Iraq was "liberated" through Western intervention, not by a popular Iraqi movement. One powerful current in today's regional discourse emphasizes liberation from excessive Western interference in Arab affairs more than liberation from undemocratic leaders.

As to possible ramifications for the future of Palestine, Ariel Sharon's government in Israel would likely view an American invasion of Iraq as an invitation to skirt the statehood issue. Unless the Bush administration shows the political will to push now for a two-state solution—a very unlikely scenario given the close links between Israeli hard-liners and administration hawks—victory in Iraq would more likely postpone than advance the creation of a democratic Palestine.

Domino democratization does sometimes occur, as in Latin America and Eastern Europe in the 1980s and 1990s. But while external influences may increase the chance of an initial change in government, what happens next depends on internal conditions. This was certainly the case in the former Soviet Union, where what at first seemed like a wave of democracy petered out in the face of deep-seated domestic obstacles. Today most former Soviet republics are autocracies.

## Conditions Matter: Middle East Realities

Even if the United States ousted Saddam Hussein and vigorously pursued political reform in the region, democratic results would be highly unlikely. Such a policy would certainly shake up the region, but the final outcome in each country would owe much more to domestic factors than to the vigor of U.S. and European reformist zeal. One of the lessons of more than a decade of democracy promotion around the world is that outsiders are usually marginal players. They become the central determinant of political change only if they are willing to intervene massively, impose a de facto protectorate, and stay for an indefinite, long term. No matter what happens in Iraq, such forceful intervention is unthinkable in most Middle East countries.

The Middle East today lacks the domestic conditions that set the stage for democratic change elsewhere. It does not have the previous experience with democracy that facilitated transitions in Central Europe. Even Egypt, which in the early part of the twentieth century had a national bourgeoisie committed to the values of liberal democracy, opted for autocracy fifty years ago. Quite a few countries in the region—Algeria, Egypt, Jordan, and Morocco among them—are liberalized autocracies whose leaders have skillfully used a measure of state-monitored political openness to promote reforms that appear pluralistic but function to preserve autocracy. Through controlled elections, divide-and-rule tactics, state interference in civil society organizations, and the obstruction of meaningful political party systems, these regimes have created deeply entrenched ruling systems that are surprisingly effective at resisting democratic change.

Nor has the Middle East experienced the prolonged periods of economic growth and the resulting dramatic changes in educational standards, living standards, and life styles that led Asian countries like Taiwan and South Korea to democratic change. The picture is instead one of socioeconomic deterioration. Even in the richest oil-producing countries, oil export revenues are no longer sufficient to subsidize rapidly growing populations at previous levels. The population of Saudi Arabia, for example, was less than 6 million in 1974 at the time of the first oil boom, but it is now 16 million and growing at one of the highest rates in the world. Through state control of the economy, furthermore, regimes have purchased the support, or at least the quiescence, of key sectors of the citizenry.

Moreover, countries of the Middle East do not benefit from a positive "neighborhood effect," the regional, locally grown pressure to conform that helped democratize Latin America. On the contrary, neighborhood norms in the Middle East encourage repressive, authoritarian regimes.

Beyond these daunting obstacles, at least three issues complicate the achievement of democracy in the Middle East:

**Islamism.** The issue is not whether Islam and democracy are incompatible in an absolute sense. Like Christianity and Judaism, Islam is far too complex a religion, with too many schools of thought, for the question even to make sense. Rather, the issue is the existence in all Middle Eastern countries, and indeed in all countries with a substantial Moslem population, of both legal and clandestine political movements that use illiberal interpretations of Islam to mobilize their followers. Since these "Islamist" movements enjoy considerable grassroots support and local authenticity, they are most likely to benefit from democratic openings. Truly free and fair elections in any country of the Middle East would likely assure Islamist parties a substantial share of the vote, or possibly even a majority, as would have happened in Algeria in 1992 had the elections not been cancelled. Democratization ironically raises the possibility of bringing to power political parties that might well abrogate democracy itself. This is a different version of the old Cold War–era fears: Communist parties in Western Europe and elsewhere would come to power through elections only to impose radical change. However, continuing to exclude or marginalize Islamist political participation would doom democracy by silencing a voice that resonates with an important segment of the public. Doing so would only provide governments with a justification for maintaining excessive controls over the entire political sphere, thereby stunting the development of other popular forces. Many governments, such as those in Algeria, Jordan, Lebanon, Morocco, Turkey, and Yemen, have tried to skirt this dilemma by giving Islamists a chance to participate in politics while at the same time preventing them from actually assuming political power, but this solution also augurs poorly for democracy.

**Conflict with Israel.** Resentment against the state of Israel, particularly against the Israeli occupation of the West Bank and Gaza, creates a measure of solidarity between Arab leaders and their citizens that is exploited regularly by autocrats to deflect attention from their own shortcomings. Until there is a two-state solution of the Israeli–Palestinian conflict that gives security and dignity to both parties, resentment will infuse all aspects of Arab politics and obscure the question of democracy.

**Perceptions of the United States.** There is a widespread perception in the Middle East that the Bush administration is embracing the cause of democracy promotion not out of real commitment, but because doing so provides a convenient justification for American intervention in Iraq and the acceptance of the Israeli reoccupation of the West Bank. Unconditional support of Israel, combined with the Sharon government's publicly stated objective of deferring Palestinian statehood, feeds a widespread feeling that the U.S. government cannot be trusted. America's long support of Arab autocracies adds to this perception, thus undermining its credibility as an advocate of change in the Middle East.


### Beyond the Mirage

The United States should promote democracy in the Middle East recognizing that quick change is a mirage. The goals must be initially modest, and the commitment to change long term.

The core elements of a democracy-oriented policy are not hard to identify: sustained, high-level pressure on Arab states to respect political and civil rights and to create or widen genuine political space; clear, consistent pressure on Arab states to carry out pro-democratic institutional, legal, and constitutional changes; and increased democracy aid that bolsters democracy activists, engages seriously with the challenge of political party development, nurtures efforts to develop the rule of law, supports serious proponents of pro-democratic institutional reforms, and supports a growing range of civil society actors, including moderate Islamists.

In the past several months, the State Department has started to frame such an effort and commit new funds to it. This new policy framework will require considerable additional high-level attention and wider support within the administration if it is not to be a futile quick fix. A serious program of long-term support for Middle East democracy would need to follow these guidelines:

- **Do not reflexively attempt to marginalize Islamist groups.** Differentiate instead between the truly extremist organizations that must be isolated because they are committed to violence and those amenable to working legally to achieve their goals. Develop strategies to encourage political processes in which moderate Islamists, along with other emerging forces, can compete fairly and over time gain incentives to moderate their illiberal ideologies. To do this, the United States needs to acquire a much better understanding of the relevant organizations in each country. It will not be easy and it entails some risk. But the only means of containing dangerous extremist groups without perpetuating wholesale repression is to open the door of legal political activity to the more moderate organizations.

- **Do not overemphasize support for westernized nongovernmental organizations and individuals with impeccable liberal credentials but little influence in their societies.** Democracy promoters need to engage as much as possible in a dialogue with a wide cross-section of influential elites: mainstream academics, journalists, moderate Islamists, and members of the professional associations who play a political role in some Arab countries, rather than only the narrow world of westernized democracy and human rights advocates.

- **Do not confuse a "sell America" campaign with democracy promotion.** The U.S. government has launched a major public relations campaign to burnish America's image in the Arab world. Whatever the value of this much-discussed effort, it has little to do with the politically nuanced task of pressuring governments on human rights and institutional reforms, and of supporting key civil groups and the like. Movement toward democracy and movement toward a more positive view of American culture and society are not synonymous.

- **Do not support lackluster institutional reform programs—such as with stagnant parliaments and judiciaries—in lieu of real political reform.** Push the liberalized autocracies of the region, such as in Bahrain, Egypt, Kuwait, Jordan, and Lebanon, beyond the superficial political reforms they use to sustain themselves. This will require pressuring such states to undertake true political restructuring, allow the development of political parties, and open up more space for political contestation.

- **Account for major differences in political starting points and potential for political change.** Shape policies accordingly. Be clear about the goal in each country: Regime change, slow liberalization, and democratization are not the same thing. Policies to achieve one goal are not necessarily appropriate for the others. In particular, a sudden regime change would probably make democratization a more remote prospect for many countries because it would too quickly tip the balance in favor of the groups that are best organized and enjoy grassroots support, Islamist organizations in most cases.

- **Review carefully everything we have done so far in the region in the name of democracy promotion.** The United States has spent more than $250 million on democracy programs in the Middle East in the past decade with little impact. Understanding the weaknesses of these prior efforts is particularly important in Egypt and the Palestinian territories, recipients of the largest amounts of such aid. Democracy assistance must not translate into more patronage for Arab governments or, conversely, support for organizations that are truly marginal in their own societies.

The idea of instant democratic transformation in the Middle East is a mirage. The fact that the Bush administration has suddenly changed its mind about the importance of democracy in the Middle East has not changed the domestic political equation in any country of the region. Furthermore, the United States has limited leverage in most Arab countries. In other regions, the United States, together with Europe and international organizations, often used the lever of economic assistance to force political reform on reluctant governments. But oil-rich countries do not receive aid. Poor countries in the region do, but the United States can hardly afford to use this aid as a weapon for political reform without jeopardizing other interests. The United States already wants a lot from Arab states. It wants help in the war on terrorism. It wants their oil. It wants cooperation in finding a solution to the Israeli–Palestinian conflict. It wants access to military installations to wage war on Iraq. It cannot afford to antagonize the very regimes whose cooperation it seeks. The United States will be forced to work with existing regimes toward gradual reform—and this is a good thing. If a tidal wave of political change actually came to pass, the United States would not be even remotely prepared to cope with the resulting instability and need for large-scale building of new political systems.

### Note

Originally published as Carnegie Policy Brief 20 (October 2002).

# CHAPTER EIGHTEEN

# Is Gradualism Possible?
# Choosing a Strategy for Promoting Democracy in the Middle East
# (2003)

THE SEPTEMBER 11, 2001, terrorist attacks against the United States have led George W. Bush's administration to reassess America's traditional acceptance of Arab autocracies as useful security partners and to engage more seriously than any previous administration with the issue of whether and how the United States can promote democracy in the Middle East. The administration's post–September 11 declarations and actions on democracy in the region have thus far followed two distinct lines, one hard and one soft. The hard line aims at regime change in countries with governments hostile to the United States. The ouster of Saddam Hussein was primarily motivated by U.S. security concerns, but some administration officials and policy experts close to the administration were also attracted by the chance to try to create democracy in Iraq and to stimulate the destabilization (and, some people hope, the democratization) of other hostile regimes in the region, notably in Iran and Syria. The soft line is directed at the Arab governments with which the United States has friendly relations. It seeks to put the United States in the role of encouraging and facilitating gradual transitions to democracy in the region, through a combination of increased aid, especially democracy-related aid, and diplomatic engagement.

As the United States attempts to develop this soft line into a workable strategy of fostering democratic change throughout the region, it confronts two major complications with regard to its own role (leaving aside the enormous difficulties inherent in trying to promote democracy in a region rife with so many formidable obstacles to such change). First, the United States lacks credibility as a pro-democratic actor. This stems from America's long-standing support for nondemocratic regimes in the region, Arab perceptions that Washington undervalues the rights of Palestinians, and various other factors.[1] Second, there is the stubborn fact that the friendly Arab autocrats serve significant American economic and security interests, and it is not clear that more democratic successor regimes would be as helpful to the United States. Beyond these two issues, however, lies a critical question that has received inadequate attention: What would a gradualist strategy for democracy in the Arab world actually be in practice?

To date, the soft line lacks definition. As State Department and U.S. Agency for International Development (USAID) officials have searched for ways to step up U.S. efforts to promote democracy in the Middle East, they have tended to put forward many ideas. All of these various ideas are appealing to one group or another in the U.S. policy community but do not necessarily add up to a coherent strategy—promoting women's rights, bolstering civil society, revitalizing education, fostering good governance, strengthening the rule of law, supporting decentralization, and so forth.

Looking at this growing domain of activities and initiatives, it is possible to see several competing strategies at work. This paper identifies and assesses these diverse strategies, examines the question of whether they constitute a coherent whole, and identifies the key choice concerning strategy that lies directly ahead.

### Political Blockage

Before discussing the contending strategies, it is useful to review the basic political situation in the region. In a small number of Arab states—Libya, Saudi Arabia, Syria, Tunisia, and the United Arab Emirates—the level of political repression is so high that there are few entry points available to the United States for programs to promote democracy. The United States could exert diplomatic pressure for political reform in these countries, but unless Washington were to back up such actions with much more substantial forms of coercive leverage, these dictatorial regimes would be unlikely to loosen their hold on power. An exception might be Saudi Arabia, where the United States, due to its long-standing close ties to the Saudi government, might have at hand some levers of real influence to encourage progress on the recently announced program of political reforms.

A majority of Arab states—Algeria, Bahrain, Egypt, Jordan, Kuwait, Lebanon, Morocco, Oman, Qatar, and Yemen—are not outright dictatorships but semi-authoritarian regimes or, as some analysts prefer, partially liberalized autocracies. U.S. (and European) efforts to promote democracy are primarily directed toward these countries. Their governments allow a certain amount of political space. In some of them, opposition parties are legal and compete in legislative elections, and independent civil society groups are allowed to exist. In others (that is, most of the Gulf states), neither parties nor independent nongovernmental organizations (NGOs) are allowed, but citizens nevertheless enjoy a limited degree of political freedom and there is some open political competition. In all of these semi-authoritarian countries, the central power holders—whether they are presidents or monarchs—remain outside the directly contested political space.

As Daniel Brumberg has argued, the political liberalization these regimes have pursued is quite different from democratization, and it would be a mistake to assume any easy or natural path from liberalization to democratization.[2] The regimes have engaged in limited, often sporadic political liberalization to relieve accumulated domestic political pressure and gain some reformist legitimacy. The reforms are a means of preserving their hold on power, not of creating democracy. That is to say, the reforms are not aimed at creating a process that would lead to the leaders eventually having to risk giving up power to some elected alternative. As Brumberg notes, liberalization in the Arab world tends to go a certain distance and then get stuck, resulting in the widespread regional syndrome of political blockage, or what he calls the trap of liberalized autocracy.

The state of the political opposition in these countries is a key factor in the partial liberalization trap. In most of these countries, the opposition falls into two parts. One part, by far the weaker of the two, consists of political activists associated with nationalist or secular traditions who advocate some liberal political ideas and whom Westerners usually call "the democrats." In most of these countries, this part of the opposition is politically weak, is unable to unite in a single party or coalition, lacks a strong base among everyday citizens, and is constantly in danger of being co-opted by the government. The stronger part of the opposition consists of Islamist forces, of diverse degrees of fundamentalism or radicalism. They tend to be well organized, dedicated, and have a significant base in the citizenry due to their network of social programs in education, health, and other services.

The willingness of many of the Islamist forces to accept a democratic political framework as something more than just a means of gaining power is uncertain at best. Their ultimate goals are even more uncertain. Arab governments use this fact—sometimes legitimately, sometimes cynically—as a justification for not further opening the political system. In turn, the continued exclusion of many Islamist groups from the inner circles of power fuels their own political radicalism, creating a negative cycle of political action and reaction that only reinforces the basic political blockage.

A few of these semi-authoritarian Arab regimes, such as Bahrain, Morocco, and perhaps Yemen, are still moving ahead with liberalizing reforms. A few others, including Egypt and Jordan, have recently been drifting backward, although in the wake of the Iraq war they and others are making some new reformist signals, seeking to gain favor in Washington. Yet all are basically stuck in a political state several steps away from authoritarianism but still very far from democracy.

## The Gradualist Scenario

At the core of any search for a strategy to promote democracy in the Middle East is the question of what transition scenario the promoters envisage. How are these semi-authoritarian regimes actually supposed to democratize? Despite all the talk in the past year about Washington's newfound desire to foster democracy in the region, there has been notably little real discussion of what the process of going from point A (blocked semi-authoritarianism) to point B (democracy) might look like.

Experience from other regions indicates that, very generally speaking, there are two paths from authoritarianism (or semi-authoritarianism) to democracy. On one path, a nondemocratic country may undergo a controlled, top-down process of iterative political change in which political space and contestation are progressively broadened to the point that democracy is achieved. On the other path, the accumulated failures of an authoritarian or semi-authoritarian regime may provoke a loss of political legitimacy, which leads to the regime being driven out of power (by spontaneous public demonstrations, an organized opposition movement, or disenchanted political elites) and to an attempt to create a democratic system to take the place of the discredited, ousted regime.

Given that many Western policy makers worry about what political forces might take over if Arab governments experienced regime collapse, the gradualist scenario is undoubtedly much more attractive to most. Presumably, it is the overall goal of most Western efforts to promote democracy in the region. It must be noted, however, that the collapse scenario has been much more common around the world than the gradual success scenario. Only a handful of countries—including Chile, Mexico, Taiwan, and South Korea (though in South Korea there was much assertive citizen activism along the way)—have managed to move to democracy through a top-down, gradualist process of political opening, in which the dictatorial regime gradually changed its stripes and left power through an electoral process. But dozens of countries in Asia, Eastern Europe, Latin America, the former Soviet Union, and sub-Saharan Africa have seen their attempted democratic transitions of the past twenty years initially defined by a crash—the crash of the incumbent dictatorial regime.

One principal characteristic of the successful gradualist transitions was that they were built on economic success. In each country, growth and development created an independent business sector and a growing middle class with an interest in and capacity to fight for a greater political say in their own affairs. The economic success also tended to moderate the opposition and undercut extremist alternatives, thereby giving the ruling elite the self-confidence to keep moving toward greater political openness.

Another critical feature of these transitions is that the process of political change was eminently political. That is to say, it did not consist only or even primarily of the step-by-step expansion of independent civil society and the technocratic reform of governing institutions. Elections were crucial to the process—not just local or legislative elections but also elections in which opposition parties were allowed to compete for the central positions of political power. In Mexico and Taiwan, elections were for years manipulated in favor of the ruling party. But over time, the elections were made fairer, and when the opposition eventually managed to win, the rulers respected the results.

On the basis of the record of experience, it is evident that though the gradualist scenario is clearly more attractive to most Western policy makers, it is difficult and has been only rarely achieved around the world. Nevertheless, the most likely alternative in the Arab world—semi-authoritarian regimes continuing to remain politically stagnant, breeding increasingly radical and empowered opposition forces, leading to eventual regime collapse and ensuing political turbulence—is unattractive enough that a gradualist strategy of promoting Arab democracy needs to be clearly identified and seriously pursued. So far, it appears that the U.S. government's efforts to promote gradualist transitions in the Arab world fit into one of three different strategies: focusing on economic reform, indirectly promoting democracy, or directly supporting democracy.

## Focusing on Economic Reform

Some U.S. officials—especially specialists who have worked in or followed the region for many years—are wary of more direct political approaches and instead recommend an "economics-first" strategy. In this view, the core driver of positive political change is most likely to be economic progress. Such progress would help a truly independent private sector emerge and shrink the corporatist states that predominate in the region, which would in turn bolster a more independent, vital civil society and media as well as competing political elites less vulnerable to co-optation and less prone to base their appeal on the widespread sense of societal failure and frustration. Greater wealth would also spawn a larger, more independent middle class with access to more travel and education and a wider range of political ideas.

In this view, therefore, the United States should concentrate its pro-reform energies in the economic domain. The prescribed economic reforms are the standard market-oriented measures that the United States and the international financial institutions advocate around the world—more privatization, fiscal reform, banking reform, tax reform, investment liberalization, and so forth. In this vein, the Bush administration has recently decided to make a major push on free trade agreements with Arab governments and has articulated the vision of a U.S.–Middle East free trade area.

The economics-first approach has several significant points of attraction. The underlying rationale is solid—there is no question that economic success does tend to make democratization more likely. Moreover, such an approach does not put the United States in the awkward, and usually resented, position of having to exert political pressure on friendly Arab governments. Economic reform is a message that is somewhat more palatable to Arab elites, and it is a subject on which the United States, due to its own economic success, has some credibility—in contrast to the serious problem of credibility plaguing U.S. declarations regarding democracy. At the same time, it should be noted that Western pushes for structural adjustment and other neoliberal reforms have been controversial and unpopular in some Arab societies (especially in those without a cushion of oil production).

Yet this approach has several serious potential limitations beyond the frequent public unpopularity of the recommended economic reform measures. The United States has already been pressing many Arab governments for years or even decades (for example, Egypt) to carry out market reforms, with only very limited success. Some governments have made progress on macroeconomic reforms, such as reducing fiscal deficits, but almost all have fallen badly short on the necessary institutional and microeconomic reforms, such as banking reform, tax reform, and modernization of the state.

Carrying out such reforms would entail a major reshaping of the way Arab states operate and their relationship with their own societies. These states have failed to follow through on such reforms out of a lack of will to confront deeply entrenched, politically protected, anti-reformist interests and a lack of desire to give up the political levers of control that statist economic structures provide. Although the idea that economic change should proceed political change is very appealing, the sticky fact remains that the lack of political reform and political accountability is precisely what undermines efforts to motivate Arab governments to undertake far-reaching economic structural reform.

Moreover, even if Arab governments actually implemented the full set of recommended market reforms, there is no guarantee that high growth and sustainable economic development would result. Many countries throughout the developing world have attempted to achieve the East Asian–style economic breakthroughs (which themselves were not really built on the kind of market reform prescriptions contained in the "Washington Consensus"). Very few have succeeded. South America is a sobering example of a region that in the 1990s accepted and implemented a significant number of the recommended market reforms yet has experienced only modest growth and is now facing political turmoil and decay rather than democratic consolidation.

Even if Arab governments actually did get serious about market reforms and those reforms led to growth and development, the positive political payoff might be at least decades away. In East Asia, the link between economic success and political change took twenty to thirty years to develop. Many observers concerned about the political viability of stagnant Arab regimes doubt that, given the rising demographic pressures and consequent political pressures, these regimes will be able to hold out that long.

**Indirectly Promoting Democracy**

The second identifiable U.S. strategy for stimulating gradualist Arab political transitions consists of promoting better governance and other state reforms as well as expanded and strengthened civil societies. These types of activities can be considered indirect promotion of democracy because they do not tackle the core processes of political contestation. Proponents of this strategy are primarily found in USAID (which began sponsoring such efforts in the region in the mid-1990s), the State Department (in the Bureau for Democracy, Human Rights, and Labor and the democracy promotion group in the Bureau for Near East Affairs), and some of the democracy promotion organizations that operate with U.S. funding. The main tool of this approach is assistance for reforming governance and developing civil society (typically sponsored by USAID and now also by the State Department under its new Middle East Partnership Initiative). U.S. policy makers have increasingly tried in the past year or two to complement such aid with diplomatic pressure on Arab governments to take seriously the challenge of improving governance and to give a real place to an independent civil society.

The most common types of work on reforming governance and the state include the following:

- strengthening the rule of law, especially through judicial reform;
- strengthening parliaments, through efforts to build better internal capacity and bolster constituency relations;
- reducing state corruption, through anticorruption commissions, legislative rationalization, and advocacy campaigns; and
- promoting decentralization, through training for local government officials and legislative actions to increase the authority of local governments.

Programs to expand civil society often consist of

- funding for NGOs devoted to public-interest advocacy, such as on human rights, the environment, and anticorruption;
- support for women's rights organizations;
- strengthening independent media; and
- underwriting formal and informal efforts to advance democratic civic education.

Such indirect aid for democracy in the Arab world has several attractive aspects. All of these types of work unquestionably touch on areas of Arab sociopolitical life that need improvement. They are a collection of what Western aid providers and policy makers tend to consider "good things" that they believe should have relevance in every region of the world. Moreover, these sorts of activities often find a narrow but real response in the host societies, heartening democracy promoters and persuading them of the value of their work. Even if there is blockage at the central political level, there may well be, for example, some judges interested in trying to improve judicial efficiency, some decent local politicians eager to learn how to better serve their constituents, or some NGO leaders with admirable talents and courage. And the democracy aid community has a well-established capacity to deliver this kind of assistance. If a U.S. embassy or USAID mission in a country wants to develop a broad portfolio of indirect aid for democracy, the mechanisms exist to do so fairly easily and quickly, provided sufficient funds are made available.

A further attraction—at least from the point of view of U.S. officials wary of stepping on the toes of friendly Arab governments—is that most of these kinds of democracy programs can be initiated (though not necessarily successfully completed) without irritating host governments. Most Arab governments are willing to tolerate these sorts of activities, within limits. They may hope that the governance programs will render the state more capable of solving citizens' problems and burnish their own legitimacy as reformist regimes, even as they drag their feet on the necessary institutional changes. They are less likely to be fond of the civil society activities but tend to put up with them, as long as such efforts are not too assertive, do not help Islamist groups, and generally give host governments some control over which groups receive the foreign support.

The nonthreatening nature of indirect aid for democracy is attractive to U.S. officials but also a sign of the central weakness of this approach. Valuable though this aid can be, there is a danger that U.S. policy makers eager to show that the United States is taking seriously the challenge of Middle Eastern democracy will expect too much from it. Efforts to improve governance and to broaden civil society work best in countries that are actually attempting to democratize—that is, where an authoritarian government has been replaced with a new elected government or else has made a decision to move seriously toward a real democratic process. These efforts are designed as ways to *further* democratic consolidation, *not* as fundamental drivers of democratization itself. They can certainly be attempted in countries engaged in limited political liberalization. But in such contexts, they are likely to fit within the boundaries of that political arrangement, perhaps widening the boundaries a bit but not altering the basic political equation. They may in fact help strengthen semi-authoritarian regimes by giving frustrated citizens the impression that important reforms are taking place, thereby bleeding off a certain amount of accumulated internal pressure for change.

To put it more bluntly, adaptable, long-surviving semi-authoritarian regimes such as those in Egypt, Jordan, and Morocco are masters at absorbing liberalizing reforms without really changing their core political structures. In such contexts, it is very possible that outside democracy promoters can work for years helping to increase judicial efficiency, augment the capacities of parliamentarians, train local mayors, nourish civic advocacy, foster greater women's rights, and promote more democratic civic education without contributing to a basic change of regime type.

### Directly Supporting Democracy

Although limited liberalization in the Arab world has thus far stopped well short of real democratization, a bridge between liberalization and democratization is not inconceivable. Building such a bridge, however, requires governments to take some important steps:

- moving toward broad, consistent respect for political and civil rights;
- opening up the domain of political contestation to all political forces that agree to play by the democratic rules of the game;

- obeying the rules of fair political contestation (above all, ceasing to rig or otherwise manipulate elections); and
- reducing the reserved political space (that is, expanding the reach of political contestation to include the country's central political power holders).

If most or all of these bridge-building steps are being taken, a country is moving from liberalization to democracy. The third direct approach to promoting gradualist democratic transitions in the Arab world seeks to use a combination of aid for democracy and diplomatic engagement to push Arab governments to begin building such a bridge in their own societies. Only a relatively small number of persons within the U.S. policy community advocate such an approach, primarily persons within the democracy aid organizations (above all, within the two political party institutes). And only fairly small-scale activities have yet been supported in this vein, though at least in two countries, Morocco and Yemen, they have been under way for some time and arguably with at least some success.

The central element of the strategy for directly supporting democracy is to encourage and pressure Arab governments to strengthen and gradually broaden the processes of organized political contestation in their countries. The most immediate focus of such efforts is normally elections—undertaking activities to make elections more meaningful. Full-fledged support in this regard would consist of various interrelated measures:

- programs to strengthen political parties—to help parties and politicians develop basic organizational skills, improve their constituency relations, improve coalition building, and the like; and where opposition political parties are not yet permitted (as in the Gulf states), urging the government through diplomacy to take the step of allowing the formation of parties;
- aid to strengthen election administration entities and push hard on governments to give such entities greater political independence;
- support for domestic and international election monitoring (resistance to election monitoring is more widespread in the Arab world than any other region and remains an area of considerable potential development);
- aid for civic groups that work to improve electoral processes by organizing candidate forums, monitoring campaign fairness, educating citizens about elections, and promoting voter turnout;
- activities to increase women's political participation;
- giving more consistent, high-level diplomatic attention to Arab elections, including real criticism when elections fall short and a reduction

of ritualistic praise for problematic electoral processes; and
- respecting the outcomes of elections, even if they are not to Washington's liking.

The United States could complement this heightened attention to elections with a broader, high-level push to encourage or pressure Arab leaders to give great respect to human rights, especially such core political and civil rights as freedom of speech, freedom of association, and due process. Many Arabs have the impression that the U.S. government pushes hard on human rights when persons connected to the United States are mistreated but remains silent when Islamists or other nonfriends of the United States suffer persecution. Correcting this double standard would send an important positive signal to Arab governments and societies.

Another broader element of assistance in strengthening the processes of political contestation could be a more serious effort by the United States to encourage Arab governments to be more politically inclusive, above all with regard to Islamists. Policies vary in the region concerning the participation of Islamist parties or organizations in formal political life, but everywhere the issue is crucial to the broader challenge of widening political contestation. The U.S. government could have much more extensive, regularized contacts with Islamists, both to get to know them better and to help them understand U.S. policy more accurately.

Opening up such contacts would not mean that the United States is approving of or embracing those groups, merely that it is acknowledging that they are a part of the political landscape. And this would send an important message of inclusiveness to Arab governments. In Egypt, for example, the current U.S. approach of having only minimal official contact with the Muslim Brotherhood and other Islamist groups reinforces the Egyptian government's policy of trying to exclude them from political life.

The strategy of directly supporting democracy is based on the idea that if the existing weak, limited processes of political contestation can be gradually infused with the principles of fairness, inclusion, honesty, and openness, governments will begin to give more real authority and power to elected parliaments and local governments, and citizens will begin to put some stock in political processes and related institutions. This in turn could encourage Arab leaders over time to reduce the political power they keep outside the processes of political contestation (that is, their own executive power) and eventually to contemplate the actual democratization of the central state.

The main attraction of the direct democracy strategy is precisely its directness—it attempts to tackle the core question of how Arab states might actually move from limited liberalization to actual democratization, something the other two strategies do not really address. Of course, even if the United States did decide to commit itself to this more activist approach, its role would still just be that of an advocate and enabler. Direct though it may be, this strategy primarily consists of pushing Arab governments to face the potential dangers of indefinite partial liberalization, identifying a road out, and urging and helping them to move along that road.

The potential payoff of this third strategy is high, but so too are its potential drawbacks and risks. If the United States actually pushed Arab leaders hard to respect human rights, be more politically inclusive, and subject their own rule to the public's choice, it would produce paroxysms of resentment among political elites in the region and alienate longtime friends. It could jeopardize the beneficial cooperation that Washington receives from friendly Arab autocrats on antiterrorist matters, on efforts to resolve the Palestinian–Israeli conflict, and on supplying oil. Some of this resentment might be mitigated by the fact that a stepped-up set of initiatives to directly aid democracy would likely be carried out by United States–based NGOs and would therefore be at least one step removed from direct U.S. governmental action. Yet even these NGOs are frequently viewed in aid-receiving countries as extensions of the U.S. government. And if such aid is to be effective, it must be backed up with significant U.S. government jawboning and pressure.

And of course the third strategy runs squarely into the deeper doubts of many in the U.S. government and elsewhere about both the possibility and desirability of any real democratization in the Middle East. Might not genuinely open political processes bring to power Islamists who would disavow democracy once in power and pursue policies inimical to U.S. security and economic interests? This question has of course animated debates over Arab political futures for many years, and the various arguments and counterarguments have been much rehearsed.

The core argument for the direct democracy strategy is that a gradual but purposeful expansion of the political space and contestation could strengthen moderates and weaken extremists on both sides of the political divide in Arab countries. According to this argument, even though this gradual process would be risky and difficult, such a frontal approach to promoting democracy in the Arab world would be less risky and problematic in the long run than letting countries continue to stagnate and fester politically.

**The Real Choice**

In theory, the three different strategies to encourage gradualist transitions to democracy in the Arab world can be seen as three parts of one integrated strategy.

In any given Arab country, the United States could simultaneously promote economic reform, increase efforts to indirectly aid democracy by assisting in reforming the state and expanding civil society, and initiate efforts to directly strengthen and broaden the established processes of political contestation.

The unfolding pattern of U.S. efforts to promote democracy in the Middle East since the early 1990s might in fact be seen as precisely the achievement of such a threefold synthesis. In the early 1990s, when the U.S. government first gave serious thought to how it might promote positive political change in the Arab world, the economic reform strategy gained favor. Then, in the second half of the decade, the United States began funding a small but growing number of programs to improve governance and foster civil society. The indirect democracy approach got a big boost after September 11, 2001—the new U.S. interest in promoting democracy in the Arab world was translated into ambitious plans to significantly increase programs to indirectly aid democracy, with the Middle East Partnership Initiative as the flagship. And then, very gradually, the U.S. government has started to support some programs that directly promote democracy—only a trickle in the 1990s but more in the post–September 11 context.

In principle, the three different approaches can indeed function as mutually reinforcing parts of one integrated strategy. In practice, however, quickly smoothing over the differences among them and insisting that U.S. policy entails pursuing all three at once gives the impression of a consensus that in fact has not yet been achieved. U.S. policy with regard to promoting democracy in the Arab world is in flux. The government is giving greater, more serious attention to the question than at any previous time. But within the many parts of the government that concern themselves with the issue—the White House, State Department, USAID, the Defense Department, and the intelligence agencies—there are many different opinions and ideas and little real consensus.

Advocates of the economic reform approach are often skeptical of the whole idea that the United States should promote democracy in the Arab world. Economic reform is their choice because it puts the day of political reckoning comfortably far off in the future and seems the least risky approach. They are usually willing to tolerate indirect democracy aid programs because they figure that such activities are unlikely to make much difference and are also relatively low risk. But they are skeptical of or actively opposed to direct efforts to promote democracy. Enthusiasts of the indirect approach accept that economic reform can have complementary value but warn against relying solely on it. They are often wary of the direct approach but are usually not opposed to at least giving it a try in limited circumstances. Advocates of the direct approach are sometimes doubtful about the economic route, seeing it as a cover for little real engagement with democracy. But they are usually favorable to indirect programs, viewing them as a natural partner of direct methods.

The crucial line is that between the direct approach and the two others. The U.S. government will undoubtedly keep trying to press for economic reform in the Arab world. And the new wave of indirect democracy aid efforts will certainly go forward. Therefore, the key question of strategy is whether the United States will decide to try to mount a major effort to support a strategy to directly promote democracy throughout the region or instead stick to the economic reform and indirect approaches.

Of course, the strategy of directly promoting democracy is not an undifferentiated tool to be applied (or not) in every country. Some countries are more ripe for such efforts than others, and direct methods may take somewhat different forms depending on the context. Morocco and Yemen, for example, have made some real progress with multiparty competition (in part with the assistance of U.S. and European elections and party programs) and could clearly benefit from continued, and indeed expanded, work in this domain. Algeria, Egypt, and Jordan are potential candidates for such efforts, although the sensitivities of their ruling elites about issues of political inclusion and rights are extremely high. A few of the small Gulf states, notably Bahrain and Qatar, may present some opportunities in this domain, although they are still grappling with starting-point issues such as whether to allow political parties and independent civic groups.

For the U.S. government to genuinely commit itself to direct methods of promoting democracy would mean a significant change of course—away from decades of support for political stasis and from deep attachments to particular rulers. It would mean taking significant political risks and expending real political capital that up to now has been used in the service of economic and security interests. This is the key choice facing the United States with regard to promoting democracy in the Middle East. Until it is clearly decided one way or the other, the growing number of U.S. policy statements and aid initiatives in the domain will lack essential strategic definition.

## Notes

Originally published as Carnegie Working Paper 39 (June 2003).

1. Marina Ottaway, *Promoting Democracy in the Middle East: The Problem of U.S. Credibility*, Working Paper no. 35 (Washington, D.C.: Carnegie Endowment for International Peace, 2003).
2. Daniel Brumberg, *Liberalization Versus Democracy: Understanding Arab Political Reform,* Working Paper no. 37 (Washington, D.C.: Carnegie Endowment for International Peace, 2003).

# CHAPTER NINETEEN

# Democracy: Terrorism's Uncertain Antidote (2003)

THE TERRORIST ATTACKS of September 11, 2001, threw into serious question a long-standing tenet of U.S. policy toward the Middle East: the assumption that nondemocratic, pro-Western regimes such as those in Egypt, Jordan, Morocco, Saudi Arabia, and Kuwait are bulwarks against Islamic radicalism. The fact that the 9–11 hijackers came from Saudi Arabia and Egypt provoked many American observers to ask whether such regimes are instead breeding grounds for terrorism. In the months immediately following September 11, U.S. policy makers began to talk about the need to pay more attention to the absence of democracy in the Arab world. In the two years since, the U.S. policy establishment has come to believe that promoting democracy in the Middle East should be a component of the war on terrorism—part of a broader effort to go beyond the active pursuit of terrorist groups to address the underlying roots of terrorism.

The most significant operative element of this new policy line has been the invasion of Iraq. In deciding to move against Saddam Hussein, President George W. Bush was motivated by a medley of security concerns, geopolitical intentions, and economic considerations. Whatever the precise weight of these different factors, one of the motivations clearly was the desire to replace the thuggish, highly repressive Iraqi dictatorship with a democratic government, both to improve the lives of Iraqis and to help spread democracy elsewhere in the region—in part as an antidote to terrorism.

The war in Iraq would spread democracy in two ways. First, some Bush aides hoped that regime change in Iraq might constitute a political shock sufficient to destabilize hostile regimes in Syria and Iran and pave the way in those countries for more open, pluralistic governments. Second, creating an example of a working democratic government in the Arab world might stimulate the pro-Western authoritarian and semi-authoritarian regimes in the region to move in a democratic direction as well.

Alongside the hard edge of military-led regime change in Iraq, the administration has unfolded a complementary soft side to the new emphasis on democracy promotion. To stimulate and support political reform in friendly Arab states, the administration has formulated an interrelated set of measures: a new aid program—the Middle East Partnership Initiative—to support democratic change; the reorientation of existing aid programs in the Arab world to sharpen their pro-democratic content; a diplomatic stance consisting of greater praise for those Arab governments that do take positive political steps and somewhat more pressure on those that do not; and a new push to promote Arab economic reform and free trade (with the hope that improved economic conditions will, over the long term, stimulate political reform).

## Obstacles to Success

This new attention on the part of the U.S. government to the near-total lack of democracy in the Middle East is a welcome development. For far too long, successive American administrations have ignored the issue, content with supporting Arab "friendly tyrants" and giving only lip service to the cause of political reform. Yet in the rush to embrace a new line, the U.S. government and the broader U.S. policy establishment need to recognize the substantial obstacles on the path to democratization.

One obstacle is the facile assumption that a straight line exists between progress on democratization and the elimination of the roots of Islamic terrorism. The sources of Islamic radicalism and the embrace of anti-American terrorism by some radicals are multifaceted and cannot be reduced to the simple proposition that the lack of democracy in the Arab world is the main cause.

Moreover, any rapid opening up of the closed political systems in Saudi Arabia or Kuwait or even Egypt could well, in the short to medium term, allow extremist groups to operate more actively and give strength to the wider Islamist organizations that sometimes feed the extremists. There may be an analogy to the much-debated relationship between the existence of democracy in countries and the proclivity of countries to go to war: Although established democracies tend not to fight wars with one another, countries setting out on the turbulent path from dictatorship to democracy are often more war-prone.

Even the successful achievement of democracy offers no guarantee that a society will not produce terrorists. More than a few established democracies have struggled with persistent terrorist threats, whether it is Spain confronting Basque terrorists, Italy facing the Red Brigades, or Great Britain grappling with the Irish Republican Army.

Second, although many people in Washington may have decided that the Middle East's democratic moment has arrived, a discernible democratic trend in the region itself is not evident. The past two years have seen mild reforms by some Arab states and increased discussion among Arab intellectuals about the need for political change. The Arab world remains dominated, however, by deeply entrenched authoritarian or semi-authoritarian governments with a proven will and capacity for survival. The recent reforms that some have undertaken— such as Bahrain's legislative elections and the Egyptian ruling party's internal reforms—are limited, adaptive initiatives designed to ensure the regimes' long-term survival. They have not altered fundamental nondemocratic features, such as unelected leadership. As Daniel Brumberg persuasively argued in the October 2002 *Journal of Democracy,* these are regimes stuck in "the trap of liberalized autocracy." They try some reforms to relieve growing pressure for participation from below, but then the political forces thereby strengthened scare the regimes from taking reform any further.

The situation is thus unlike, and much more difficult than, the prevailing circumstances in other regions where the United States made a major push for democracy in past decades, such as Latin America in the 1980s or Eastern Europe in the late 1980s and early 1990s. Internally generated movements toward democracy already existed in these areas, with significant regional demonstration effects. In taking on the challenge of promoting democracy in those regions, the United States was reinforcing a growing domestic dynamic of change rather than trying to create one almost from scratch. For example, the United States supported Solidarity in Poland and the Civic Forum in Czechoslovakia during their periods of anti-totalitarian struggle, but it did not create them.

Positive results are not guaranteed even where an internal impetus for democratic change asserts itself, a breakthrough occurs, and the United States sides with the forces of change. In the early 1990s, the new states of the former Soviet Union took what looked at the time like dramatic steps toward democracy. Today, most of that region is a democratic wasteland dominated by harshly authoritarian regimes in some countries and seriously backsliding leaders in others.

Third, the United States faces a tremendous problem of credibility in asserting itself as a pro-democratic actor in the Middle East. Confronted with the notion that the Bush administration is now committed to democracy in the region, many Arabs react with incredulity, resentment, and outright anger. They have a very hard time taking the idea seriously, given Washington's longtime backing of authoritarian governments in the region, what they believe is insufficient U.S. support for Palestinian rights, and a war in Iraq that most Arabs feel was an illegitimate imposition of American political force on Arab territory. As the U.S. Advisory Group on Public Diplomacy in the Arab and Muslim World highlighted in its October 2003 report, "hostility toward America [in the Muslim world] has reached shocking levels."

The credibility problem renders real partnership with the Arab world extremely difficult, yet such partnerships have been key to successful democracy promotion efforts elsewhere. The lack of credibility is serious but not immutable. Over time American policy makers and aid officials can overcome ingrained suspicions and skepticism, as they did to some degree in Latin America from the mid-1980s through the 1990s. But such a transformation of attitudes can be at best only slowly achieved. It will require long-term consistency between democratic word and deed, as well as the steady commitment of major resources for at least a decade or two. And real progress with the credibility gap probably cannot be achieved without a substantial rebalancing of the U.S. approach to the Israeli–Palestinian conflict, which appears unlikely to occur under the Bush administration.

## The Difficult Early Steps

The postwar situation in Iraq highlights just how difficult trying to build democracy in the Arab world is, even with the unusually high degree of influence over Iraqi domestic affairs gained by the American-led invasion and occupation. More than half a year after Saddam's ouster, a new Iraqi political system has only barely begun to take shape. From the early maneuverings and machinations of the Iraqi Governing Council, as well as the varied sociopolitical pressures roiling beneath the surface of the Coalition Provisional Authority's rule, it is evident how long and hard it will be to resolve the sharply different interests and intentions of the various ethnic and religious strata of Iraqi society in a manner compatible with a pluralistic, liberal political order.

It is probable that Iraq eventually will have a political system considerably better for its people than Saddam's regime, although the possibility of an eventual lapse into destructive civil conflict exists. But the diplomatic, political, and economic costs for the United States of helping Iraq get there will end up being much, much higher than initially anticipated. This is evident in the tremendous hostility the war has provoked toward the United States in the Muslim world and in many other places, the troubling fact that recruitment for Al Qaeda and other radical Islamist terrorist organizations has reportedly spiked since the war, and the huge price tag that the war and occupation have already incurred.

The challenge of spreading democracy to the rest of the region is equally problematic. Given Iraq's history of political repression and violence, its divided society, and its centralized economic resources, an exemplary democratic order will not likely emerge in the next decade or two. The more probable political outcome is a choppy, poorly functioning pluralism or a moderately authoritarian regime. The power of an Iraqi democratic model for its neighbors is thus very uncertain.

Even if Iraq manages to succeed democratically, the demonstration effect will be limited, given a model whose first steps consist of foreign invasion, followed by a short but frightening period of chaos and violence, then a long foreign occupation. Unlike the regional demonstration effects of democratic breakthroughs in Latin America and Eastern Europe, this is not a political model rooted in what a people can do for themselves. It hinges on the much less appealing example of what the application of enormous foreign military force and subsequent political intervention and economic aid can make possible.

**The Soft Side**

The soft side of the new democracy policy for the Middle East is also just beginning to take root. The constituent elements all make sense, but none is likely to have any rapid or decisive effect. Stepping up democracy aid through the Middle East Partnership Initiative and bolstering the democracy component of existing aid programs will allow greater support for worthwhile initiatives in the realms of civil society development, women's rights, rule of law strengthening, and political participation. But as the experience with such aid in other regions makes clear, democracy support programs only have a moderate impact at best, mildly reinforcing whatever domestic reform trends exist. They often bounce off regimes determined to resist fundamental change.

Greater economic reform in the Arab world and more open trade relations with the United States represent valuable goals, but not a formula for near-term political change. For twenty years Washington has been pushing the Egyptian government to implement basic market reforms, with only partial success. It is unclear whether or how the Bush administration will overcome Arab states' proven unwillingness to jeopardize the support of core protected constituencies through disruptive reform measures. And the one Arab country that has made real progress on market reforms—Tunisia—has experienced no positive spillover effect in the political realm. Despite an impressive recent record of economic performance, Tunisia remains one of the most repressive Arab states.

U.S. diplomatic pressure for political change is a potentially critical element of a pro-democratic policy. And administration officials are beginning to push a bit more openly and directly on political reform issues with some of the American-friendly regimes in the region, such as Egypt and Jordan. Bush aides point to the president's August 2002 letter to Egyptian President Hosni Mubarak expressing U.S. dissatisfaction with Egypt's strong-arm treatment of human rights activist Saad Eddin Ibrahim as evidence of a new, tougher line. So far the letter stands more as an exception than a new rule. The relationships between Washington and Arab capitals are still very much oriented to the status quo.

The stubborn fact remains that the United States depends on many of these regimes for extensive security cooperation on antiterrorism, at least limited support for U.S. diplomatic efforts in the Israeli–Palestinian conflict, and, in the case of the Gulf states, access to the largest oil reserves in the world. The Bush administration's newfound desire for democratization in these countries is balanced against a deep caution about not producing cataclysmic change. These societies have strong Islamic movements and a very uncertain capability to move rapidly from paternalistic patterns of political control to genuine pluralism and openness without losing control completely.

**Feet on the Ground**

The Bush administration is attempting what some policy makers and observers hope might become an historic shift in U.S. Middle East policy toward a pro-democratic stance. The Bush team's willingness to shake up old ways of U.S. diplomacy in the Arab world is commendable. So is its adamant rejection of noxious culturalist arguments about the supposed incompatibility of Arab culture and liberal democracy. Yet casting out unhelpful habits of the past and rejecting vulgar culturalism are not a license for downplaying hard facts on the ground.

It is true that there is no inherent reason why the Arab world cannot join the global democratic trend. Yet there are very real, deeply rooted historical, sociopolitical, and economic reasons why the democratization of Arab societies will prove unusually slow, difficult, and conflictive. Similarly, there are substantial reasons why U.S. policy cannot swing to a forceful pro-democratic orientation without some major trade-offs with regard to near-term security and economic interests.

The place of a pro-democracy effort in the broader campaign against terrorism will not be simple or straightforward. Many elements of the Bush administration's antiterror effort in other parts of the world, such as the increased support to friendly nondemocratic regimes in Central and South Asia, already cut against democracy concerns. The attempted democratization of Iraq to date has provided only uncertain and mixed results with respect to reducing terrorism. Similar tensions and complexities inevitably will continue to arise to the extent the United States pushes its new democracy agenda in the rest of the Arab world.

To be effective and sustainable, the U.S. effort to promote democracy in the Middle East will require a sharp sense of nuance and balance, a strong dose of humility, and a willingness to invest heavily and stay the course for decades in the face of much discouragement along the way. And though it has been launched from the shell of the war on terrorism, the effort can succeed only if it eschews some of the signature elements of that campaign to date, such as the dubious philosophy of "you're either with us or against us" and the misguided notion that creating fear in the Arab world breeds respect.

## Note

The Carnegie Endowment gratefully acknowledges the permission of *Current History* to reprint this article, which originally appeared in *Current History*, vol. 102, no. 668 (December 2003).

SECTION SIX

# *Afterword*

ALTHOUGH FADDISH IDEAS and initiatives frequently afflict the field of democracy promotion, the overall enterprise is not a fad. It is here to stay as a significant element of foreign aid, diplomacy, and international relations more generally, for several reasons.

To start, democracy has become part of the development consensus. From the 1960s through the 1980s, the international donor community that arose as a response to the challenge of fostering socioeconomic development in the poorer countries of the world paid relatively little attention to the political side of the development equation. To the extent aid providers did concern themselves with the politics of the aid-receiving countries, democracy was usually not the objective. The aid providers often believed that a strong, even dictatorial, hand was necessary in poor countries to build states and forge economic progress. Democracy might come about later, once substantial development was achieved, but it was best not pursued too soon.

That thinking changed fundamentally in the 1990s. Democracy's "third wave" forced developmentalists to confront the fact that citizens in many developing countries were interested in—and demanding—political freedom and pluralism. Moreover, in reaction to accumulated frustration with the negative developmental consequences of unaccountable, unrepresentative governments in many countries, the development community embraced the idea that good governance is necessary for development. And when good governance was spelled out as more accountable, participatory, and representative governance, the links with democracy were obvious. Accordingly, a new credo has emerged in the development community, the proposition that democracy and development go hand-in-hand. And although in organizational terms democracy promotion remains a somewhat separate body of activities from socioeconomic development work, the notion that promoting democracy is consistent with or even integral to the overall challenge of fostering development has gained wide acceptance in Western policy circles.

The new credo linking democracy and development risks being overstated by a policy community eager to believe that all good things go together. Life is rarely so neat in practice. China stands as a powerful contrary example, a country that has achieved remarkable economic growth for twenty years without democracy or Western-style rule of law. And it is an example that strongmen leaders in some other East Asian countries, as well as in Central Asia, the Caucasus, the Middle East, and Africa would like to emulate. Of course the question remains unresolved of how long China can sustain its economic progress without a real political opening. And the fact that a few authoritarian governments have been able to make significant economic progress does not negate the fact that for most developing countries more accountable, participatory, and representative governments would be helpful for development.

Democracy promotion is taking root not just because it has become part of the development consensus but also because an increasing number of people within the established democracies believe that democracy is a good thing in and of itself for people in other parts of the world. In other words, they have gravitated to the view that promoting democracy is an intrinsically good thing to do. The end of the Cold War was crucial in this regard. It helped end the attachment of some Western intellectual and policy elites to politically relativistic thinking with respect to developing countries. And it reduced the understandable tendency of people in developing countries to see any political aid offered from the outside as being inevitably linked to ulterior, nondemocratic motives.

A striking feature of the growth of democracy promotion work has been the extremely wide range of governments and other institutions getting involved. Some Americans still tend to think of democracy building as a uniquely American foreign policy concern. But today almost every established democracy engages in at least some diplomatic and aid efforts to support democracy in other countries. All of the major Western bilateral aid agencies now have departments devoted to the promotion of some combination of democracy, good governance, and human rights. Many international institutions concerned with political affairs, starting with the United Nations, now take on democracy issues.

Some of the wealthier new democracies, such as Chile, Poland, and Taiwan, are also establishing democracy-promotion programs. Although these many pro-democratic activities do not represent a high priority for most of the governments and international organizations involved, they are nevertheless growing and being institutionalized. European spending on democracy aid, for example, has in recent years exceeded what the United States contributes to this domain.

A changed view in the United States and Europe of the relationship between democracy and security also adds to the grounding of democracy promotion in Western policy circles. During the Cold War, the United States and its main European partners faced a deep tension between the effort to check the Soviet Union and the stated goal of defending freedom around the world. Many of their anti-Soviet allies were dictatorships, and the anti-Soviet policy often involved supporting the abridgement of democracy in other countries. With the end of the Cold War, that central tension lifted and Western policy makers embraced the idea that at least in principle, democracies make better security partners for the West than nondemocracies.

Nevertheless, tensions and contradictions between democracy and security keep arising. The United States and other major democratic powers have continued to maintain friendly, often even cozy relationships with authoritarian regimes in various parts of the world for the sake of economic and security interests. Their willingness to devote substantial resources and sustained, high-level diplomatic attention to the task of democracy promotion is still often quite limited. Even so, the idea that the advance of democracy directly benefits Western security interests does carry some weight.

The U.S. war on terror has complicated this issue. It has prompted the United States to seek closer relationships with quite a few nondemocratic governments in Central Asia, South Asia, the Middle East, and elsewhere, for the sake of useful security cooperation. Yet it has also impelled the United States and Europe to think seriously for the first time about trying to promote democracy in the Middle East, out of the belief that opening up stagnant Middle East autocracies will help undercut the sources of radical Islamism. These two conflicting imperatives have produced confusion and sometimes incoherence in U.S. policy as well as rising accusations of hypocrisy from observers in other countries. Although the war on terror has resulted in the downgrading of democracy concerns toward some important countries, it does not constitute a reversal of the underlying acceptance by the mainstream Western policy establishment that democracy promotion is at least one part of the overall security agenda.

That democracy promotion will continue in the decades ahead does not mean it will necessarily evolve into a strong, coherent field. It may well remain marked by persistent uncertainty both about its methods and the degree of its impact. This is not because of any special deficiencies on the part of democracy promoters. It is due to the central, unavoidable fact that trying to help another society fundamentally change and improve its political life, whether through aid programs, diplomatic carrots and sticks, or any other approach, is tremendously difficult. The principles of democracy are quite clear. The processes for achieving them are not. How can Argentina overcome its debilitating, chronic problem of an irresponsible, feckless political elite? What might allow Nigeria to ameliorate the gross, deeply entrenched patterns of corrupt governance that keep strangling its chances for successful democratization? From where in Uzbek society will an impulse for democracy arise strong enough to overcome a long, powerful tradition of authoritarian rule? How can Pakistan revive some sort of democratic political life in the face of a military deeply entrenched in politics, discredited civilian political parties, and surging sociocultural pressures and divisions? There are simply no ready answers for such questions—and similar questions can be posed for the dozens of countries struggling with democratization. There are no recipes or formulas that can be neatly applied by well-intentioned outside actors looking to help.

I often hear people within the democracy-promotion community explain the lack of certainty about the methods and impact of democracy building by arguing that democracy promotion is a young field compared with socioeconomic development aid. Over time, they contend, democracy promotion will mature into a more well-elaborated field, perhaps even a proto-science. I certainly hope it will advance in learning and sophistication, but I do not think we should expect, or even aim for anything like a science. To start with, democracy promotion is hardly a young field when one considers the efforts by the United States in the early twentieth century to construct democratic governments in Central America and the Caribbean after its various military interventions there. And some parts of British and French colonialism in the late nineteenth and early twentieth centuries could be construed as democracy building. Moreover, even though socioeconomic development aid has been extensively pursued for more than 40 years, one could hardly say that it is near to becoming a science. Fundamental debates and uncertainties still regularly roil the field, whether about aid effectiveness, the validity of the core formula of market-led reform, or other major issues. Significant learning has certainly occurred about promoting socioeconomic development, but like democracy building, it inevitably involves the often irrational and unpredictable impulses and ideas of human societies, and as such is not wholly or even largely susceptible to the certainty of pure science.

We can be fairly confident that democracy promotion will continue. But we can unfortunately not be certain that democracy will actually succeed in the dozens of countries around the world that moved away from dictatorship in the last 25 years. There are many fewer outright authoritarian regimes today than in the 1970s or 1980s, and some of those that remain probably have a limited lifespan. But as I wrote in "The End of the Transition Paradigm," most of the countries in the third wave have ended up in a gray zone between democracy and dictatorship. And the gray zone is not a way station in which countries are necessarily moving forward to consolidated democracy or backward to authoritarianism. Rather, it is a political state of its own that often achieves significant stability.

The different political syndromes and conditions within the gray zone can be disaggregated in varying ways, and a growing number of writers on comparative democratization are at work on that. The unifying core of these different political syndromes is a hollowing out of the attempted democratization. The institutional forms of democracy, especially elections, are at least partially achieved, but the democratic substance that is supposed to be built through these forms—above all the effective representation of interests and open, genuine competition for power—is undermined in different ways. The third wave was an exhilarating trend, but consolidating democracy is proving extremely difficult for countries with weak or absent traditions of pluralism; shaky or sometime rapacious states; large numbers of poor, marginalized, and unhappy citizens; and other debilitating structural conditions. And on top of these conditions are a whole set of acute problems or crises that strike many of these countries—international criminal networks, especially tied to drug trafficking, that prey on weak states; health crises such as the HIV-AIDS epidemic that devastate the social fabric; economic crises that undercut the economic position of large number of citizens; and so forth.

All of this means that decades of extremely hard work are ahead on the democracy promotion front. Helping countries turn democratic forms into democratic substance is a deep, broad task. It will entail greatly sharpening existing forms of aid. And it demands going far beyond conventional aid to take on issues such as reducing entrenched concentrations of economic power; activating and politically integrating poor, marginalized sectors (even if their political views and demands do not match the international community's standard development model); and rejuvenating stale, often deeply problematic, political elites. Such tasks will require not only more resources, but just as importantly, more flexibility and risk taking in the use of what resources are put to work. And they will likely require a greater level of interventionism, better ties between the political and economic sides of development aid, and almost an entirely different set of expectations about the timescale of the efforts needed and the kinds of results that can be reasonably expected.

In response to these enormous challenges, the field of democracy promotion may coalesce in a positive way, if a number of constructive developments come together: Coordination and cooperation among the growing number of organizations engaged in the field will need to increase. Diplomats and aid practitioners must more consistently and effectively support each other in democracy-related efforts. Real bridges must be built between socioeconomic development aid and democracy promotion. A new generation of people with substantial practical experience in democracy building must bring higher levels of knowledge and professionalism to the domain and take up positions of responsibility in aid organizations, foreign ministries, and international institutions. Politicians, civic activists, and government officials in countries on the receiving end of democracy promotion efforts must learn to better use such assistance. And the academic community must produce increasing amounts of critical, reflective analysis of democracy promotion that is conceptually challenging and practically relevant.

Yet it is also possible to imagine a negative scenario in which the field of democracy promotion does not coalesce and does not rise to the challenge. The developments that could lead to this negative scenario include: if democracy aid becomes overly systemized by aid bureaucracies and ends up stuck in routinized, cookie-cutter approaches; if the positive policy link between democracy and security is eclipsed by older patterns of reliance on the promised stability of authoritarian friends; if the United States and Europe fail to achieve a sense of partnership in their democracy efforts and pursue their own separate lines; if democracy support funds get thrown in large amounts at crises, in rushed, unsustainable ways, pulling needed funds away from less high-profile, more sustained efforts in other countries; or if ordinary citizens and political elites in countries struggling with democracy turn their political frustrations into blame on external actors and create a new trend of heightened sovereignty and resistance to democracy promotion.

No one factor will determine whether the field of democracy promotion ends up moving more in a positive direction or a negative one. Like democratization itself, democracy promotion is an eminently human endeavor, subject to countless complexities and pitfalls. The recurrent temptations for advocates of democracy promotion, temptations such as hubris, teleology, and exclusivity, must be given a wide berth. Any sustained experience of promoting democracy on the ground quickly makes crystal clear some simple, sobering facts. It is slow, hard work. There are no guarantees it will succeed. And no one has a unique or exclusive purchase on the subject. But those who try to push democracy forward day by day, place by place, also know without a doubt that it is the right thing to do.

# Bibliography on Democracy Promotion

## GENERAL

Allison, Graham T., Jr., and Robert P. Beschel, Jr. "Can the United States Promote Democracy?" *Political Science Quarterly*, vol. 107, no. 1 (Spring 1992): 81–98.

Bivens, Matt. "Aboard the Gravy Train," *Harper's* (August 1997).

Boot, Max. "Neither New Nor Nefarious: The Liberal Empire Strikes Back," *Current History*, vol. 102, no. 667 (2003): 361–6.

Brinkley, Douglas. "Democratic Enlargement: The Clinton Doctrine," *Foreign Policy,* no. 106 (Spring 1997): 111–27.

Burnell, Peter. "Good Government and Democratization: A Sideways Look at Aid and Conditionality," *Democratization*, vol. 1, no. 3 (Autumn 1994): 485–503.

Burnell, Peter, ed. *Democracy Assistance: International Co-operation for Democratization*. London: Frank Cass, 2000.

Carothers, Thomas. "Why Dictators Aren't Dominoes," *Foreign Policy* (July/August 2003): 59–60.

_____. "Democracy, State, and AID: A Tale of Two Cultures," *The Foreign Service Journal* (February 2001): 21–6.

_____. *Aiding Democracy Abroad: The Learning Curve*. Washington, D.C.: Carnegie Endowment for International Peace, 1999.

_____. "Democracy Assistance: The Question of Strategy," *Democratization*, vol. 4, no. 3 (Autumn 1997): 109–32.

_____. *Assessing Democracy Assistance: The Case of Romania*. Washington, D.C.: Carnegie Endowment for International Peace, 1996.

_____. "Aiding Post-Communist Societies: A Better Way?" *Problems of Post-Communism* (September/October 1996): 15–24.

_____. "The NED at Ten," *Foreign Policy*, no. 95 (Summer 1994): 123–38.

_____. *In the Name of Democracy: U.S. Policy Toward Latin America in the Reagan Years*. Berkeley: University of California Press, 1991.

Chua, Amy. *World on Fire: How Exporting Free Market Democracy Breeds Ethnic Hatred and Global Instability*. New York: Doubleday, 2003.

Cox, Michael, G. John Ikenberry, and Takashi Inoguchi. *American Democracy Promotion: Impulses, Strategies, and Impacts*. Oxford: Oxford University Press, 2000.

Crawford, Gordon. "Foreign Aid and Political Conditionality: Issues of Effectiveness and Consistency," *Democratization*, vol. 4, no. 3 (Autumn 1997): 69–108.

_____. "Promoting Democracy from Without: Learning from Within (Part I)," *Democratization*, vol. 10, no. 1 (Spring 2003): 77–98.

_____. "Promoting Democracy from Without: Learning from Within (Part II)," *Democratization*, vol. 10, no. 2 (Summer 2003): 1–20.

_____. *Foreign Aid and Political Reform: A Comparative Analysis of Democracy Assistance and Political Conditionality*. Leeds, U.K.: Palgrave, 2001.

Crawford, Gordon, with Iain Kearton. "Evaluating Democracy and Governance Assistance." Leeds, U.K.: Centre for Development Studies, February 2002.

Creative Associates International. *A Retrospective of A.I.D.'s Experience in Strengthening Democratic Institutions in Latin America, 1961–1981*. Washington, D.C.: USAID, September 1987.

Crook, Elizabeth Fletcher. "Political Development as a Program Objective of U.S. Foreign Assistance: Title IX of the 1966 Foreign Assistance Act," Tufts University Ph.D. thesis, 1970 (unpublished).

Dalpino, Catharin E. *Anchoring Third Wave Democracies: Prospects and Problems for U.S. Policy*. Washington, D.C.: Institute for the Study of Diplomacy, Georgetown University, 1998.

_____. *Deferring Democracy: Promoting Openness in Authoritarian Regimes*. Washington, D.C.: Brookings Institution Press, 2000.

Dalpino, Catharin E., and Mike Jendrzejczyk. "Has the Clinton Administration Done a Good Job of Promoting Democracy in Asia?" *The CQ Researcher,* vol. 8, no. 27 (July 24, 1998).

Dawisha, Karen, ed. *The International Dimension of Post-Communist Transitions in Russia and the New States of Eurasia*. Armonk, N.Y.: M. E. Sharpe, 1997.

Diamond, Larry. "Promoting Democracy in Africa: U.S. and International Policies in Transition," in John W. Harbeson and Donald Rothchild, eds., *Africa in World Politics: Post-Cold War Challenges*. Boulder, Colo.: Westview Press, 1995.

_____. "Promoting Democracy," *Foreign Policy,* no. 87 (Summer 1992): 25–46.

_____. *Developing Democracy: Toward Consolidation*. Baltimore: Johns Hopkins University Press, 1999.

_____. *Promoting Democracy in the 1990s: Actors and Instruments, Issues and Imperatives.* Washington, D.C.: Carnegie Commission on Preventing Deadly Conflict, 1995.

Ethier, Diane. "Is Democracy Promotion Effective? Comparing Conditionality and Incentives," *Democratization*, vol. 10, no. 1 (Spring 2003): 99–120.

European Stability Initiative. "Rhetoric and Reform: A Case Study of Institution Building in Montenegro 1998–2001," *ESI Report* (June 27, 2001).

Farer, Tom J., ed. *Beyond Sovereignty: Collectively Defending Democracy in the Americas*. Baltimore: Johns Hopkins University Press, 1996.

Finkel, Steven E. "Can Democracy Be Taught?" *Journal of Democracy*, vol. 14, no. 4 (October 2003): 137–51.

Fisher, Jeff. "Elections and International Civilian Policing: History and Practice in Peace Operations," White Paper. Washington, D.C.: International Foundation for Elections Systems, June 2002.

Geddes, Barbara. *Politician's Dilemma: Building State Capacity in Latin America*. Berkeley: University of California Press, 1994.

Gershman, Carl. "The United States and the World Democratic Revolution," *The Washington Quarterly,* vol. 12, no. 1 (Winter 1989): 127–40.

Golub, Stephen. "Assessing and Enhancing the Impact of Democratic Development Projects: A Practitioner's Perspective," *Studies in Comparative International Development,* vol. 28, no. 1 (Spring 1993): 54–70.

Green, Jerrold D. "USAID's Democratic Pluralism Initiative: Pragmatism or Altruism?" *Ethics and International Affairs*, vol. 5 (1991): 215–31.

Grindle, Merilee S., ed. *Getting Good Government: Capacity Building in the Public Sector of Developing Countries*. Cambridge, Mass.: Harvard Institute for International Development, 1997.

Halperin, Morton H., and Kristen Lomasney. "Guaranteeing Democracy: A Review of the Record," *Journal of Democracy,* vol. 9, no. 2 (1998): 134–47.

Hendrickson, David C. "The Democratist Crusade: Intervention, Economic Sanctions, and Engagement," *World Policy Journal*, vol. 11 (Winter 1994/1995): 18–30.

Hook, Steven W. "'Building Democracy' through Foreign Aid: The Limitations of United States Political Conditionalities, 1992–96," *Democratization*, vol. 5, no. 3 (Autumn 1998): 156–80.

Huntley, James Robert. *Pax Democratica: A Strategy for the 21st Century*. New York: St. Martin's Press, 1998.

International Institute for Democracy and Electoral Assistance. *Democracy and Deep-Rooted Conflict: Options for Negotiators*. Stockholm: 1998.

_____. *The International IDEA Handbook on Democracy Assessment*. Stockholm: 2001.

Joyner, Christopher C. "The United Nations and Democracy," *Global Governance,* vol. 5 (1999): 333–57.

Kearns, Ian. "Western Intervention and the Promotion of Democracy in Serbia," *Political Quarterly*, vol. 70, no. 1 (January/March 1999): 23–30.

Landsberg, Chris. "Promoting Democracy: The Mandela-Mbeki Doctrine," *Journal of Democracy*, vol. 11, no. 3 (July 2000): 107–21.

Lasota, Irena. "Sometimes Less is More," *Journal of Democracy*, vol. 10, no. 4 (October 1999): 125–8.

Leftwich, Adrian, ed. "Governance, Democracy and Development in the Third World," *Third World Quarterly*, vol. 14, no. 3 (1993): 605–24.

_____. *Democracy and Development: Theory and Practice*. Cambridge, U.K.: Polity Press, 1996.

Lowenthal, Abraham F., ed. *Exporting Democracy: The United States and Latin America*. Baltimore: Johns Hopkins University Press, 1991.

Meernik, James. "United States Military Intervention and the Promotion of Democracy," *Journal of Peace Research*, vol. 33, no. 4 (November 1996): 391–420.

Mendelson, Sarah E. "Democracy Assistance and Political Transition in Russia," *International Security*, vol. 25, no. 4 (Spring 2001): 68–106.

Moore, Mick, and Mark Robinson. "Can Foreign Aid Be Used to Promote Good Government in Developing Countries?" *Ethics and International Affairs,* vol. 8 (1994): 141–58.

Moss, Todd J. "U.S. Policy and Democratisation in Africa: The Limits of Liberal Universalism," *The Journal of Modern African Studies,* vol. 33, no. 2 (1995): 189–209.

Muravchik, Joshua. *Exporting Democracy: Fulfilling America's Destiny.* Washington, D.C.: American Enterprise Institute Press, 1991.

Olsen, Gorm Rye. "Europe and the Promotion of Democracy in Post–Cold War Africa: How Serious Is Europe and for What Reason?" *African Affairs*, vol. 97, no. 388 (July 1998): 343–67.

_____. "Promotion of Democracy as a Foreign Policy Instrument of 'Europe': Limits to International Idealism," *Democratization*, vol. 7, no. 2 (Summer 2000): 142–67.

Ott, Dana, and Melissa Rosser. "The Electronic Republic? The Role of the Internet in Promoting Democracy in Africa," *Democratization*, vol. 7, no. 1 (Spring 2000): 137–56.

Ottaway, Marina. "Think Again: Nation Building," *Foreign Policy* (September/October 2002): 16-24.

_____. *Africa's New Leaders: Democracy or State Reconstruction?* Washington, D.C.: Brookings Institution Press, 1999.

_____. *Democracy Challenged: The Rise of Semi-Authoritarianism*. Washington, D.C.: Carnegie Endowment for International Peace, 2003.

Ottaway, Marina, and Theresa Chung. "Debating Democracy Assistance: Toward a New Paradigm," *Journal of Democracy,* vol. 10, no. 4 (October 1999): 99–113.

Packenham, Robert A. *Liberal America and the Third World: Political Development Ideas in Foreign Aid and Social Science*. Princeton, N.J.: Princeton University Press, 1973.

Palmer, Ambassador Mark. *Breaking the Real Axis of Evil: How to Oust the World's Last Dictators by 2005*. New York: Rowman & Littlefield, 2003.

Papić, Dr. Žarko, et al. *International Support Policies to South-East European Countries: Lessons (Not) Learned in B-H*. Sarajevo: Muller, 2001.

Pinkney, Robert. "Can, and Should, Europe Export Democracy to Africa?" *Democracy and Nature*, vol. 5, no. 2 (July 1999): 325–42.

Pinto-Duschinsky, Michael. "The Rise of 'Political Aid,'" in Larry Diamond, Marc Plattner, Yun-han Chu, and Hung-mao Tien, eds., *Consolidating the Third Wave Democracies*. Baltimore: Johns Hopkins University Press, 1997: 295–324.

Pridham, Geoffrey, Eric Herring, and George Sanford, eds. *Building Democracy? The International Dimension of Democratisation in Eastern Europe*. New York: Leicester University Press, 1997.

Quigley, Kevin F. F. "Political Scientists and Assisting Democracy: Too Tenuous Links," *PS, Political Science & Politics*, vol. 30, no. 3 (September 1997): 564–67.

_____. *For Democracy's Sake: Foundations and Democracy Assistance in Central Europe*. Washington, D.C.: Woodrow Wilson Center Press, 1997.

Quinn, Frederick. *Democracy at Dawn: Notes from Poland and Points East*. College Station, Tex.: Texas A&M University Press, 1998.

Riccardi, Andrea. "Promoting Democracy, Peace, and Solidarity," *Journal of Democracy*, vol. 9, no. 4 (Fall 1998): 157–67.

Robinson, William I. *Promoting Polyarchy: Globalization, US Intervention, and Hegemony*. Cambridge, U.K.: Cambridge University Press, 1996.

Samuels, David. "At Play in the Fields of Oppression," *Harper's* (May 1995).

Santiso, Carlos. "International Co-operation for Democracy and Good Governance: Moving Toward a Second Generation?" *European Journal of Development Research*, vol. 13, no. 1 (June 2001): 154–80.

_____. "Sisyphus in the Castle: Improving European Union Strategies for Democracy Promotion and Governance Conditionality," *The European Journal of Development Research*, vol. 15, no. 1 (June 2003): 1–28.

Scott, James. "Transnationalizing Democracy Promotion: The Role of Western Political Foundations and Think-tanks," *Democratization*, vol. 6, no. 3 (Autumn 1999): 146–70.

Scott, James, and Kelly Walters. "Supporting the Wave: Western Political Foundations and the Promotion of a Global Democratic Society," *Global Society*, vol. 14, no. 2 (April 2000): 237–57.

Sharp, Gene. *From Dictatorship to Democracy: A Conceptual Framework for Liberation*. Boston: Albert Einstein Institution, 2002.

Smith, Tony. *America's Mission: The United States and the Worldwide Struggle for Democracy in the Twentieth Century*. Princeton, N.J.: Princeton University Press, 1994.

Tomasevski, Katarina. *Between Sanctions and Elections: Aid Donors and Their Human Rights Performance*. London: Pinter Publishers Ltd., 1997.

USAID. "Conducting a DG Assessment: A Framework for Strategy Development." Washington, D.C.: USAID Office of Democracy and Governance, November 2000.

Vasquez, Ian. "Washington's Dubious Crusade for Hemispheric Democracy," *Policy Analysis*, no. 201. Washington, D.C.: CATO Institute, January 12, 1994.

Vener, Jessica I. "Prompting Democratic Transitions from Abroad: International Donors and Multi-Partyism in Tanzania," *Democratization*, vol. 7, no. 4 (Winter 2000): 133–62.

von Hippel, Karin. *Democracy by Force: U.S. Military Intervention in the Post-Cold War World.* Cambridge, U.K.: Cambridge University Press, 2000.

Wedel, Janine R. *Collision and Collusion: The Strange Case of Western Aid to Eastern Europe, 1989–1998.* New York: St. Martin's Press, 1998.

Whitehead, Laurence, ed. "Concerning International Support for Democracy in the South," in Robin Luckham and Gordon White, eds., *Democratization in the South: The Jagged Wave.* Manchester, U.K.: Manchester University Press, 1996: 246–50.

———. *The International Dimensions of Democratization: Europe and the Americas.* Oxford, U.K.: Oxford University Press, 1996.

Wiarda, Howard J. *Cracks in the Consensus: Debating the Democracy Agenda in U.S. Foreign Policy.* The Washington Papers, vol. 172. Westport, Conn.: Praeger Publishers, 1997.

Youngs, Richard. "Democracy Promotion: The Case of European Union Strategy," Brussels: Centre for European Policy Studies, October 2001.

———. "European Approaches to Democracy Assistance: Learning the Right Lessons?" *Third World Quarterly*, vol. 24, no. 1 (2003): 127–38.

———. "European Union Democracy Promotion Policies: Ten Years On," *European Foreign Affairs Review*, vol. 6, no. 3 (Autumn 2000): 355–73.

Zakaria, Fareed. "The Rise of Illiberal Democracy," *Foreign Affairs,* vol. 76, no. 6 (November/December 1997): 22–43.

———. *The Future of Freedom: Illiberal Democracy at Home and Abroad.* New York: W.W. Norton, 2003.

## CIVIL-MILITARY RELATIONS

Betz, David J. "The Persistent Problem of Civil-Military Relations in East and Central Europe: A Briefing Note on Democratic Control of Armed Forces." Geneva: Geneva Centre for the Democratic Control of Armed Forces, July 2002.

Bland, Douglas L. "Patterns in Liberal Democratic Civil-Military Relations," *Armed Forces and Society*, vol. 27, no. 4 (Summer 2001): 525–40.

Burk, James. "Theories of Democratic Civil-Military Relations," *Armed Forces and Society*, vol. 29, no. 1 (Fall 2002): 7–29.

Cope, John A. *International Military Education and Training: An Assessment*, McNair Paper, no. 44. Washington, D.C.: Institute for National Strategic Studies, October 1995.

Donnelly, Chris. "Civil-Military Relations in the New Democracies," *Journal of Communist Studies and Transition Politics*, vol. 17, no. 1 (March 2001): 7–10.

Forman, Johanna Mendelson, and Claude Welch. *Civil-Military Relations: USAID's Role.* Washington, D.C.: USAID Center for Democracy and Governance, July 1998.

Huntington, Samuel, P. "Reforming Civil-Military Relations," *Journal of Democracy,* vol. 6 (1995): 9–17.

Mares, David R. *Civil-Military Relations: Building Democracy and Regional Security in Latin America, Southern Asia, and Central Europe.* Boulder, Colo.: Westview Press, 1998.

Rhame, Thomas G. "Security Assistance Programs: Promoting Democracy in the Post–Cold War Era," *Army*, vol. 46, no. 6 (June 1996): 25–31.

Ulrich, Marybeth Peterson. "U.S. Assistance and Military Democratization in the Czech Republic," *Problems of Post-Communism*, vol. 45, no. 2 (March/April 1998): 22–32.

Watts, Larry L. "Reforming Civil-Military Relations in Post-Communist States: Civil Control vs. Democratic Control," *Journal of Political and Military Sociology*, vol. 30, no. 1 (Summer 2002): 51–70.

## CIVIL SOCIETY

Abramson, David M. "A Critical Look at NGOs and Civil Society as Means to an End in Uzbekistan," *Human Organization*, vol. 58, issue 3 (Fall 1999): 240–50.

Berman, Sheri. "Civil Society and the Collapse of the Weimar Republic," *World Politics*, vol. 49, no. 3 (April 1997): 401–29.

Blair, Harry. "Civil Society and Building Democracy: Lessons from International Donor Experience," in Amanda Bernard, Henny Helmrich, and Percy B. Lehning, eds., *Civil Society and International Development.* Paris: North-South Centre of the Council of Europe and Development Centre of the Organization for Economic Cooperation and Development, 1998.

_____. "Jump-Starting Democracy: Adult Civic Education and Democratic Participation in Three Countries," *Democratization*, vol. 10, no. 1 (Spring 2003): 53–76.

Bratton, Michael, and Philip Alderfer. "The Effects of Civic Education on Political Culture: Evidence from Zambia," *World Development,* vol. 27, no. 5 (1999): 807–24.

Brysk, Alison. "Democratizing Civil Society in Latin America," *Journal of Democracy*, vol. 11, no. 3 (July 2000): 151–65.

Diamond, Larry. "Rethinking Civil Society: Toward Democratic Consolidation," *Journal of Democracy,* vol. 5, no. 3 (July 1994): 4–17.

Doherty, Ivan. "Democracy Out of Balance: Civil Society Can't Replace Political Parties," *Policy Review*, no. 106 (April–May 2001): 25–35.

Edwards, Bob, Michael W. Foley, and Mario Diani, eds. *Beyond Tocqueville: Civil Society and the Social Capital Debate in Comparative Perspective.* Hanover, N.H.: University Press, 2001.

Edwards, Michael, and David Hume. *Beyond the Magic Bullet: NGO Performance and Accountability in the Post–Cold War.* West Hartford, Conn.: Kumarian Press, 1996.

Encarnación, Omar G. "Tocqueville's Missionaries: Civil Society Advocacy and the Promotion of Democracy," *World Policy Journal*, vol. 17, no. 1 (Spring 2000): 9–18.

_____. *The Myth of Civil Society: Social Capital and Democratic Consolidation in Spain and Brazil.* New York: Palgrave McMillan, 2003.

Foley, Michael W. "Laying the Groundwork: The Struggle for Civil Society in El Salvador," *Journal of Interamerican Studies and World Affairs,* vol. 38, no. 1 (1996): 67–104.

Foley, Michael W., and Bob Edwards. "The Paradox of Civil Society," *Journal of Democracy*, vol. 7, no. 3 (July 1996): 38–52.

Forman, Johanna Mendelson. "Promoting Civil Society in Good Governance: Lessons for the Security Sector." Geneva: Geneva Centre for the Democratic Control of Armed Forces, 2002.

Fowler, Alan. "Non-governmental Organizations as Agents of Democratization: An African Perspective," *Journal of International Development*, vol. 5, no. 3 (1993): 325–39.

Fullinwider, Robert K., ed. *Civil Society, Democracy and Civic Renewal*. Lanham, Md.: Rowman & Littlefield Publishers, 1999.

Hadenius, Axel, and Fredrik Uggla. "Making Civil Society Work, Promoting Democratic Development: What Can States and Donors Do?" *World Development*, vol. 24, no. 10 (1996): 1621–39.

Hann, Chris, and Elizabeth Dunn, eds. *Civil Society: Challenging Western Models*. New York: Routledge, 1996.

Hansen, Gary. *Constituencies for Reform: Strategic Approaches for Donor-Supported Civic Advocacy Programs*, USAID Program and Operations Assessment Report no. 12. Washington, D.C.: USAID, February 1996.

Haynes, Jeff. *Democracy and Civil Society in the Third World: Politics & New Political Movements*. Cambridge, U.K.: Polity Press, 1997.

Hearn, Julie. "Foreign Aid, Democratisation and Civil Society in Africa: A Study of South Africa, Ghana and Uganda," Institute of Development Studies discussion paper no. 368. Sussex, U.K.: Institute of Development Studies, March 1999.

Henderson, Sarah L. *Building Democracy in Contemporary Russia: Western Support for Grassroots Organizations*. Ithaca, N.Y.: Cornell University Press, 2003.

Hudock, Ann C. *NGOs and Civil Society: Democracy by Proxy?* Cambridge, U.K.: Polity Press, 1999.

Hulme, David, and Michael Edwards, eds. *NGOs, States and Donors: Too Close for Comfort?* New York: St. Martin's Press, 1997.

Jenkins, Rob. "Mistaking 'Governance' for 'Politics': Foreign Aid, Democracy and the Construction of Civil Society," *Civil Society: Histories and Possibilities*. Cambridge: Cambridge University Press, 2001.

Jünemann, Annette. "From the Bottom to the Top: Civil Society and Transnational Non-Governmental Organizations in the Euro-Mediterranean Partnership," *Democratization*, vol. 9, no. 1 (Spring 2002): 87–105.

Keane, John. *Civil Society: Old Images, New Visions*. Stanford, Calif.: Stanford University Press, 1998.

Luong, Pauline Jones, and Erika Weinthal. "The NGO Paradox: Democratic Goals and Non-democratic Outcomes in Kazakhstan," *Europe-Asia Studies*, vol. 51, no. 7 (1999): 1267–84.

Macdonald, Laura. *Supporting Civil Society: The Political Role of Non-governmental Organizations in Central America*. New York: St. Martin's Press, 1997.

McMahon, Patrice C. "Building Civil Societies in East Central Europe: The Effect of American Non-Governmental Organizations on Women's Groups," *Democratization*, vol. 8, no. 2 (Summer 2001): 45–68.

Mendelson, Sarah E., and John K. Glenn, eds. *The Power and Limits of NGOs: A Critical Look at Building Democracy in Eastern Europe*. New York: Columbia University Press, 2002.

National Democratic Institute. *Increasing Citizen Participation through Advocacy Efforts: A Guidebook for Program Development*. Washington, D.C.: 2000.

Ndegwa, Stephen N. *The Two Faces of Civil Society: NGOs and Politics in Africa*. West Hartford, Conn.: Kumarian Press, 1996.

Ottaway, Marina. "Strengthening Civil Society in Other Countries," *The Chronicle Review* (June 2001).

Ottaway, Marina, and Thomas Carothers. *Funding Virtue: Civil Society Aid and Democracy Promotion*. Washington, D.C.: Carnegie Endowment for International Peace, 2000.

Pearce, Jenny. "Civil Society, the Market and Democracy in Latin America," *Democratization*, vol. 4, no. 2 (Summer 1997): 57–83.

Pietrzyk, Dorota I. "Democracy or Civil Society?" *Politics*, vol. 23, no. 1 (February 2003): 38–45.

Quigley, Kevin F. F. "Towards Consolidating Democracy: The Paradoxical Role of Democracy Groups in Thailand," *Democratization*, vol. 3, no. 3 (Autumn 1996): 264–86.

Reilly, Charles A., ed. *New Paths to Democratic Development in Latin America: The Rise of NGO-Municipal Collaboration*. Boulder, Colo.: Lynne Rienner, 1995.

Richter, James. "Promoting Civil Society? Democracy Assistance and Russian Women's Organizations," *Problems of Post-Communism*, vol. 49, no. 3 (January/February 2002): 30–41.

Rieff, David. "Civil Society and the Future of the Nation-State," *The Nation* (February 22, 1999): 11–16.

Robinson, Mark. "Strengthening Civil Society in Africa: The Role of Foreign Political Aid," *IDS Bulletin*, vol. 26, no. 2 (April 1995): 70–80.

Sabatini, Christopher, Gwendolyn Bevis, and Steven Finkel. *The Impact of Civic Education Programs on Political Participation and Democratic Attitudes*. Washington, D.C.: Management Systems International, January 27, 1998.

Siegel, Daniel, and Jenny Yancey. *The Rebirth of Civil Society: The Development of the Nonprofit Sector in East Central Europe and the Role of Western Assistance*. New York: Rockefeller Brothers Fund, 1992.

Taylor, Lucy. "Textbook Citizens: Education for Democracy and Political Culture in El Salvador," *Democratization*, vol. 6, no. 3 (Autumn 1999): 62–83.

USAID. "Approaches to Civic Education: Lessons Learned." Washington, D.C.: USAID Office of Democracy and Governance, July 2002.

Van Rooy, Alison, ed. *Civil Society and the Aid Industry*. London: Earthscan Publications, 1998.

White, Gordon. "Civil Society, Democratization and Development (I): Clearing the Analytical Ground," *Democratization*, vol. 1, no. 3 (Autumn 1994): 56–84.

## DECENTRALIZATION

Beaumont, Enid. "Democracy and Public Administration Reform Linked," *Public Manager,* vol. 28, no. 1 (Spring 1999): 47–50.

Blair, Harry. *Assessing Democratic Decentralization: A CDIE Concept Paper.* Washington, D.C.: USAID, November 6, 1995.

Campbell, Tim E. J. *Innovations and Risk Taking: The Engine of Reform and Local Government in Latin America and the Caribbean.* Washington, D.C.: World Bank, 1997.

Cohen, John, and Stephen B. Peterson. *Administrative Decentralization: Strategies for Developing Countries.* West Hartford, Conn.: Kumarian Press, 1997.

Crook, Richard Charles, and James Manor. *Democracy and Decentralization in South Asia and West Africa: Participation, Accountability, and Performance.* Cambridge, U.K.: Cambridge University Press, 1998.

Hadenius, Axel. "Decentralization and Democratic Governance: Experiences from India, Bolivia and South Africa." Stockholm: Swedish Ministry of Foreign Affairs, Expert Group on Development Issues, 2003.

Heller, Patrick. "Moving the State: the Politics of Democratic Decentralization in Kerala [India], South Africa, and Porto Alegre," *Politics and Society*, vol. 29, no. 1 (March 2001): 131–63.

International Institute for Democracy and Electoral Assistance. *Democracy at the Local Level: The International IDEA Handbook on Participation, Representation, Conflict Management and Governance.* Stockholm: 2001.

Johnson, Ronald W. *Decentralization Strategy Design: Complementary Perspectives on a Common Theme,* USAID document no. PN-ABW-981. Washington, D.C.: USAID, August 1995.

Manor, James. *The Political Economy of Democratic Decentralization.* Washington, D.C.: World Bank, 1999.

O'Brien, David, and Luciano Catenacci. "Towards a Framework for Local Democracy in a War-Torn Society: The Lessons of Selected Foreign Assistance Programmes in El Salvador," *Democratization*, vol. 3, no. 4 (Winter 1996): 435–58.

Sabatini, Christopher. "Decentralization and Political Parties," *Journal of Democracy*, vol. 14, no. 2 (2003): 138–50.

USAID Center for Democracy and Governance. *Handbook on Programming for Democratic Decentralization.* Washington, D.C.: May 2000.

## ELECTIONS

Anglin, Douglas G. "International Monitoring of the Transition to Democracy in South Africa, 1992–1994," *African Affairs,* vol. 94, no. 377 (1995): 519–43.

Bjornlund, Eric. "Democracy Inc.," *The Wilson Quarterly* (Summer 2001): 18–21.

Bjornlund, Eric, Michael Bratton, and Clark Gibson. "Observing Multiparty Elections in Africa: Lessons from Zambia," *African Affairs*, no. 91, no. 384 (July 1992): 405–31.

Carroll, David J., and Robert A. Pastor. "Moderating Ethnic Tensions by Electoral Mediation: The Case of Guyana," *Security Dialogue*, vol. 24, no. 2 (1993): 163–73.

Elklit, Jørgen, ed. *Electoral Systems for Emerging Democracies: Experiences and Suggestions.* Copenhagen: Danish Ministry of Foreign Affairs, 1997.

Elklit, Jørgen, and Andrew Reynolds. "The Impact of Election Administration on the Legitimacy of Emerging Democracies: A New Research Agenda." Notre Dame, Ind.: Helen Kellogg Institute for International Studies, September 2000.

Elklit, Jørgen, and Palle Svensson. "What Makes Elections Free and Fair?" *Journal of Democracy,* vol. 8, no. 3 (July 1997): 32–46.

Estok, Melissa, Neil Nevitte, and Glenn Cowan. *The Quick Count and Election Observation: An NDI Guide for Civic Organizations and Political Parties.* Washington, D.C.: National Democratic Institute, 2002.

Evered, Timothy C. *United Nations Electoral Assistance and the Evolving Right to Democratic Governance.* Livingston, N.J.: Center for U.N. Reform Education, 1996.

Fisher, Jeff. "Electoral Conflict and Violence: A Strategy for Study and Prevention," White Paper. Washington, D.C.: International Foundation for Election Systems, 2001–2002.

Garber, Larry, and Glenn Cowan. "The Virtues of Parallel Vote Tabulations," *Journal of Democracy,* vol. 4, no. 2 (April 1994): 95–107.

Goodwin-Gill, Guy S. *Free and Fair Elections: International Law and Practice.* Geneva: Inter-Parliamentary Union, 1994.

Herman, Edward S., and Frank Brodhead. *Demonstration Elections.* Boston: South End Press, 1984.

Hirschmann, David. *Managing Democratic Electoral Assistance.* Washington, D.C.: USAID, 1995.

International Institute for Democracy and Electoral Assistance. *International Electoral Standards: Guidelines for Reviewing the Legal Framework of Elections.* Stockholm: 2002.

_____. *The International IDEA Handbook of Electoral System Design.* Stockholm: 2002.

Koenig-Archibugi, Mathias. "International Electoral Assistance," *Peace Review,* vol. 9, no. 3 (September 1997): 357–64.

Kumar, Krishna, ed. *Postconflict Elections, Democratization, and International Assistance.* Boulder, Colo.: Lynne Rienner, 1998.

Lyons, Terrence. *Voting for Peace: Postconflict Elections in Liberia.* Washington, D.C.: Brookings Institution Press, 1999.

McCoy, Jennifer, Larry Garber, and Robert Pastor. "Pollwatching and Peacemaking," *Journal of Democracy,* vol. 2, no. 4 (Fall 1991): 102–14.

National Democratic Institute for International Affairs. *How Domestic Organizations Monitor Elections: An A to Z Guide.* Washington, D.C.: 1995.

Nevitte, Neil, and Santiago A. Canton. "The Role of Domestic Observers," *Journal of Democracy,* vol. 8, no. 3 (July 1997): 47–61.

Norris, Robert, and Patrick Merloe. *Media Monitoring to Promote Democratic Elections: An NDI Handbook for Citizen Organizations.* Washington, D.C.: National Democratic Institute, 2002.

Padilla, David, and Elizabeth Houppert. "International Election Observing: Enhancing the Principle of Free and Fair Elections," *Emory International Law Review,* vol. 7, no. 1 (Spring 1993): 73–132.

Pastor, Robert A. "The Role of Electoral Administration in Democratic Transitions: Implications for Policy and Research," *Democratization,* vol. 6, no. 4 (Winter 1999): 1–27.

_____. "Mediating Elections," *Journal of Democracy,* vol. 9, no. 1 (January 1998): 154–63.

Reilly, Benjamin. "International Electoral Assistance: A Review of Donor Activities and Lessons Learned," Working Paper no. 17. The Hague: Netherlands Institute of International Relations (Clingendael), June 2003.

_____. *Democracy in Divided Societies: Electoral Engineering for Conflict Management.* Cambridge, U.K.: Cambridge University Press, 2001.

Sisk, Timothy, and Andrew Reynolds, eds. *Elections and Conflict Management in Africa.* Washington, D.C.: U.S. Institute of Peace Press, 1998.

USAID. "Managing Assistance in Support of Political and Electoral Processes." Washington, D.C.: USAID Office of Democracy and Governance, January 2000.

## LEGISLATURES

Baaklini, Abdo I., and James J. Heaphey. *Legislative Institution Building in Brazil, Costa Rica, and Lebanon.* Beverly Hills, Calif.: Sage Publications, 1976.

Lippman, Hal, and Jan Emmert. *Assisting Legislatures in Developing Countries: A Framework for Program Planning and Implementation,* USAID document no. PN-ACA-902. Washington, D.C.: USAID, October 1997.

McCannell, Ryan S. *Legislative Strengthening: A Synthesis of USAID Experience.* Washington, D.C.: USAID, May 1995.

USAID. "USAID Handbook on Legislative Strengthening." Washington, D.C.: USAID Office of Democracy and Governance, February 2000.

## MEDIA

Githongo, John. "Civil Society, Democratization and the Media in Kenya," *Development,* vol. 40, no. 4 (1997): 41–5.

Gross, Peter. *Mass Media in Revolution and National Development: The Romanian Laboratory.* Ames: Iowa State University Press, 1996.

Howard, Ross. "International Media Assistance: A Review of Donor Activities and Lessons Learned," Working Paper no. 19. The Hague: Netherlands Institute of International Relations (Clingendael), June 2003.

Janus, Noreene, and Rick Rockwell. *The Latin American Journalism Project: Lessons Learned.* Washington, D.C.: USAID, November 1998.

Myers, Mary. "The Promotion of Democracy at the Grass-roots: The Example of Radio in Mali," *Democratization,* vol. 5, no. 2 (Summer 1998): 200–16.

O'Neil, Patrick H., ed. *Communicating Democracy: The Media and Political Transitions.* Boulder, Colo.: Lynne Rienner, 1998.

_____. *Post-Communism and the Media in Eastern Europe.* Portland, Ore.: Frank Cass, 1997.

USAID. "The Role of Media in Democracy: A Strategic Approach." Washington, D.C.: USAID Office of Democracy and Governance, June 1999.

## MIDDLE EAST

Afkhami, Mahnaz. "Promoting Women's Rights in the Muslim World," *Journal of Democracy,* vol. 8, no. 1 (January 1997): 157–66.

Brumberg, Daniel. "Democratization in the Arab World? The Trap of Liberalized Autocracy," *Journal of Democracy* (October 2002).

_____. "Liberalization Versus Democracy: Understanding Arab Political Reform," Working Paper no. 37. Washington, D.C.: Carnegie Endowment for International Peace, 2003.

Byman, Daniel. "Constructing a Democratic Iraq: Challenges and Opportunities," *International Security,* vol. 28, no. 1 (Summer 2003): 47.

Carapico, Sheila. "Foreign Aid for Promoting Democracy in the Arab World," *Middle East Journal,* vol. 53, no. 3 (Summer 2002).

Daguzun, Jean-Francois. "France, Democratization and North Africa," *Democratization,* vol. 9, no. 1 (Spring 2002): 135–48.

Dawisha, Adeed, and Karen Dawisha. "How to Build a Democratic Iraq," *Foreign Affairs,* vol. 82, no. 3 (May/June 2003): 36.

Gillespie, Richard, and Laurence Whitehead. "European Democracy Promotion in North Africa: Limits and Prospects," *Democratization,* vol. 9, no. 1 (Spring 2002).

Haass, Richard. "Toward Greater Democracy in the Muslim World," *The Washington Quarterly,* vol. 29, no. 3 (Summer 2003): 137–48.

Haddadi, Said. "Two Cheers for Whom? The European Union and Democratization in Morocco," *Democratization,* vol. 9, no. 1 (Spring 2002): 149–69.

Hamarneh, Mustafa. "Democratization in the Masreq: The Role of External Factors," *Mediterranean Politics,* vol. 5, no. 1 (Spring 2000): 77–95.

Hawthorne, Amy. "Can the United States Promote Democracy in the Middle East?" *Current History* (January 2003): 21–6.

_____. "Middle Eastern Democracy: Is Civil Society the Answer?" Carnegie Paper no. 44. Washington, D.C.: Carnegie Endowment for International Peace, March 2004.

Henry, Clement M. "Promoting Democracy: USAID, at Sea or Off to Cyberspace?" *Middle East Policy,* vol. 5, no. 1 (1997): 178–90.

Jost, Kenneth, and Benton Ives-Halperin. "Democracy in the Arab World: Will U.S. Efforts to Promote Democracy Succeed?" *Congressional Quarterly Researcher*, vol. 14, no. 4 (January 30, 2004): 73–99.

Khan, Muqtedar. "Prospects for Muslim Democracy: The Role of U.S. Policy," *Middle East Policy*, vol. 10, no. 3 (Fall 2003): 79–89.

Kibble, David G. "Monarchs, Mosques, and Military Hardware: A Pragmatic Approach to the Promotion of Human Rights and Democracy in the Middle East," *Comparative Strategy*, vol. 17, no. 4 (October 1998): 381–91.

Muravchik, Joshua. "Bringing Democracy to the Arab World," *Current History*, vol. 103, no. 669 (January 2004): 8–10.

Ottaway, Marina. "Promoting Democracy in the Middle East: The Problem of U.S. Credibility," Working Paper no. 35. Washington, D.C.: Carnegie Endowment for International Peace, March 2003.

_____. "Women's Rights and Democracy in the Arab World," Carnegie Paper no. 42. Washington, D.C.: Carnegie Endowment for International Peace, March 2004.

Salmoni, Barak. "America's Iraq Strategy: Democratic Chimeras, Regional Realities," *Current History,* vol. 103, no. 669 (January 2004): 17–20.

Takeyh, Ray. "Faith-Based Initiatives: Can Islam Bring Democracy to the Middle East?" *Foreign Policy* (November/December 2001): 68–70.

_____. "Uncle Sam in the Arab Street," *The National Interest*, no. 75 (Spring 2004): 45–51.

Windsor, Jennifer L. "Promoting Democracy Can Combat Terrorism," *The Washington Quarterly*, vol. 26, no. 3 (Summer 2003): 43–58.

Wittes, Tamara Cofman. "Arab Democracy, American Ambivalence: Will Bush's Rhetoric about Transforming the Middle East Be Matched by American Deeds?" *The Weekly Standard*, vol. 9, no. 23 (February 23, 2004): 34–7.

Wood, Pia Christina. "French Foreign Policy and Tunisia: Do Human Rights Matter?" *Middle East Policy*, vol. 2 (June 2002): 92–110.

Youngs, Richard. "The European Union and Democracy Promotion in the Mediterranean: A New or Disingenuous Strategy," *Democratization*, vol. 9, no. 1 (Spring 2002): 40–62.

## POLITICAL PARTIES

Burnell, Peter, and Alan Ware, eds. *Funding Democratization*. Manchester, U.K.: Manchester University Press, 1998.

Muravchik, Joshua. "U.S. Political Parties Abroad," *The Washington Quarterly*, vol. 12, no. 3 (Summer 1989): 91–100.

Phillips, Ann L. "Exporting Democracy: German Political Foundations in Central-East Europe," *Democratization*, vol. 6, no. 2 (Summer 1999): 70–98.

Pinto-Duschinsky, Michael. "Foreign Political Aid: The German Political Foundations and Their U.S. Counterparts," *International Affairs*, vol. 67, no. 1 (1991): 33–63.

USAID. "USAID Political Party Development Assistance." Washington, D.C.: USAID Office of Democracy and Governance, April 1999.


## RULE OF LAW

Alvarez, José. "Promoting the 'Rule of Law' in Latin America: Problems and Prospects," *George Washington Journal of International Law and Economy*, vol. 25 (1991): 287–332.

Biebesheimer, Christina, and J. Mark Payne. "IDB Experience in Judicial Reform: Lessons Learned and Elements for Policy Formation." Technical Papers Series. Washington, D.C.: Inter-American Development Bank, Sustainable Development Department, November 2001.

Blair, Harry, and Gary Hansen. *Weighing in on the Scales of Justice: Strategic Approaches for Donor-Supported Rule of Law Programs,* USAID Program and Operations Assessment Report no. 7. Washington, D.C.: USAID, 1994.

Chua, Amy L. "Markets, Democracy, and Ethnicity: Toward a New Paradigm for Law and Development," *Yale Law Journal,* vol. 108, no. 1 (October 1998): 1–107.

Ciurlizza, Javier. "Judicial Reform and International Legal Technical Assistance in Latin America," *Democratization*, vol. 7, no. 2 (Summer 2000): 211–30.

Dezalay, Yves, and Bryant G. Garth. *Global Prescriptions: The Production, Exportation, and Importation of a New Legal Orthodoxy.* Ann Arbor: University of Michigan Press, 2002.

Domingo, Pilar, and Rachel Sieder, eds. *Rule of Law in Latin America: The International Promotion of Judicial Reform.* London: Institute of Latin American Studies, University of London, 2001.

Elster, Jon. "Constitution-Making in Eastern Europe: Rebuilding the Boat in the Open Sea," *Public Administration,* vol. 71 (Spring/Summer 1993): 169–217.

Faundez, Julio, ed. *Good Government and Law: Legal and Institutional Reform in Developing Countries.* New York: St. Martin's Press, 1997.

Gardner, James. *Legal Imperialism: American Lawyers and Foreign Aid in Latin America.* Madison: University of Wisconsin Press, 1980.

Golub, Stephen. "The Growth of a Public Interest Law Movement: Origins, Operations, Impact and Lessons for Legal System Development," in G. Sidney Silliman and Lela Garner Noble, eds., *Organizing for Democracy: NGOs, Civil Society and the Philippine State.* Honolulu: University of Hawaii Press, 1998: 254–79.

———. "Beyond the Rule of Law Orthodoxy: The Legal Empowerment Alternative," Working Paper no. 41. Washington, D.C.: Carnegie Endowment for International Peace, 2003.

Hammergren, Linn A. *The Politics of Justice and Justice Reform in Latin America: The Peruvian Case in Comparative Perspective.* Boulder, Colo.: Westview Press, 1998.

_____. *Code Reform and Law Revision,* USAID Document no. PN-ACD-022. Washington, D.C.: USAID Center for Democracy and Governance, 1998.

_____. *Institutional Strengthening and Justice Reform,* USAID Document no. PN-ACD-020. Washington, D.C.: USAID Center for Democracy and Governance, 1998.

_____. *Judicial Training and Justice Reform,* USAID Document no. PN-ACD-021. Washington, D.C.: USAID Center for Democracy and Governance, 1998.

_____. *Political Will, Constituency Building, and Public Support in Rule of Law Programs,* USAID Document no. PN-ACE-023. Washington, D.C.: USAID Center for Democracy and Governance, 1998.

Hoeland, Armin. "The Evolution of Law in Eastern and Central Europe: Are We Witnessing a Renaissance of 'Law and Development'?" in Gessner Bolkmar, Armin Hoeland, and Csaba Varga, eds., *European Legal Cultures.* Dartmouth, N.H.: Aldershot, 1996.

Huggins, Martha. *Political Policing: The United States and Latin America.* Durham, N.C.: Duke University Press, 1998.

Jarquin, Edmundo, and Fernando Carrillo, eds. *Justice Delayed: Judicial Reform in Latin America.* Washington, D.C.: Inter-American Development Bank, 1998.

Jensen, Erik G., and Thomas C. Heller, eds. *Beyond Common Knowledge: Empirical Approaches to the Rule of Law.* Stanford, Calif.: Stanford University Press, 2003.

Krasnov, Mikhail. "Is the 'Concept of Judicial Reform' Timely?" *East European Constitutional Review,* vol. 11, nos. 1/2 (Winter/Spring 2002): 92–4.

Lawyers Committee for Human Rights. *Building on Quicksand: The Collapse of the World Bank's Judicial Reform Project in Peru.* New York: April 2000.

McClymont, Mary, and Stephen Golub. *Many Roads to Justice: The Law-Related Work of Ford Foundation Grantees Around the World.* New York: Ford Foundation, 2000.

Méndez, Juan E., Guillermo O'Donnell, and Paulo Sérgio Pinheiro. *The (Un) Rule of Law & the Underprivileged in Latin America.* Notre Dame, Ind.: University of Notre Dame Press, 1999.

Merryman, John Henry. "Comparative Law and Social Change: On the Origins, Style, Decline and Revival of the Law and Development Movement," *American Journal of Comparative Law,* vol. 25, no. 3 (1977): 457–91.

Neild, Rachel. *Themes and Debates in Public Security Reform: A Manual for Civil Society.* Washington, D.C.: Washington Office on Latin America, 1998.

Oakley, Robert B., Michael J. Dziedzic, and Eliot M. Goldberg, eds. *Policing the New World Disorder: Peace Operations and Public Security.* Washington, D.C.: National Defense University Press, 1998.

Russell, Peter H., and David M. O'Brien. *Judicial Independence in the Age of Democracy: Critical Perspectives from around the World.* Charlottesville: University of Virginia Press, 2001.

Sajó, András. "Universal Rights, Missionaries, Converts, and 'Local Savages,'" *East European Constitutional Review,* vol. 6, no. 1 (Winter 1997): 44–9.

Sevastik, Per, ed. *Legal Assistance to Developing Countries.* Dordrecht, The Netherlands: Kluwer Law, 1997.

Sharlet, Robert. "Legal Transplants and Political Mutations: The Reception of Constitutional Law in Russia and the New Independent States," *East European Constitutional Review*, vol. 7, no. 4 (Fall 1998): 59–68.

USAID. "Guidance for Promoting Judicial Independence and Impartiality." Washington, D.C.: USAID Office of Democracy and Governance, January 2002.

Washington Office on Latin America. *Elusive Justice: The U.S. Administration of Justice Program in Latin America.* Washington, D.C.: May 1990.

Widner, Jennifer A. *Building the Rule of Law: Francis Nyalali and the Road to Judicial Independence in Africa.* New York: W. W. Norton & Company, 2001.


## TRADE UNIONS

Buchanan, Paul G. "The Impact of U.S. Labor," in Abraham F. Lowenthal, ed. *Exporting Democracy: The United States and Latin America, Themes and Issues.* Baltimore: Johns Hopkins University Press, 1991: 155–87.

Cook, Linda J. *Labor and Liberalization: Trade Unions in the New Russia.* New York: Twentieth Century Fund Press, 1997.

Spalding, Hobart A. "The Two Latin American Foreign Policies of the U.S. Labor Movement: The AFL-CIO Top Brass vs. Rank-and-File," *Science & Society,* vol. 56, no. 4 (Winter 1992/1993): 421–39.

Welch, Cliff. "Labor Internationalism: U.S. Involvement in Brazilian Unions, 1945–1965," *Latin American Research Review*, vol. 30, no. 2 (1995): 61–89.

# Index

283

# About the Author

Thomas Carothers is founder and director of the Democracy and Rule of Law Project at the Carnegie Endowment. A leading authority on democratization and democracy promotion, he has worked on democracy programs for more than fifteen years with many American, European, and international organizations and carried out extensive field research on democratization around the world. He has written or edited five books on democracy promotion, including *Aiding Democracy Abroad: The Learning Curve* (Carnegie Endowment, 1999) and *Funding Virtue: Civil Society Aid and Democracy Promotion* (Carnegie Endowment, 2000), co-edited with Marina Ottaway. He has also published many articles on the subject in major journals and newspapers. He is a recurrent distinguished visiting professor at the Central European University in Budapest and serves on the boards of various democracy promotion organizations.

Prior to joining the Carnegie Endowment, Carothers was an attorney at Arnold & Porter in Washington, D.C., and served in the Office of the Legal Adviser of the U.S. Department of State. He has also been an International Affairs Fellow of the Council on Foreign Relations and a Guest Scholar at the Woodrow Wilson International Center for Scholars. He is a graduate of Harvard Law School, the London School of Economics, and Harvard College.

He is currently coediting a book with Marina Ottaway on promoting democracy in the Middle East.